Ava Gardner

"She was looking into my eyes with that way she had of looking that made you wonder whether she really saw out of her own eyes. They would look on and on after everyone else's eyes in the world would have stopped looking. She looked as though there were nothing on earth she would not look at like that, and really she was afraid of so many things."

Ernest Hemingway
The Sun Also Rises

"She is wild and innocent, pledged to love
Through all disaster..."

Robert Graves
Collected Poems

Gilles Dagneau

Ava Gardner

The Barefoot Contessa

edited and translated by
Sandra Eiko Tokunaga

GREMESE
INTERNATIONAL

Film Series
Monographs on entertainment artists for schools and universities.

Special thanks to:

Manola Laille, Ronald Grant, Chuck Painter, Stéphane Bourgoin, Olivier Eyquem, Brigitte Olivier, Patrice Tehio, Virginie Pesselet, Frédéric Boueil, Catherine Hamel, Okon Jones, Frédéric Dagneau, Jean-Max Causse, Marie Tual, Patrick Brion, Roberto Perazzone, Marion Cres, Aline Bertoni, Raymond Lefèvre, Michèle Snapes, Christopher Miles, Renée Vincent, Jean-Paul Merkens, Jean-Christian Offerlé, Nathalie Vuthilan, Pierre Vachet.

Original title:
Ava Gardner
belle, sauvage, innocente
2002 © Gremese

Photo credits:
The photos in this book come from collections owned by the Cinémathèque Française, National Film Archive, Cahiers du Cinéma and the Author's personal collection.
Photos appearing on pp. 142, 182 and 185: "Antenne 2". Photo on p. 75: Photocave. Photo on p. 145: Lorimar Television. Photo on p. 133: Robert Cohen. Photo on p. 182: Walter Limot.
The Publisher has made all efforts possible to locate the names of the people who have taken the photos that appear in this book and indicate them to the reader. If this has not been possible in all cases, please excuse any possible errors or omissions. The Publisher is prepared to complete any missing details in future new editions of this book. The Publisher is also prepared to recognize rights as per Article 70 of the 1941 law 633.

Photocomposition:
Graphic Art 6 s.r.l. – Rome

Printed in Italy

2016 © Gremese International s.r.l.s. – Rome, Italy

EAN 978-88-7301-780-6

Contents

A scene from
The Sun Also Rises
(1957), directed by
Henry King.

Ava the rebel

The scene: London sometime during the eighties. In one of the city's many parks. Two nondescript elderly ladies walk slowly side by side with their little Welsh Corgi. The two women had met in 1948 when one of them, Reenie, had been taken into the service of the other, Ava Gardner.

They seem to arouse no general interest except perhaps that of a photographer who suddenly aims his zoom in their direction for two or three stolen photos that might appear in the gossip columns. Photos we wished we had never seen, so painfully do they wound our memory. Their captions reveal the disturbing state of health of the woman once known as *"The world's most beautiful animal"*. Ava Gardner has painfully survived two strokes. Ava and Reenie, lost in their reminiscing, wander a bit too far.

> *Ava:* I'm kinda tired.
> *Reenie:* I am too. You think we can make it to that bench over there?
> *Ava:* I don't think I can, Reenie. Let's sit down and rest a bit.[1]

The two friends doze on the lawn. When they awake, their limbs are so sore they can't even move. There is no other alternative but to roll over to the nearest tree and try to get up. This disturbing scene worries the little dog Morgan, named after Ava's right-hand man Jess Morgan. This is the final scene in the life of the Corgi's mistress. The dog bursts into a fit of barking. Ava and Reenie get the giggles.

> *Ava:* Reenie, did you ever think we would come to this?
> *Reenie:* No, never, never, never.[1]

The idea of death does not frighten Ava Gardner, who once remarked, "You know, if I had my life to live all over again, I'd live it exactly in the same way. Maybe a few changes here and there, but nothing special. Because the truth is I've enjoyed my life. I've had a hell of a good time."[2] As reassuring as this might sound, the end was no less diminishing, childish, or terrifying in its banality. Like a false note in the perfectly harmonious image journalists had always tried to keep alive of a rich life, though one that had turned its back on happiness.

Ava Gardner refused to give a meaning to her life. She claimed she liked living in a superficial and frivolous way, though in fact her life hid very deep losses and true wounds. Indeed, Ava lived her life as a reaction against a destiny that had been imposed upon her despite herself: against Hollywood, its lifestyle, its production system, against journalists eager to magnify her misadventures and volcanic passions, against the eyes of men. An entire life that had been undermined by too many conflicts. A life marked by ruptures and brutal, rash reactions.

Ava Gardner the woman, as opposed to the star, died shortly after this incident in the park, leaving her legend to live on. Yet she would not have cared at all about becoming a legend, for she detested the image that we all adored. As the old doctor in *55 Days at Peking* declares sadly to Natasha, Ava's character, *"If you die, Natasha, all the light will be gone from this place."* Yet Ava would not listen to any of this, not even to Natasha for that matter. Ava had no consideration for her image whatsoever. An image she bore like a burden, a complete fabrication of the movies, that ghost industry which had made her a star to the detriment of the actress, a myth rather than a woman:

With a musician in *The Barefoot Contessa*.

I've always felt a prisoner of my image, felt that people preferred the myths and didn't want to hear about the real me at all. Because I was promoted as a sort of siren and played all those sexy broads, people made the mistake of thinking I was like that off the screen. They couldn't have been more wrong.[2]

A few months later an AFP press release announced the news:

LONDON 25 JANUARY 1990 – One of the greatest stars of Hollywood, Ava Gardner, died of pneumonia in her home in London at the age of 67, Claude Mills, one of her friends, announced. According to Mr. Mills, the actress died Thursday morning in her sleep. She had been living in London for many years and loved the city very much. She had a quieter life here than she would have had in the United States. People in the neighborhood had got used to seeing her walking her dog in the park and didn't bother her. The actress' body will be taken back to Smithfield, North Carolina, where she will be laid to rest beside her parents, Mr Mills added.

"Adieu Pandora, Adieu Contessa!," "Good bye, Ava," "A Queen is Dead," "Ava Leaves Us," "Death of a Goddess," the newspapers headlined the next day. *"Hollywood has lost its last myth,"* remarked one Paris daily. *"The film noir fit her like a glove - a woman of fatal passions, she never stopped proving that she could act",* so rightly commented another national newspaper. For the last time, Ava appeared on the front pages of all the popular magazines. In a sublime black-and-white photo by Norman Parkinson, the effect of her strapless gown and cape emphasized the lines of her neck, shoulders and breasts. As for *Paris Match*, it explained its cover dedicated to the legendary couple Gardner-Sinatra: *"In the tumult of her love life, the only man who ever counted."*

The sky was overcast at Sunset Memorial Park Cemetery in the small town of Smithfield. A dome of umbrellas sheltered some five hundred friends, family members and onlookers who had come that Monday 29 January to pay their final respects to Ava Gardner. No famous celebrities, but a mysterious limousine with tinted windows. Frank Sinatra, it was rumored. After the service, celebrated by Reverend Francis Bradshaw of the Methodist Church of Smithfield, the fine rain finally stopped and gradually the sun reappeared from behind the clouds. A scene that evoked the burial of Maria Vargas in *The Barefoot Contessa*. Director Joseph Mankiewicz, who had cast Ava in this landmark film, commented on the actress' philosophy of life: "I don't think that Ava ever put all of her body or soul into her roles. She devoted them to her life. That was the way she wanted to be happy."

Ava Gardner had not acted in any film for almost four years after a stroke in September 1986 had left her partially paralyzed. She appeared for the last time in *Maggie*, a 60-minute pilot for a television series that Warner never produced. Bedridden in her London home in Knightsbridge, she devoted herself to her memoirs. Ava had often been solicited by publishers to write her life story and had declined countless proposals. She finally decided to take advantage of the opportunity to set the record straight. "If I don't give my side of the story," she explained, "it'll be too late, and then some self-appointed biographer will step in and add to the inaccuracies, the inventions, and the abysmal lies that already exist."[2]

And so she began:

I was born Ava Lavinia Gardner on Christmas Eve 1922, in Grabtown, North Carolina. Not Brogden, not Smithfield, like so many of the books say, but poor old Grabtown. Precisely. God knows why it got that name: there was no place to grab, and hardly any town at all... I came into this world at ten o'clock at night, and I've often thought that that was the reason I turned into such a nocturnal creature. When the sun sets, honey, I feel more, oh, alert. More alive. By midnight, I feel fantastic. Even when I was a little girl, my father would shake his head and say, "Let's just hope you get a job where you work nights." Little did he know what was in store for me.[2]

No did Ava. Being a movie star had never been a need, a dream, or even a vague wish for Ava Gardner. If this was what she in fact became, it was due to the kind of fate that watches over all great destinies and determines the course of an entire existence. And also thanks to Ava's incomparable beauty, which Hollywood experts

only had to highlight to reveal the myriad facets that could then be adapted to her roles.

As a teenager Ava did not show the least desire to escape her modest milieu and was taking a course to become a secretary. One day in 1932 her mother, Mollie Gardner, a frank and hardworking woman, took Ava to the movies to see Clark Gable. He was her mother's fetish actor and was starring in *Red Dust*. Little did Ava know that twenty years later she would be co-starring with the legendary actor herself in John Ford's remake *Mogambo*.

A publicity photo taken for *The Killers*, directed by Robert Siodmak in 1946.

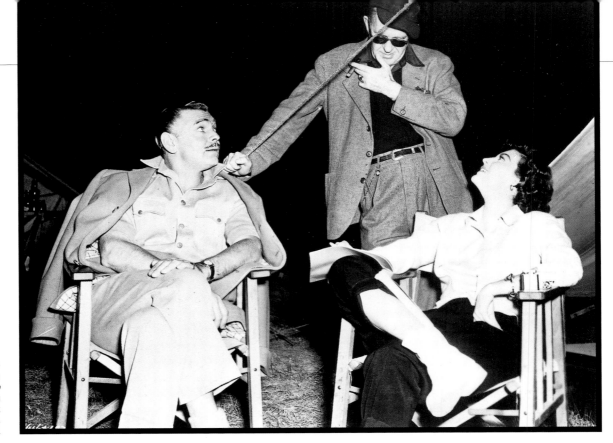

A pause during the shooting of *Mogambo* (1953). Standing between Clark Gable and Ava, director John Ford.

Though the silver screen left Ava indifferent, Ava soon attracted Hollywood. One day her brother-in-law displayed her alluring picture in his shop window in New York. She was seventeen. Ava immediately conquered her first heart as soon as a passerby, Barney Duhan, set eyes on her photo. Barney was a young employee at MGM and absolutely had to get a date with the model. Ava's shock wave traveled at lightning speed right out to California and the heartland of America's film industry with its talent for transforming emotion into dollars.

"Tell New York to ship her out! She's a good piece of merchandise!" George Sidney is reputed to have said as head of casting at Metro-Goldwyn-Mayer. Ava's undeniable sex appeal and the young girl's luminous beauty prevailed in the decision, over her diction which was disastrous, and her acting ability, which was considered zero.

Ava had hardly signed what she termed that "damned contract" when MGM's good fairy already began to reveal its true face. The Studio seemed more like a wicked witch whose wand was used mainly to keep a colony of starlets in tow on grandiose kitsch sets. Among these girls there was Ava, probably the most unmotivated of all.

Docile and innocent, Ava bent to the golden rule "seen but not heard" and let herself be imprisoned, a consenting victim in that marvelous enticing Southern Californian mirage. They taught her to walk, to pose, and above all to smile. In this total in-house apprenticeship, acting was an optional.

Her elder sister Beatrice, "Bappie", who had gotten her into all of this in the first place, urged Ava to accept the gifts multimillionaire Howard Hughes lavished on her. Bappie told her sister to just sit back and enjoy the sumptuous life that was suddenly welcoming her with open arms. Yet the real dream was being lived by Bappie, who could enjoy it all vicariously. Despite it all, Ava remained faithful to herself and her tastes, particularly when it came to men. And it was absolutely out of the question to surrender to Howard Hughes. Ava was not a prostitute. The heroine who had inspired the heavens of Hollywood never found the intimate happiness to make the dream truly complete.

Ava was almost embarrassingly beautiful. She had a luminous, sculptural beauty that in its haughtiness surpassed all description. A beauty that was a dominating force by its sheer obviousness. Beauty she cast out like a

Ava Gardner, the eternal traveler. Here at Le Bourget Airport near Paris in 1956.

challenge to the many pretenders who vied to prove they were worthy. Beauty that never ceased to rouse senses and flatter egos when finally they had conquered the object of their desire. "Her big lively eyes, high cheekbones, and that dimple in her chin drove them mad," remembered prince Ali Khan.

From the very onslaught, events in Ava Gardner's private life prevailed over her career, much to the glee of reporters. Ava was far from a revelation on the screen in those early days and her first appearances were not the topic of lengthy criticism. In fact, she did not know how to do anything except be beautiful.

Ava's role in 1942 essentially consisted of being the wife of America's most popular actor, Mickey Rooney. In 1944 she was the wife of bandleader Artie Shaw. Indeed it was not until 1946, in *The Killers,* that Ava truly got her first serious acting role, and by that time she already had two marriages behind her:

I was greener than grass about everything. I'd never acted or been photographed, I was awkward and scared stupid. Half the time on the set, I was trying not to bawl just because I didn't know how to do what they wanted. All my energy went into just not collapsing, since I didn't know what I was supposed to do.[2]

This shy little extra had married two big stars, one right after the other, and these men's values and aspirations were not at all those of the nice young men back in North Carolina. Ava's "simple country girl"[2] values came up against the licentious morals of the Hollywood fauna. Ava's first failed romances plunged her into crisis. Indeed, she had never conceived of love outside the eternal bonds of marriage.

Ava was aware of how restricting her beauty was, of how it could cause her to be misunderstood. What was there beyond her beauty? A personality, an intelligent mind, a soul? Artie Shaw, who considered his fifth wife Ava rather dumb and uncultured, had her read Tolstoy, Mann, Shakespeare, all in a jumble, and managed to do nothing but give her a complex. "I don't think I would have ever fallen in love with you if you weren't so beautiful," he once confessed.

In Hollywood's dream factory, would Ava manage to truly exist as a person and be more than just another pin-up? Her beauty was an obstacle to her own happiness. It gave her no alternative but to become a star. But the status of a star brings isolation. It crowns, but does not necessarily bring acceptance. Ava had tremendous difficulty in being recognized as a true actress.

John Huston was not at all bothered with psychology when it came to directing Ava. During the shooting of *The Night of the Iguana* in 1963, in an attempt to better understand her character Maxine, she had asked whether the woman was in fact in love or not with the former priest played by Richard Burton. "Don't worry sweetheart," replied Huston, "just stand there and be beautiful. That's all you have to do."[3]

John Huston shot a furious Ava in the sequence, now a classic, of her midnight swim. He was getting back at her for a twenty-year-old grudge when a very young Ava had dodged his advances by throwing herself fully dressed into his villa pool. Ava, as many stars, was a male fantasy come true.

She suffered from knowing that on the screen she was merely the expression of what she inspired in the minds of producers, screenwriters, directors – that is, of their desires and dreams. She was a larger-than-life image projected to create strong erotic impact just within the bounds of the Hays Code. The Code was a strict standard of ethics and aesthetics that laid down what could or could not be shown, and was the trademark of MGM's films. Based on this, symbolism, transfer and distorted meanings became terms of an erotic language.

Even the fabrics used for Ava's costumes participated in the suggestiveness needed to dodge censorship: the shimmering black satin of Ava's dress in *The Killers* made her a "black mare of the devil."[4] Publicity for *The Barefoot Contessa* was also built on this concept, declaring her *"The most beautiful animal in the world."* In *Mogambo* Ava was given the nickname "Honey Bear" to suggest a sweet and inoffensive plaything. Each time, however, the aim was to propose a sexual horizon offered by a mindless woman of pleasure who acts just as an animal does, that is, purely by instinct.

Speaking of the heroine Maria Vargas in *The Barefoot Contessa,* a woman torn from her own world to be made into a movie star, Ava remarked:

She learned very early in life that you shouldn't expect too much from men. They took advantage of her poverty. They took advantage of her sensitivity. They took advantage of her desire for love. Like Maria, I've been let down by love. But all the hurts left in a woman like Maria and me never destroy our capacity, our need for love.[5]

To exist only through the eyes of men or those of the public. That was the price to pay. But Ava Gardner was rather indifferent to glory and the American idea of

14

Pandora, the bearer of a mythic name, cannot escape her destiny. She enters the legend of the Flying Dutchman. Here in Albert Lewin's *Pandora and the Flying Dutchman* (1950).

success, though she was one of its most striking representatives. In the beginning she went along with much that Metro-Goldwyn-Mayer wanted for her. But over the years the young woman's character grew more assertive. Ava was a star despite herself, disappointed and dissatisfied with being a sex symbol rather than an actress, and she eventually rebelled against the Hollywood bosses.

As a rebel she provocatively inflicted her caprices, carrying these conflicts over into her private life too, with her third husband Frank Sinatra. And also in her dealings with the press. Indeed she had ended up hating journalists, for they reflected her movie queen image that was such a heavy burden, and so very diminishing, and in the end so pathetic.

"She remains," summed up one journalist, "that boundless adventurer whose freedom... shows how some stars manage to be greater than the movie industry to which they have given themselves, by not letting it completely dominate them."[6] Just as Maria, Ava was also elu-

1942.
Ava does not know
how to do much
more than just
be beautiful.

The forceful
Victoria Jones in
Bhowani Junction.

psychological support, which for Ava Gardner became the worse thing she could ever have turned to. Unlike many actors and actresses who lost themselves to drinking beyond the point of no return, alcohol protected Ava. Ava was not Marilyn. Ava demanded excitement, drink, noise and rage rather than withdrawal into depression.

Spain was the most obvious demonstration of her determination to free herself from the bonds of Hollywood. She began to seriously consider moving to Spain in 1950 during the shooting of *Pandora and the Flying Dutchman*. This idea reflected a search for an identity, a way of creating a new persona in a new place. After Garbo, Ava was the second star to leave Hollywood.

It was a very personal and rather mysterious decision. Ava saw in this obscure country – for Spain at the time had not yet opened up to tourism – a refuge from the agonies of her formidable celebrity. She felt an affinity with Spanish culture, loved bullfighting and flamenco. Yet to what degree Ava had a true taste for Spain and its culture was uncertain. "I think she liked flamenco so much," said Reenie, "because it annoyed everybody else, I really do."[2]

Alcohol was a refuge, Spain was a place of exile. Both were escapes, whether psychological or geographical. Ava Gardner's life resembled a wanderlust of body and soul. "I have always loved travel. I'm a gypsy. Two suitcases and a ticket and I'm content,"[8] she once admitted.

Ava's destinations were more and more numerous in her search for a home port. Some good films? They were few and far between in her rather unwieldy filmography: 72 films over 45 years. This was without any career management or planning, nor good business sense, whether under MGM from 1941 to 1958, or under self-management after that. Free or not to make her decisions, as a young actress or in her later years, admittedly Ava Gardner had never been capable of managing her career. Nor her personal life, for that matter.

Under the Studio's tyrannical stranglehold Ava of course had little freedom. The secret of a fulfilled career is a combination of talent, aptitude, good luck, the capacity to adapt to the system and its constraints, and a good deal of willpower. It is rather doubtful whether Ava Gardner ever showed much tenacity. She often treated her career in an astonishingly offhanded manner. An ideal filmography, of course, is also pleasant to imagine, without the flops (due to studio decisions and also personal errors of judgment). This would have comprised about a dozen titles, linked by a theme run-

sive. Her belief was that she was "too free to become attached to happiness."[7]

Just as Maria, Ava fled those who thought they could buy her. She took a distance from the world that had created her. Alcohol, yes alcohol helped. She did not choose alcohol, but it corresponded to a lifestyle that was normal for Hollywood society. Ava went along with it, helped by Artie Shaw, who was not content to simply elevate her to the rank of a well-mannered and cultured woman. Alcohol was a dangerous ning like a silver thread through the body of works, each intimately bound to the actress's own life.

A few great names in cinema and literature did help Ava show a bit of what she could do. They offered her the possibility of delving into the depths of her soul and led to her own self-analysis. Ava in real life eventually grew to resemble the heroines of Ernest Hemingway, Albert Lewin, John Huston, Joseph Mankiewicz, George Cukor and Stanley Kramer.

These were characters destined to wander eternally, victims of thwarted or impossible love, and overcome by an intense sense of failure. They were lost, desperate characters who surrendered themselves blindly to their passions. Characters too beautiful or too demanding to be satisfied with simply being a common mortal, and who found refuge in a nocturnal existence that was either totally disconnected from reality or beyond the threshold of death.

In the painful moments of a tumultuous love life and a career that refused her the only recognition to which she truly aspired, though she deserved it – that of serious actress – Ava liked to dream of quiet homespun joys. Yet was this not simply a utopia? Was Ava in fact made for anything other than what she became? Ava, fundamentally dispassionate and never very interested in cinema, was always on the fringe of this world, constantly unfulfilled, in perpetual craving as she quested after a vague happiness that remained forever elusive. A woman so uncertain of her desire that she could find her true equilibrium only in her desire for this uncertainty.

Though Ava Gardner tirelessly repeated how she was not a good actress, how she could not have cared less about her roles, how all she wanted was enough money so that she did not have to make another movie again, she still liked to go over the good reviews that proved the indisputable merit of her work.

Fewer stars so disparaged the profession. How many times had Ava declared that she despised every moment of filming? At those times she seemed to forget that she was, and would always be, the magnificent and disturbing Pandora, the pathetic Cynthia of *The Snows of Kilimanjaro*, the immortal barefoot Contessa, the devastating Victoria Jones of *Bhowani Junction*.

Ava never believed in herself or in her capacity to move people. As her life drew to an end in comfortable seclusion in London, one winter evening she called Michael Winner who had directed her in *The Sentinel*: "I'm watching *The Barefoot Contessa* on TV – I was pretty, wasn't I?"

How long was it before she finally recognized the cinematic heritage which film buffs around the world could thank her for? Ava Gardner finally found grace in her own eyes. Reconciled with herself, with her beauty and talent, she could depart, her spirit at rest.

Apprenticeship: 1941-1945

Ava Gardner was quite young when she was suddenly plunged into a world for which she was totally unprepared. Emotionally she still looked to her mother for guidance, and professionally Ava was to become a secretary. The radical change in the course of her life demanded a new very special apprenticeship.

Between *H.M. Pulham Esquire* in 1941, to her role in the film which gave Ava her first true acting break, *Whistle Stop* in 1945, she appeared in about twenty all but forgotten productions. These were films mainly intended as vehicles for the big stars such as Lionel Barrymore, Norma Shearer, Van Heflin, Van Johnson, Gene Kelly, Joan Crawford, or John Wayne. Ava's roles could all be shot in only one or two days.

In 1942, with the United States' official entry into the war, film directors were requisitioned by the army and artists sent to entertain the troops. The studios turned to producing either propaganda or escapist entertainment. The titles of these films: *Joe Smith American, Hitler's Madman, Pilot N° 5, Reunion in France, Music for Millions, Two Girls and a Sailor,* were all a sign of the times. And Ava made her modest contribution.

One of the first films to be born out of this patriotic wave, *Ghosts on the Loose*, gave Ava her first chance to act. Despite idiotic lines galore, her performance in the film nevertheless prompted MGM to cast her in bit parts in *Three Men in White* (1943), *Maisie Goes to Reno* (1944), and *She Went to the Races* (1945). Her name began to appear here and there in reviews. Yet Ava never truly managed to draw the press away from publicizing the sensational adventures and misadventures of her private life and seriously consider her qualities as an actress.

It all began during the summer of 1939, when Ava's mother Mary Elizabeth Gardner and her youngest daughter Ava went to visit "Bappie" who was living in New York. Ava had called her eldest sister Bappie, instead of Beatrice, ever since she could remember. Ava was the last of the children still living at home with her mother. The two had moved to Rock Ridge in North Carolina after Ava's father, Jonas Gardner, had died the year before. Ava was the youngest child in the big family. She was seven years younger than Myra, and nineteen years younger than Bappie. Her other sisters and brothers were Elsie Mae, Inez, Raymond, and Jonas Melvin, whom they all called Jack.

All of Ava's brothers and sisters were now married. The eldest child Bappie, however, was a freewheeling woman with a mind of her own. She had decided to start a new life far from the reproachful eyes of her parents, who frowned upon her recent divorce. Their father Jonas was an Irish Catholic, the fourth generation of tobacco farmers. And their mother Mary Elizabeth, whom everyone called Mollie, was a no-nonsense hardworking woman from a family of Scottish Baptists.

The Gardners were staunch churchgoing puritans. Jonas, in fact, had helped build the Brogden church and Mollie generously helped out at Sunday school. As in all God-fearing families, divorce was simply not a word in their vocabulary. Bappie first thought of moving to Richmond, but was then lured by the attractions of New York. There she found a job, and eventually married Larry Tarr,

Between 1941 and 1945, Ava posed for some one hundred photos and appeared in twenty or so minor films, most of which were made to entertain the troops.

whose father had created the Tarr Photographic Studios, located on a bustling street in Manhattan.

Tarr's photographer's eye was attracted to the fresh good looks of his sister-in-law Ava, whom he affectionately called "Dollface". The young girl inspired him to take some Southern Belle type pictures in the style made so popular by Vivien Leigh as Scarlett O'Hara. Ava posed wide-eyed in a straw hat demurely tied in a bow under her chin. Larry Tarr placed a sepia print of the photo in his shop window. The shop was ideally located at the corner of 5th Avenue and 63rd Street. The photo immediately drew the attention of passersby. One of them, Barney Duhan, explained:

> I was running late for a party, and thought what lousy luck it was with my looks and my income that I didn't have a date for the party. I saw the picture – and said, out loud, "Gee, wouldn't she be a fantastic date! Maybe I can get her telephone number!" So I went to a telephone on the corner and called the shop where the picture was.[9]

Barney Duhan claimed to be a talent scout and hinted that Metro-Goldwyn-Mayer (the studio in fact had just produced *Gone With the Wind*) might be interested in this girl with such fantastic looks. Ava, however, was no longer in New York and had gone back to North Carolina for her second year of secretarial studies at Atlantic Christian College. When Bappie heard the news she was of course very excited for her sister, but not truly surprised. She had always been convinced that Ava had all it took to make it in a profession where looks really counted. In fact, every time her sister had visited her in New York she had tried to find her work as a model, though without any luck.

Bappie's husband, who loved New York's nightlife, had sometimes taken young Ava on his rounds. One night they had met a small band of jazz musicians looking for a lead singer. Larry Tarr had even paid for a demo with Ava singing the one and only song she knew: *Amapola*. Larry had always been just as convinced as his wife that Ava had the makings of a big star. So, little did it matter when Barney Duhan later turned out to be an errand boy in the law department of Loew's Inc. instead of an important talent scout. They saw him above all as a sign of destiny.

With Bappie's help, Tarr worked all night making blow ups of Ava's best pictures and the next morning dropped them off at MGM's New York offices. All of this excitement left Ava completely indifferent. Acting simply did not interest her. Singing, on the other hand, was her real passion. She had been very disappointed

when the bandleader had not contacted her after receiving the demo.

Ava had just graduated from secretarial school and had hopes of getting her first office job when friendly, easygoing Marvin Schenck, head of talent at MGM, offered to see her. The reading did not go well. Ava had such a heavy southern accent that Marvin Schenck could hardly even understand her when she said she was "Aavah Gahd-nuh". As she read her part to a dumbstruck Schenck trying to feed her her lines, Ava did not seem to have the slightest idea what was expected of her.

Al Altman did not have any more luck when it came to directing her in a screen test. He had her sit down, cross her legs, glance right, left, get up, walk across the room and pick up a vase. "She was lousy. I told her, 'Look up, Ava, look down, smile.' She couldn't do anything. We all looked at each other and shook our heads. She was hopeless," the director remembered. Yet as Silas Seadler had to admit, "Maybe she looked hopeless when Al shot it. But when we ran the test – you never saw anything like it. She just took our collective breaths away."[9]

The series of screen tests were concluded by the traditional interview. Ava relaxed and opened up a little. She talked about her five brothers and sisters, the surprise in the family when she was born on Christmas Eve, 24 December 1922. She explained she was from a small town in North Carolina, and that she had been called Ava after her aunt Ava on her father's side. Her mother had given her the middle name Lavinia because she liked the way the two names sounded together.

Aware of how tremendously handicapped she would be with her accent and diction, Marvin Schenck sent a silent test back to Hollywood. George Sidney was then in charge of hiring new talent. He was directing the shorts for the series *Our Gang* and *Pete Smith* in which Ava later made her screen debut. He was as enthusiastic as the New York office about Ava and told them to have her sent to Hollywood right away. Ten years later, it was George Sidney who got her cast as Julie La Verne, the alcoholic woman in *Show Boat*.

Ava was offered one of the standard six-month contracts at 50 dollars a week, which was considered enough to give the Studio exclusivity over a future star. Though a movie career was not one of Ava's big dreams, being a secretary had never been a burning ambition either. So, Ava thought, why not just go and "breathe the same air as Clark Gable!"[2] Ava's mother Mollie, who was seriously ill, beamed with pride when she was shown Ava's screen tests. She decided to let her daughter leave for Holly-

wood under the condition, however, that Bappie accompany her.

The sister who had so scandalized the family with her divorce, now left her job as supervisor in the handbag section of a department store. She seized this opportunity to make good her separation from her second husband Larry Tarr, since he had to stay and run the family photography business in New York. Undoubtedly, at this point, it was Bappie who was more attracted to Hollywood than Ava.

After what seemed an endless journey across the United States, the Gardner sisters finally arrived and stepped off the train into the blazing California sun. They were met by Milton Weiss, head of publicity at Metro-Goldwyn-Mayer. It was 23 August 1941. One of Milton Weiss' rituals upon the arrival of any new recruit was to take her on a tour of the lot.

MGM was at the height of its glory at that time and had the biggest stars in the business under contract such as Greta Garbo, Clark Gable, Joan Crawford, Spencer Tracy, and James Stewart. MGM's films had the biggest production budgets in the industry too. The ten Oscars for its *Gone With the Wind* had crowned it indisputably king and attracted the finest artistic talent anywhere. Yet the Studio was also on the eve of its decline. The ominous effects of the Anti-Trust Law and television were already preparing to deal a disastrous blow to its supremacy. And soon the war would be wreaking havoc in its European market.

Nevertheless, for the moment, production was still in full swing. The twenty-seven sound stages in Culver City were working non-stop. On one of these they were shooting *Babes on Broadway*. As soon as Ava stepped onto the sound stage, a strange androgynous creature came up to her like a dwarf version of Carmen Miranda. From under a huge bright basket of exotic fruit peered a face smeared with makeup. It was only after a long pause that she recognized Mickey Rooney.

Rooney personified the MGM spirit par excellence: ingenious, dynamic, enterprising and funny. The hero of comedies and musicals, he was a dynamo of the bursting youth and energy of his twenty years. He was very short and not particularly handsome, but his unfailing smile and unbridled imagination were irresistible. In his popular series *Andy Hardy* (1938-1946), a mirror of wholesome respectable America, with the inseparable Judy Garland by his side, he played Judge Hardy's smart-aleck wisecracking son. He was always getting himself into trouble and inevitably turning to Dad to bail him out.

The actor Rooney was from a family of vaudevillians and got his start in the movies at the age of six. He was so much of a performer down to his toes that in everyday life "there wasn't a minute when he wasn't on stage."[2] Though an inexhaustible life of the party, he was excruciating to live with. He seemed to compensate for the insecurity of his shortness by a 24-hour frenzy.

Ava remembered the call she got at the Plaza Hotel that same evening she had been introduced to him on the set of *Babes on Broadway:* "Hello Miss Gardner, this is Mickey Rooney. What about dinner tonight?"[2] And Mickey, with his contagious enthusiasm, knew just how to dazzle the budding starlets of the Studio. Ava did finally accept his invitation, though it took fifteen days of non-stop calls from Rooney. How could she not be impressed with those dates out on the town in the most elegant restaurants and in vogue night spots in the city? Ava tried not to look too enthralled when Mickey Rooney introduced her to some of his friends such as Lana Turner, Judy Garland, Esther Williams, Kathryn Grayson, or Elizabeth Taylor.

In the meantime, Ava and Bappie were obliged to move into reasonably priced lodgings at the Hollywood Wilcox. Bappie found a job in a department store, and Ava began her long apprenticeship at MGM. Every morning she got up at dawn to catch the several buses that finally got her to the Studio on time. Extremely conscious of her complete ignorance of what it meant to be a movie star, Ava was still quite oblivious to the tremendous impact she produced on men. "She can't act, she can't talk, she's terrific!" was the way MGM's big boss Louis B. Mayer had summed it up.

Indeed Ava was stunningly beautiful. Her simplicity and total lack of pretense only heightened this beauty. The Studio was well known for its assembly line treatment used to produce a chain of look-alike dolls that conformed to the MGM aesthetic model (George Cukor's spoof *A Star Is Born* remains memorable). Ava had absolutely no need to be remade. She acquiesced to much of the procedure, but put her foot down when it came to plucking out her eyebrows and replacing them with a thin pencil line. Sydney Guilaroff, MGM's master hairstylist, who later became Ava's friend, confidant and occasional lover recalled:

She had so much elegance and natural beauty that instinctively she resisted MGM's elaborate makeup process, consenting only to a light coat of pancake. She applied her own lipstick and added a little mascara to her eyelashes, then powdered down. She rather liked a sheen on her face, a natural tone value, and I admired and encouraged her for that.[10]

"I thought Ava was the prettiest girl I'd ever seen," Ava's childhood friend recalled. "Her voice was so deep and husky that everybody thought she had a cold or laryngitis, but we soon learned it was her natural voice."[11] Gertrude Vogeler was the voice coach at Metro. In this department Ava had everything to learn. She was virtually incapable of reciting a single line from a script. This elderly sympathetic woman, whose dedication even went as far as letting starlets in difficulty stay at her home, offered Ava all of her support and kindness.

Hollywood was a spawning ground for aspiring actresses kept under contract to ensure a steady flow of extras to the MGM studios. As Robert Parrish so aptly evoked in his book,[12] this pool of beauties was also unofficially tapped by male members of cast and crews alike for other needs. During shootings, it was not unusual for an extra to be assigned to a producer or a director as a "personal companion". The bitter realization of *The Barefoot Contessa* heroine Myrna comes to mind when producer Kirk Edwards alludes to prostitution. Nevertheless, in Ava's case, Arlene Dahl remembered:

> One game she did not play was the couch game. She never had to and she never did. She was not promiscuous, she was true – true blue. When she was married, she was married. She didn't fool around; there was never any scandal about her. She was exactly the opposite of the roles she played.[2]

Ava had always had a romantic idea of love and marriage based on the model of her parents: "... no matter how much fun I was having, I was not going to bed with any man until I was married to him. Sex before marriage was definitely out."[2] And Mickey Rooney was prepared to do anything, even to get officially engaged to Ava, for her favors. He soon realized however that this also meant convincing, that is, charming, her chaperon Bappie too. He immediately set to work and won her over. Bappie, older and more world-wise was determined not to miss out on anything this exciting new movie world could bring. She used her influence to persuade her younger sister to give Rooney a chance. On Christmas 1941 Ava celebrated her nineteenth birthday and gave in to both her sister and the actor.

One of Ava's first roles was in *We Were Dancing*, a simple walk-on part in which she crosses the lobby of a hotel. This film was the high point in the career of Norma Shearer, one of cinema's greatest pre-war stars. The actress' career was entirely managed by her husband, producer Irving Thalberg, whom she married in 1927. After his death in 1936 she gave up acting.

Ava married Mickey Rooney just before *We Were Dancing* was released in the United States in 1942. Everyone considered Ava a basely calculating woman who had married Rooney only for her own professional ambitions. As far as they were concerned Ava was just another dumb starlet ready to do anything for success. Ava Gardner accepted to become Ava Rooney on 10 January 1942, barely five months after her arrival in Hollywood, simply because she could not take Mickey Rooney's spoiled brat performance any longer. His non-stop harassment had finally convinced Ava that perhaps he was truly in love with her. She discovered too late, however, that once he had gotten what he wanted, he was back with his buddies again boasting about his exploit.

"The plain facts are that being Mrs. Rooney *never* gave me a single boost in the direction of stardom. Mickey *never* tried to make me an actress, *never* taught me anything, and *never* got me an acting job."[2] Today the question that comes to mind is rather how could the tall, majestic Ava have married this little man whose Andy Hardy movies so buoyed the hearts of all America? At the time though, people were wondering quite the reverse. That is, how could a national idol like Mickey Rooney so disappoint his public by marrying a complete unknown? This was the attitude for many years and was even encouraged by Ava herself, who continued to declare that she was not a true actress. And thus the image continued to be nurtured of an Ava whose success was due entirely to the men she married.

Though MGM strongly opposed the marriage, Mickey Rooney eventually cajoled the paternal Louis B. Mayer into giving his grudging approval. The Studio, however, long held this against Ava. Perhaps the many years she was kept from truly showing what she could do were in part due to Louis B. Mayer's feelings of vengeance. He tyrannically ruled over the careers of his actors and actresses and also over every aspect of their private lives. All marriages were submitted for approval to the big boss. Contracts included rigorous morals clauses and Ava was obliged, for example, to never do anything "to prejudice the producer or the motion picture industry in general."[2]

Would not her marriage to Mickey Rooney seriously jeopardize his image? Would his female fans ever forgive

10 January 1942. Scandal at Metro-Goldwyn-Mayer: international star Mickey Rooney marries Ava Gardner, a nineteen-year-old extra.

him for marrying a mere extra? Did he not risk losing his faithful female audiences who, during wartime, would make up more than half his theatre audience?

The wedding took place in strict privacy, in a Presbyterian church in Ballard, a small town at the foot of the Santa Ynez mountains. This was the first of Mickey Rooney's eight marriages, and was entirely under the control of MGM. Bappie, Mickey Rooney's parents, his step-father and the actor's publicist Les Petersen attended. Les Petersen decided how everything was to be done, right down to how the photos should be taken to hide how much shorter the groom was than the bride (Ava towered a head over Mickey). Les' delicate task was to keep an eye on Mickey whose penchant for girls, booze and gambling was familiar to everyone close to him. In fact, in real life he was the antithesis of the screen personality which Les Peterson was hired to uphold. It was imperative that the public continue to believe that Mickey lived just as in his films, according to the irreproachable morals that had won him a special Oscar.

Ava and Mickey's marriage was announced to the press in the midst of tragic world events: just one month before, the Japanese had attacked the American naval base at Pearl Harbor. Germany and Italy had declared war on the United States. MGM was participating in the war effort by organizing for its artists to entertain the troops. The couple's honeymoon was also (business obliged) combined with a cross-country promotion of Rooney's new film *Life Begins for Andy Hardy*.

The newlyweds made a detour through North Carolina's capital of Raleigh where Ava's sister Inez was caring for their mother, now in critical condition. It was a very special and moving visit despite the bitter sadness caused by the press. It looked down on Ava's background and made it even worse by headlining that the Cinderella marriage united "the daughter of a poor tenant farmer and the greatest star of Hollywood." No one close to Ava could see any truth in this exaggerated version of her family background.

When the flourishing tobacco era began to wane, the Gardners had of course suffered the effects of falling prices. Ava's father Jonas was forced to leave sharecropping and go to work in a sawmill. He also got a job as a maintenance man at the old Brogden school. This was a training school for teachers where Mollie helped with the meals. Of course, during the Depression, the school was then shut down. The family moved to Newport News in Virginia and Mollie found employment in a boarding house for shipyard workers. Despite these difficulties, which were also shared by millions of Americans during those years, the Gardner family never suffered poverty.

The newlyweds' trip wound up in Washington for a reception to celebrate President Roosevelt's birthday. Ava felt as if she were in a dream: "Six months ago I was in Wilson, North Carolina, worrying about what sort of secretarial job I might get, and there I was in the White House being introduced to the President of the United States and the First Lady. It was unbelievable - absolutely unbelievable!"[2]

MGM eventually resigned itself to Mickey Rooney's marriage and decided to make *The Courtship of Andy Hardy* in which Andy Hardy gets married. Ava Gardner appeared in a bit part as a box office cashier in one of the filler shorts of the series *Our Gang / Mighty Lak a Goat* (1942). "How many?" she asks four children who concoct a stain remover that smells so badly that even the actors in the film leave the screen. In this little film, a precursor of the visual invention used in the *Purple Rose of Cairo*, Ava gratifies us with a crinkling of her nose as she impatiently closes her till.

Ava was of course not mentioned in the credits of this film debut, nor did her name appear for other bit parts such as King Vidor's *H.M. Pulham Esquire* (in which Ava played a wealthy socialite); *This Time for Keeps* (where she is glimpsed in a car); *Kid Glove Killer* (as she waits on cars in a drive-in); or in *Sunday Punch* (as a spectator at a boxing match). A single line of dialogue exchanged with Lionel Barrymore in *Calling Dr. Gillespie*, another film of the popular series, drew her for an instant out of her mutism when she announced: "Doctor Gillespie, the other patient has just arrived."

Ava soon discovered the great abyss between the screen character Andy Hardy and the real-life actor who portrayed him. Mickey Rooney certainly did not let marriage cramp his style and, as Ava soon realized, he was an inexhaustible skirt chaser. As soon as he was sure that Ava was his, he went back to his bad habits. When his young wife was urgently hospitalized for appendicitis, Mickey saw the perfect chance to have some of his new girlfriends over to share his empty bed. Ava was hurt and angry but said nothing until the evening when a drunken Mickey went too far and, boasting to some friends, proudly shared the list of his conquests from his telephone book to everyone.

During the first year of their marriage, Ava and Mickey Rooney separated twice. In April, Ava went to live with her sister again, and Bappie eventually managed

Two years after signing an exclusive contract with MGM, Ava is approached by an unknown producer to appear in *Ghosts on the Loose* (directed by William Beaudine in 1943). It was a film in the series *East Side Kids*. Here with Blanche Payson.

to get the newlyweds to make up. The couple moved to Bel Air to a bigger house on Stone Canyon Road. Nevertheless, Mickey seemed to live everywhere except at home. When it was not a movie, it was his girlfriends, or boozing with buddies, playing golf or going to the horse races, and by that winter the couple were again separated. It was a difficult year for Ava whose beliefs had been badly shaken and who did not have much confidence in herself as an actress either.

Only Sydney Guilaroff, who carefully studied all her rushes, had words of encouragement for her when he told her, "You're a natural-born actress and one day you're going to be a great star."[10] In the meantime, Ava posed for photos in the most varied settings and seasons, and continued appearing in films that reflected the world situation. *Hitler's Madman*, directed by Douglas Sirk, showed her in one of her rare appearances as a blond when she was part of a group of stu-

dents promised to German soldiers. In *Reunion in France*, directed by Jules Dassin, Ava was Marie, a sales girl at Montanot's. Joan Crawford, a good client in difficulty, goes to beg for a job at the famous haute couture shop. The story was set during the war in occupied Paris. All of the characters speak German, including Ava, from what we can gather from the one line she stammers rather unconvincingly.

Ava Gardner and Mickey Rooney's divorce was made official on 21 May 1943 in Los Angeles by Judge Thurmond Clarke. The grounds against Mickey Rooney were "extreme mental cruelty". Ava kept such gifts as her car, jewelry and furs. She waived the claim she had on half of Mickey's property and settled for twenty-five thousand dollars. By a bitter twist of fate, Ava's mother Mollie died that very same day of cancer, making it one of the saddest days in Ava's life.

In Hollywood it was common practice for actors

In this first bit part, Ava was a model submissive young bride. Here with Rick Vallin (the groom) and surrounded by the boisterous incorrigible "Kids" after the wedding, in *Ghosts on the Loose*.

and actresses under contract to be loaned out to other studios and to be cast in movies by other producers. Though Ava hated this policy, in fact ironically her best films were eventually made thanks to this practice. Apart from the rare exceptions such as *The Great Sinner* and *Show Boat*, and above all George Cukor's *Bhowani Junction*, produced by MGM, the Studio had never shown much interest in seriously promoting her career. Ava had been under contract with the major for almost two years when she was loaned out to make *Ghosts on the Loose* for the small-time outfit Monogram. Though far from a masterpiece, *Ghosts on the Loose* had the distinction of giving Ava her first true role. She was the heroine Betty in this silly low-budget East Side Kids comedy, shot in only one week with no retakes:

Ghosts on the Loose was a piece of sweet, unsophisticated rubbish. But it did give me one sudden thrill that I've never forgotten. And although it's happened a hundred times since then, the feeling of that first wonderful moment never returned. Bappie and I were walking in an area of Los Angeles where the theatres didn't show the best of movies. I don't think they even showed B pictures – the movies they played were of the XYZ variety. But suddenly Bappie gripped my arm and said excitedly, "Ava! Look!" High up, outside one of the movie houses, there was this huge blazing sign in electric lights:

GHOSTS ON THE LOOSE
with Ava Gardner

Oh, my God, I couldn't believe it. Who in the world had decided to put those words up there I'll never know. Per-

In Richard Thorpe's *Two Girls and a Sailor* (1944) Ava falls asleep on her partner's shoulder (Frank Sully). She is exhausted after performing in four shows daily at the Deyo Sisters' club (on her right, Jimmy Durante).

haps it was because I'd been married to Mickey; I certainly didn't have any star status of my own. But at that moment I didn't really care about the how's or the why's. My name was up in lights for the very first time in my life. I've got to say it was a thrill. Then it wore off, and I've never had that feeling again. Ever.[2]

Of course all of this publicity seems excessive when in fact the East Side Kids were the real stars of the movie from beginning to end. As Aurélien Ferenczi recalled:

The success of Wyler's *Dead End* had inspired a series of neighborhood comedies, tragicomic teenage gang adventures. So there was *Dead End Kids*, and then, after the first group broke up, *East Side Kids*.[13]

Given the world situation at the time, the Kids dis-

cover a Nazi unit whose hideout is next door to Jack's house. He is a newly married young man and has just bought the house. The Kids, who want to fix up the place for him, find themselves accidentally in the Nazi's hideout. The ghostly face of Bela Lugosi appears and disappears in the oval frame of a painting hanging on the wall to try to dissuade the Kids from pursuing their investigation. Everything is a pretext for burlesque comedy right up to the unmasking with its message: Nazism is a contagious disease from which we must guard ourselves. Otherwise we risk developing swastikas on our faces like oozing sores.

The recent discovery[14] of Ava Gardner in this film amuses more than saddens. Betty is a docile woman catering to her husband's every desire. The script gave her some pretty submissive lines ("Anything you want to

In Willis Goldbeck's *Three Men in White* (1944), Jean Brown uses her charms to distract Dr. Adams (Van Johnson) from his professional obligations.

do is alright with me."), which were quite the opposite of the essence of her future roles. The wedding ceremony was a rare occasion in Ava Gardner's filmography. Never again would any of her films give her the opportunity of such a scene.

The role of Jean Brown in *Three Men in White* came closest to anticipating Ava Gardner's future direction. After 1943, which was devoted to more fleeting appearances as cashier, receptionist or check girl, respectively in *Lost Angel*, *Swing Fever*, *Two Girls and a Sailor*, MGM decided to cast its new recruit as a seductress in another movie in the Dr. Gillespie series. In *Three Men in White*, Dr. Gillespie tests the integrity of one of his promising interns (Van Johnson) to see if he has the necessary force of character for the medical profession. The test consists

in seeing whether the young man can resist two seductresses, a young nurse, played by Marilyn Maxwell, and a patient, Ava Gardner.

In one of the scenes Ava (Jean Brown) comes to the emergency ward in the middle of the night. Van Johnson soon discovers that behind the alcoholic she is pretending to be, is concealed the true self-sacrificing soul of a devoted daughter with an invalid mother under her care. Charles Higham remembered:

> Her performance was charming: under Lillian Burns' scrupulous guidance, she was convincingly beat up and besotted as an alcoholic, and played the scenes of seduction with a cool, poised sense of comedy.[9]

With *Three Men in White*, which was released in the

United States in April 1944, came the first reviews which mentioned Ava Gardner: "Marilyn Maxwell and Ava Gardner, two of the smoothest young sirens to be found, are superb, and should delight the studio with their histrionic conduct here," chimed *Hollywood Reporter*. Yet three months later, upon the release of *Maisie Goes to Reno*, in which Ava Gardner plays a haughty and arrogant millionairess, Bosley Crowther of the *New York Times* launched a very negative campaign against Ava, whom he described as "abominable, weak, sultry but stupid."

Ava was discouraged at the end of 1944 and was quite aware of the mediocrity of *Three Men in White*: "I thought it was a pretty bad picture," she wrote to a friend, "but I liked my part".[11] She was torn by her divorce and a tense, ambiguous, and downright violent relationship with Howard Hughes. Ever since seeing her in the film, Hughes had fallen hopelessly in love with her. At times Ava seriously considered giving up Hollywood and going back home to North Carolina. She yearned to find a job as a secretary and marry a nice ordinary young man. However, she opted for another way out and took refuge in the night. Herman Hover, the former manager of Ciro's, said:

Ava was the most constant and the most intense customer I ever had. She'd come in with the whole gang, or sometimes stag – she was one of the few Hollywood girls who'd dream of going stag – and she'd dance and talk to the bandleader and drink a few, and then she'd want to go on to a party afterward. She never misbehaved or got unseemly. Often I'd have her up to my big house in Beverly Hills with Lana Turner and other party-loving stars and we'd start all over again at three o'clock in the morning. No sex, just a lot of lewd jokes and laughter and fun.

From left to right: Roland Dupree, Ann Sothern, Paul Cavanagh, and Marta Linden in a scene from Harry Beaumont's *Maisie Goes to Reno* (1944).

Opposite page: With James Craig and Frances Gifford posing in the studio for the promotion of Willis Goldbeck's *She Went to the Races* (1945).

33

More than her very basic acting, it is Ava's beauty, her elegance and her presence that subjugates viewers in *She Went to the Races*. Here again with James Craig.

Then everyone would drag themselves off at dawn, Ava looking as good as new.[9]

It was during one of these parties that Frances Heflin, the wife of the actor Van Helfin, introduced Artie Shaw to Ava. He was just out of the army, thirty-five and an attractive man and brilliant musician. He was entirely self-educated and terribly macho. Ava fell in love with him at once: "I suppose that Artie was the first intelligent, intellectual male I'd ever met, and he bowled me over."[2]

It was 1945. Ava Gardner had now been under contract with MGM for four years. Her salary had risen to 200 dollars a week. And though by then she had made twenty-two films, Ava's career was still yet to begin.

At the time, Philip Yordan was not yet the well-known pen name used for many stories by screenwriters who had been blacklisted for anti-American activities by the Commission in force at the time. He was simply a young

man getting started in his career and looking for work. His agent Charles Feldman had just acquired the rights for a screen adaptation of *Whistle Stop*. The derisory price (7,500 dollars) seemed in itself good enough reason for Charles Feldman to take an interest in the novel. The other was his encounter with the German-Jewish producer in exile in the United States, Seymour Nebenzal. Indeed, Nebenzal was looking for low-budget projects. Neither of the two men was aware of what *Whistle Stop* was about. A short while later Philip Yordan discovered that the novel was about prostitution and the incestuous relationship between a brother and sister. These were, in other words, themes that were totally impossible to make into a movie.

Philip Yordan completely re-wrote the story of this mysterious woman. After two years in Chicago, Mary returns to her hometown laden with gifts obviously offered by her lovers, or rather, clients. This was the only perceptible trace of the original novel's content. Mary has decided to leave her former troubled life behind. The

The European promotion of *Whistle Stop* ignores George Raft (center) and uses Ava Gardner's newly acquired celebrity, referring to her as "the disturbing star of *The Killers* and *Singapore*". On the left, Jimmy Conlin.

screen adaptation conceals the brother-sister relationship. Kenny (played by George Raft), is a hoodlum who Mary puts back on the road to respectability. Yet they had not found the actress to play Mary, and shooting was to begin in a few short weeks. Producer Seymour Nebenzal and writer Philip Yordan were getting desperate:

> We couldn't find anybody suitable, which was a polite way of saying no one wanted to play the part. Nebenzal and I on our dates used to go to the Mocambo every night. All of the "in" movie crowd did. You could see everyone there. And Ava was there all the time. Nebenzal saw her there one night and said, "She's doing nothing at Metro, she looks great, why don't we use her?" I said: "Fine!" I should argue? 5,000 to Metro, and the dame was ours.[9]

It is worth noting that it was two European exiled emigrés (Nebenzal and the French director of Russian descent Léonide Moguy), sensitive to Ava's wild beauty, who were the first to give the actress her real chance. Léonide Moguy felt that MGM's training made its actresses stilted and that most American women appeared frigid. Did Ava exude a sensuality that was too obvious and threatening for MGM? Most probably. In *Whistle Stop*, Léonide Moguy let her true nature be revealed. It was not easy for Ava, fresh from her training at the Studio, to now work along completely opposite principles. Léonide Moguy was extremely patient as he directed Ava, who betrayed her inexperience constantly.

The novice actress visibly did not have the slightest idea of how to approach the role of Mary. She tried her hardest to adopt the best attitude at the right moment. Yet Ava's facial expressions in the closeups betray her uncertainty whenever she must express anything other than the simple fact of being beautiful.

Philip Yordan recalled the nightmare of those first days of filming when the producer called him on the set to re-write the opening of the film:

> I had written a scene in which Ava arrived from Chicago with a mink coat and a ring, and Raft was asking her who had given her these presents. Originally, it was a bitter, rather sophisticated sequence. But it was obvious that neither Raft nor Ava had the slightest idea how to speak the lines. I asked Moguy to call an early lunch break and I sat down and rewrote the entire scene in monosyllables. The dialogue then ran as follows: "What's that?" "A ring." "Where did you get it?" "Chicago." "From whom?" "A man." "What man?" etc. It was ghastly. Only by casting the lines in the most primitive terms could Raft or Ava learn to speak them.[9]

Whistle Stop nevertheless confirmed the intense impact that Ava Gardner was capable of producing. One scene in particular was the basis of a future role: Mary seizes the framed portrait of her rival which is on a dresser in the bedroom. Kenny tears it from her hands.

Mary: I suppose you've been pretty busy since I've been gone?
Kenny: And I'm gonna keep busy.
Mary: Are you?

Mary goes up to Kenny, puts her arms around him and as they kiss the camera slips down to the framed picture Kenny lets fall, completely melting in Ava's arms. This is all Ava Gardner needs to do to get to a man's heart. *Whistle Stop* defined the two contrasting poles of the Ava Gardner character: the femme fatale and the woman who helps restore the man she has chosen to love. At times vamp, at times a sincere woman devoted body and soul to him, as the future Pandora. At the time, *Variety* observed that Ava had given her best portraying her character, a woman in search of possessing her man.

By the time the film was released in Europe, Ava had made three other films. Publicity cashed in on them to promote *Whistle Stop*: "Ava Gardner, the disturbing star of *The Killers* and *Singapore*." The billings promised: "a great international film by the famous French director Léonide Moguy." So many superlatives could not have made its success more doubtful. *Whistle Stop* remained an insignificant mannered noir film that was soon all but forgotten. Ava Gardner's presence is the only element of interest. It was an artistic reference for the actress of her ability to act. Despite her weaknesses, Ava Gardner could finally aspire to serious roles. The opportunity was offered to her the following year.

On the horizon of her private life, too, there seemed to be a glimmer of hope. On 17 October 1945 she married Artie Shaw in Beverly Hills.

Ava is the object of everyone's desires in *Whistle Stop* (1945).

Dawn: 1946-1949

With *The Killers*, which truly launched her career, Ava Gardner gained new status under the aegis of Universal. Indeed, though Metro-Goldwyn-Mayer had kept her under exclusive contract since 1941, Ava was never mentioned in any of the Studio's credits. Out of the eight films she made from 1946 to 1949, her name appeared in only four. Universal produced three of them and RKO one.

It seemed that MGM was reluctant and embarrassed to lay claim to a creature with such a strong sexual charge, a profile which had been established since *Whistle Stop* and confirmed with *The Killers*. This image, upon which Ava had based her notoriety, placed her outside the pale of popular musical comedies and family movies. Instead she was forced to play only supporting roles for her own studio (to Deborah Kerr in *The Hucksters*, and Barbara Stanwyck in *East Side, West Side*), though MGM's competitors were billing her in leading roles that co-starred her for example with Fred MacMurray (*Singapore*), Robert Walker (*One Touch of Venus*), or Robert Mitchum (*My Forbidden Past / Carriage Entrance*).

Ava was so extraordinarily photogenic that this made up for her still apparent weaknesses as an actress. It was obvious that she had talent, and with each film she moved with increasing ease before the camera. Though MGM had contributed nothing to fostering the actress' career, as Ava's fame began to grow, the Studio suddenly began to boast of her triumphs. It was then that MGM decided to bring together for the first time on the screen one of the most passionate couples in American film, Ava Gardner and Gregory Peck, in *The Great Sinner*.

Ava's hits and flops of those days depended mainly on the quality of the scripts and the directors' interest. None of Ava's films from 1946 to 1949 could equal the artistic quality achieved in *The Killers*. Nevertheless, *One Touch of Venus* is still considered one of her best films of the period. This was as much for Ava's performance – she acted in this comedy with such brio – as for the fine directing. For the first time Ava could now be considered a complete actress.

One of Hollywood's most prominent independent producers at the time, Mark Hellinger, had been looking for backers for a screen adaptation of the story by Hemingway *Men Without Women* (*The Killers*) ever since its publication in 1927. The cost of the rights (50,000 dollars) had discouraged anyone he had approached. Though Universal had also shown complete indifference to the project initially, in 1946 it suddenly decided to finance the *The Killers* project. The studio had taken over International Pictures and now aimed at promoting quality film.

The story in the original work was entirely contained in the first ten minutes of the film. Here it relates how two killers track down and murder "the Swede", a taciturn man living in a small town in New Jersey. Film history has revealed that John Huston (not mentioned in the credits) conceived the development of the masterful technical opening. The film confirmed the excellent duo Robert Siodmak and cameraman Elwood Bredell after their collaboration on *Phantom Lady*. The film's black and white photography, with its long shadows and low-angled lights, created a disturbing atmosphere that drove

"I always felt a prisoner of my image." *Opposite page:* Ava in Robert Siodmak's *The Killers* (1946).

a tense screenplay rich in suspense-filled action. John Huston based one of the film's highpoints, the robbery of a factory payroll, on the real life confession of gangster Dutch Schultz. With studio screenwriter Anthony Veiller, who had been assigned to *The Killers*, Huston conceived the character of private detective James Reardon. He wove a complex plot filled with subterfuge and double-crossings, and developed a flashback structure reminiscent of *Citizen Kane*.

The role of Kitty Collins was specially created to enrich the film version of *Men Without Women*. As gangster Jim Colfax's woman, she convinces "the Swede" to take part in the hold-up. In fact she gets him to double-cross the gang and flee with her, taking the loot with them. Kitty eventually reveals her true plan, however, to cut the gangster out too. All that was left now was to find the actress to play Kitty Collins.

Mark Hellinger, who had seen *Whistle Stop*, decided to develop and fine tune the training that Nebenzal and Léonide Moguy had begun with Ava Gardner a few months before. Hellinger was an emigré just as Nebenzal and Moguy were. He teamed up with director Siodmak, an exile who had fled Nazi Germany. Hellinger was sensitive to Ava's personality, which was completely ignored at MGM. Ava saw in *The Killers* the opportunity to show what she could really do as an actress:

> I was very excited at the opportunity. I liked the odd but interesting twists of Kitty's character, the lack of emotional security she felt in her early years, and the way this contributed to what she turned into later... I liked Mark Hellinger at once... He trusted me from the beginning and I trusted him.[2]

Ava Gardner needed terribly to be reassured. Her marriage to Artie Shaw had drawn her into a select circle of West Coast intellectuals. The elite in fields such as music, literature, and psychoanalysis flocked to the couple's Bedford Drive mansion. Artie Shaw, who loved making a brilliant impression in society, seemed like he could converse on virtually any subject under the sun. He was appalled by his new wife's lack of culture and education. Ava once remarked:

> You don't know what it's like to be as young as I was then and know you're uneducated, to be afraid to talk to people because you're afraid even the questions you ask will be stupid. My shame at my ignorance had even caused me to lie to Artie about my age when we first met.[2]

Opposite page:
A mythic couple,
Burt Lancaster and
Ava Gardner, at the
dawn of their
careers in
The Killers (1946).

The noir film
reveals Ava
Gardner. After
Whistle Stop,
The Killers confirms
her aptitude for
playing the femme
fatale.

Convinced of his wife's intelligence, Shaw decided to bring his wife up to standard by getting her to read a list of suggested books. He also initiated her into the game of chess. His constant criticism finally convinced her to enroll in UCLA for correspondence courses. "I can still remember showing my report card to everyone on the set of *The Killers* and bragging about my B+. The company didn't know whether to laugh or cry,"[2] she commented.

Robert Siodmak did not share producer Mark Hellinger's enthusiasm. The prospect of directing an inexperienced actress understandably made him nervous. During the shooting, before each scene Siodmak subjected Ava to intense psychological preparation. He admitted later that he had given her a rather rough time to get her to express the hysteria that gradually grips her character in the film's final scene as Kitty rushes to her dying husband, the criminal Olfax.

Today, compared to some of her other films, Ava's performance in *The Killers* seems weak and not truly up to her best. Her efforts to live up to the role are all too obvious and she is visibly self-conscious. She poses rather than acts. Kitty Collins' purposely exaggerated sophistication limited the possibilities for character development. Only Ava's suggestive bearing in the (by now famous) black satin dress has remained immortalized, the satin shimmering and glinting over her curves, caressing the actress' every move. Though the role was simplistic, it projected the image of a dangerously beautiful woman in a film dominated by men (Ava of course was absent from any of the action scenes essential to the plot). This laid the foundations for the emblematic figure that shaped Ava Gardner's reputation for the next five years. This characterization was then taken one step further and enriched with a fatal element in *Pandora and the Flying Dutchman*. Ava recognized the importance of her role as Kitty:

Until I played Kitty Collins, I had never worked very hard in pictures, never taken my career very seriously. I felt no burning ambition to become a real actress. I was just a girl who was lucky enough to have a job in pictures. Playing Kitty changed that, showed me what it meant to try to act, and made me feel that I might have a little talent in that area after all.[2]

The Killers was also responsible for one of the most important encounters of her career. Indeed, Ernest Hemingway, usually so tough, declared that the film was the best adaptation of one of his works ever. Ava certainly had something to do with this generous evaluation. She became the novelist's fetish actress. After this film, she went on to portray two of his most famous heroines: Cynthia in *The Snows of Kilimanjaro*, and Lady Brett Ashley in *The Sun Also Rises*. Years later, John Huston also projected his fascination for Ava onto the screen in *The Life and Times of Judge Roy Bean*. This came after one of her greatest roles, which Huston offered her in 1963, in *The Night of the Iguana*.

The unhoped for success of *The Killers* catapulted Ava Gardner to international fame, along with her co-star Burt Lancaster, just making his film debut. It marked the turning point in Robert Siodmak's career and he later directed a series of films in the same vein. Mark Hellinger became the official producer for Universal as a result of his part in the success. Today the film is often cited as a classic of the noir genre. Nevertheless, the film's exciting American release in August 1946 offered little consolation to Ava, who was again plagued by another romantic disappointment. Separated from Artie Shaw, she took refuge at a friend's home:

He disregarded my smallest wish and humiliated me every chance he got, until I was barely able to hold back my tears. I worshipped the man, but that period was one of the worst I ever endured.[2]

The encounter with Kitty Collins (Ava Gardner), which will be fatal to the hero (Burt Lancaster).

In 1947 in Jack Conway's *The Hucksters*, Ava Gardner is the partner of "the King", Clark Gable, the fetish actor of Ava's mother. From left to right, Clark Gable, Ava Gardner, Deborah Kerr, Gloria Holden, and Adolphe Menjou.

Ava's marriage to Mickey Rooney had failed because the two were hardly more than immature teenagers. Her marriage to Artie Shaw was a different story. The domineering personality and cruel treatment of this husband twelve years her senior had created infinitely more suffering. "Still and all, Artie was one of the deep hurts of my life,"[2] Ava was later to admit. Shaw had asked for the divorce and it was made official on 25 October 1946, just a year and a week after they were married. From that date on Ava would never be the same.

The triumph of *The Killers* did nothing to encourage MGM to show more interest in Ava. Of course her contract was renegotiated to 1,250 dollars a week, but the film chosen for her in early 1947, *The Hucksters*, billed her fifth. Ava's name came after Clark Gable and Deborah Kerr. Kerr had just arrived from England to make her Hollywood debut. And even the two supporting actors Adolphe Menjou and Sydney Greenstreet appeared before Ava.

Was this the reason Ava did not want to accept the part? In the corridors of MGM it was rumored that the actress was in fact terrified by the idea of playing opposite Clark Gable. Then he too turned down the role.

Gable feared the negative image that playing the scoundrel Victor would project to the public. After the great actor's long absence from the screen, the King was looking for popularity. He demanded a re-write of the story and made Victor into an honest young man trying to make a career in advertising. Kay Dorrance, in the original work an adulterous wife, was transformed into a war widow. The casting of Deborah Kerr for the part could not have been more perfect. Clark Gable wanted to reassure Ava about being in the film. She recalled:

> Clark, who'd pushed for me for the part, actually came to our modest apartment to talk to me, me a little nobody, about the role. But that was Clark: down-to-earth, informal, liking people, helping them and all done with style... Clark didn't really have to encourage me to play Jean Ogilvie. MGM had already marked me for it and MGM owned me body and soul. I had to get permission from Louis B. Mayer for everything I did.[2]

For MGM, just the fact that Ava was in the same movie with the King already promised extraordinary promotion for her. Gracious and enveloping, Ava played her part as an actress, singer and Clark Gable's ex-mistress, as she came and went magically on the screen to the

writer's whims. The film begins with Ava on Clark's arm, as an enthusiastic, affectionate and seductive young woman. This bloom of innocence continues until the cabaret sequence in which Gable celebrates a little victory at work with his friends. Ava sings *Don't Tell Me*, then joins Clark's table. Ava's role consists in sparking a little romantic duel between Deborah Kerr and herself and wreaking havoc in the certitudes of Clark Gable's heart.

The screenplay gave Ava two other chances to try to seduce Clark: one in a train as he travels to Los Angeles, the other at her place when she invites him to dinner. Ava takes advantage of this tête-à-tête to try to entice him one last time, but in vain. Clark stays faithful to the severe Deborah Kerr, to whom Ava relinquishes the film's final romantic moonlight scene. Ava Gardner later said she was intimidated by the legendary actor, whom she could not help seeing as her mother's movie heartthrob. Both Gable and Gardner shared the same fragility: Clark because he was an actor in decline, Ava because she was taking her first steps in a career that already promised to be difficult. Ava and Clark later made two other films together, *Lone Star* and *Mogambo*, and became bound by an unshakeable friendship. When the film was released, Clark declared in an interview how excellent and promising his co-star Ava Gardner was as an actress. Charles Higham[9] relates that Ava had Clark's words recorded and that she played them over and over again.

The Hucksters was a studio film typical of so many of the time. It seemed just one more of those slick boring box office hits, equal to the bestsellers upon which they were based. Nevertheless, it definitely had an important impact on Ava's celebrity. The actress was starting to get good reviews and prompted *Newsweek* to declare that the film owed much to Ava Gardner's performance. This was somewhat of an exaggerated homage since there was also the performance by precise and irreproachable Deborah

Kerr. She was a British actress par excellence when it came to the craft of acting.

Though Ava had been under contract with MGM since August 1941, the Studio had no particular interest in developing her career. The Studio therefore saw no problem in agreeing with producer Jerry Bresler to loan Ava to Universal for two consecutive films: *Singapore* and *One Touch of Venus*. Of course, Ava had absolutely no say in the negotiations and was as little in control of her future as the heroine Linda in *Singapore*. Linda, suffering from amnesia, has a totally new life created for her.

In *Singapore* a Japanese bomb attack separates Linda and Matt Gordon (Fred MacMurray) on the day of their engagement. Five years later, Matt Gordon returns to Singapore to recover rare pearls he had hidden during the rout. Linda has made a new life for herself and is now married to an English plantation owner. Ava's acting in *Singapore* was tinged with despair. Her pleading voice betrayed her great weariness. Had life dealt her a bad hand? Was she Linda, the ex-fiancée of a sailor and adventurer, or Mrs. Van Leyden, the wife of an English plantation owner? Ava seemed to be questioning her own true identity. Had she been born Ava Lavinia Gardner or "Lucy Ann Johnson", as the Studio's press releases claimed? This name, a sheer invention by MGM, was intended to give Ava the proper ancestry considered worthy of a star. From this point of view, *Singapore* truly appeared to be an allegory of the destiny which Hollywood had forced upon Ava.

With its simplistic plot, *Singapore* did not escape any of the clichés of those B-movies made with exotic overtones. There was everything: the trafficking of rare pearls, an infallible hero, a hilarious studio reconstruction of Singapore's seedier neighborhoods, the usual juicy supporting roles which were a regular fare of the genre. There was the fat boss with a big cigar who oozes

43

With Fred MacMurray in John Brahm's *Singapore* (1947).

Opposite page: Another shot from *The Hucksters*, with Clark Gable.

44

corruption, or the lazy gentleman crook portrayed by George Lloyd. Worth mentioning were also the retired couple on a trip to the Far East with their indispensable humor. She, a wide-eyed chubby tourist brimming with childish excitement complete with overdone squeals, and he, good-natured and affable, who spends most of his time apologizing for his wife.

Singapore also belonged to the post-war American films replete with dubious orientalism. Disdained today, these films were the delight of a generation of movie-goers hungry for adventure. It was a time when cinema was above all a popular pastime that drew huge crowds to the Sunday matinees. Though the screenplays did not do them justice, these films reflected undeniable technical and artistic know-how. This is demonstrated in their studied lighting and excellent black-and white-photography. The light filtering through closed shutters that casts jagged shadows across the bodies of its characters has become a figure of style. It is inevitably used in contemporary film as a tribute to colonial cinema.

Singapore owed much to the diligent contribution of salaried employees of the Hollywood studio who often remained anonymous. Costume designer Michael Woulfe cleverly compensated for the lack of color by his patterns and use of contrasts. He bundled Ava up in dresses clasped to the neck and did not free her breasts (veiled in chiffon) until the ball scene, with a gown that would herald the unforgettable dresses of *Pandora and the Flying Dutchman*, and later *The Snows of Kilimanjaro*.

Ava's co-star, the broad shouldered and monolithic Fred MacMurray, was the antithesis of Burt Lancaster in *The Killers*. MacMurray's wide shoulders were precisely those of all infallible heroes, stubbornly immune to any self-questioning, whether in affairs of love or otherwise. Determined and obtuse, he could never be perturbed by passion. During those post-war years, the image of the sovereign hero was tenacious. Linda surrendered to it just as Ava Gardner, who also adored virile men.

In late 1947, while Ava was on tour promoting *The Killers,* Mark Hellinger introduced her to Howard Duff in New York. Duff was a promising young actor whom Universal had recently cast in *The Naked City* directed by

MacMurray and Ava in another scene from *Singapore*.

Jules Dassin. Howard Duff, though not very famous today, at the time was enjoying rising popularity after having been discovered in an earlier film by Jules Dassin, *Brute Force*. It was a period when Ava had withdrawn into a life of dissolution and was already beginning to show obvious signs of instability. She had her own table at Ciro's, one of the most in vogue clubs at the time and, as Howard Duff remarked:

> She was incredibly restless. If we were in one place, she wanted to be in another. She was never satisfied. Quickly I understood how mercurial and changeable she was, maddening, exasperating one minute, adorable the next, a mixture of qualities that baffled and infuriated me. But sexually she had me hooked from the outset.[9]

This time Ava ignored her usual principles and did not want to marry Howard Duff, who was still involved with Yvonne De Carlo: "I loved him, but not deeply enough to start down that route. Let's have fun, I said. And we sure did."[2] Her unhappy experiences in marriage had changed her. From now on Ava espoused the morals that typified the showbiz world which had become her own.

Nevertheless, she also continued to believe that the most beautiful day of her life would be when she could turn her back on all of it. She yearned to live life as she truly desired, with someone whom she really loved. According to Howard Duff:

> We went to nightclubs constantly, especially Ciro's. She was a night person. But when she was working she disciplined herself completely. She liked to give the impression that she didn't care about her roles, but she was in fact pretty damn serious and dedicated. I had to drive her home early. She was always first at the studio and into makeup. She drove herself without mercy.[9]

The year 1948 was filled with intense activity. Ava made three films in quick succession. She even intervened personally to convince Louis B. Mayer to let her make another film for Universal after that: *One Touch of Venus*. He was against it and as a pretext argued that shooting would start soon on *The Bribe*. When it turned out that they did not even have the script ready yet, Ava was free to play Venus, the goddess of love. It was a role made for her.

46

Ava (here with
Robert Walker)
reveals her talent
for comedy in the
adaptation of a
Broadway success,
William A. Seiter's
One Touch of Venus
(1948).

Apart from *The Little Hut* made in 1956, this was her only venture into comedy. Or rather into the – completely mad – universe of screenwriter Frank Tashlin. Here he adapted a Broadway hit to the screen. Later he would be famous for discovering Jerry Lewis and revealing the voluptuous curves of Jayne Mansfield.

The charm and delight of *One Touch of Venus* was created by the encounter between a deliciously uninhibited creature, Venus, and Eddie Hatch, a timid and reserved young man played by Robert Walker. Venus is actually a statue transformed by a kiss into a real human being. She is therefore completely unaware that some pleasures might actually be forbidden in this world. She sets about "torturing" with questionable, though well-meaning persistence, the utterly helpless Robert Walker. His feeble attempts are almost burlesque as he flees both this delightful woman and the police.

Universal Studios had already launched Ava Gardner's version of the femme fatale in *The Killers*. This major was decidedly bold and chose not to slip back into a genre which was now intimately bound to her personality. Indeed, *One Touch of Venus* brought a true breath of fresh air just when a darker image was expected. Sparkling eyes replaced Ava's veiled and languorous looks, quick light movements superseded the poses of the vamp, conscious of her magnetism.

Ava Gardner swept through the entire 82 minutes with the grace of an angel. Her sculptural beauty so reflected the perfection of Venus that one wondered whether the model had inspired the masterpiece or the

other way around. The directing and mise en scene of *One Touch of Venus* were perpetual invention. Respect for unity of time (the action takes place during a period of 24 hours) brought a dynamism which strengthened Ava's keenly perceptive acting. She appeared as a radiant, frivolous, and innocent butterfly.

Unfortunately *One Touch of Venus* was a commercial failure. It was erroneously billed as a musical comedy, though the film only featured two songs (*Speak Low*, a duet with Ava Gardner and Dick Hames, and *My Heart Is Showing*, an original song written for the film). Moreover, the low-budget production was in black and white just when audiences were growing eager for dazzling spectacles in color. The film was nevertheless delicious and charming. It revealed a rare facet of Ava's character. Her flawless mastery of space, the pace of her acting, her graceful twirling movements expressed quite obviously a slightly perverse and terribly seductive innocence. *One Touch of Venus* was in fact the first film in which Ava's talent as an actress was affirmed.

MGM intended to reclaim its star Ava Gardner with the series film *The Bribe* made in 1948. Yet it was a

Above:
Robert Walker in vain tries to resist the charms of an enterprising Venus.

Below:
From left to right, James Flavin, Robert Walker, Ava Gardner, and Tom Conway in *One Touch of Venus*.

In this scene from *The Bribe* (1948), MGM very obviously models Ava's role after the character she created in the Universal production *The Killers* (1946).

in romantic roles he detested, agreed with Ava Gardner in considering *The Bribe* among his worst films. Largely in voiceover, his deep sonorous voice delivered an insipid narration. Indeed, only the film's cast of great actors can bring enjoyment in watching these old reels today. Charles Laughton, in the film's other unforgettable role, was perfect as the despicable J.J. Bealer, and of course Ava actively contributed to the viewers' pleasure.

She appears out of the darkness, illuminated by the flame of a match which is immediately consumed in the hearts of the late night audience. Elizabeth is a night-club singer whose suave silkiness is unfaltering. It is immediately clear that the vamp created by Robert Siodmak in *The Killers* was a model for this new character. Robert Taylor, a federal agent on a mission, soon falls hopelessly in love with her, despite his suspicions. Is she actually double-crossing someone (just as Kitty Collins had in *The Killers*)? Is she also involved in illegal trafficking? Will she drive the hero to desperation?

The Bribe was intended to be a hit like *The Killers*. Ava sang *Situation Wanted* (if she did want to work for a man, which one?). She wore a black satin dress so similar to the famous garment in *The Killers* that it looked almost straight off the set of Universal. The only change made by wardrobe mistress Irene was to switch the strap originally on Ava's left shoulder to her right one.

For street clothes Ava Gardner wore blouses with a more traditional flair that generously bared her shoulders, or thick skirts with woven waistbands. Despite these rather modest outfits, Ava managed to bring charisma to these clothes designed to reflect the drabness of her character's life. Penniless Elizabeth lives on an island and is trapped in a relationship she is desperately trying to flee. Poverty forces her to do menial jobs. Her husband Tug turns to petty crime.

Director Robert Z. Leonard, one of MGM's directors on contract, had been reproached for a career that had been summed up in a famous comment as "forty-five years of mediocrity interrupted by a few good ideas."[16] Ava Gardner could have been made to scrub the floor, an image as incongruous as it was seductive. Stars were usually made to stay on their Olympus. It was not until 1964, in fact, that Sophia Loren in *Marriage Italian Style* played the role of a housewife.

Of course, such a film was not expected of Robert Z. Leonard. The director did the best he could, in the MGM spirit, within the bounds of the extremely basic script. *The Bribe* had much in common with *Singapore*. Its plot revolved around trafficking, though of airplane engines instead of pearls. The two films both shared an

disappointment. The French title was promising and guaranteed adventure. The film's opening images set the scene on an island off Central America hit by violent lightning and a tremendous special-effects storm. Once again the B-movie formula was set into motion. The usual clichés resurfaced intact through a conventional story expressed by the usual studio aesthetics and a script based on the traditional flashback principle.

In film history no praise can do justice to the actors of these exotic adventures. They heroically transcended their roles and gave credibility to impossibly lukewarm plots. Robert Taylor, whose unwilling career was forged mainly

With John Hodiak and Robert Taylor in the exotic adventure *The Bribe.*

With Robert Taylor, a discreet affair that continued in their private lives during the entire filming of *The Bribe.*

With Robert
Taylor in *The Bribe*.

exotic setting, though in countries on different latitudes. There was Charles Laughton in a role that recalled the villain Mauribus (Thomas Gomez), and a symphonic music score intended to heighten the dramatic intensity of action scenes. This also helped to distract from the bad special effects and back projections.

Leonard successfully evoked the suffocating tropical heat, thanks to his excellent sense of detail (we can almost feel the characters' intense thirst); good dialogue ("This wretched country! If you ain't fried, you boil in your own juice.") and the creative lighting by Joseph Ruttenberg. Walls were endlessly swept by glinting fans, tropical rains, long shadows. A disabled Charles Laughton, obese and sweaty, evoked a climate that only the natives knew how to live with. Less sensitive to the heat, Ava was happy to ever so slightly open her deep neckline to get the most of a cooling fan. She delicately dabbed a small drop of sweat with her handkerchief as it began to bead near her right earlobe. This graceful delicate gesture was a good demonstration of how studied it was. Compared to the polished acting of Robert Taylor and Charles Laughton, Ava's beauty in fact remained her strongest quality.

Ava Gardner and Robert Taylor prolonged in private what in the beginning was the element of a classic script that demanded a hero be in love with the heroine. The shooting of *The Bribe* resulted in a fleeting, passionate love affair between the two. At the time, Robert Taylor was still married to Barbara Stanwyck, though they were on the verge of divorce. As for Ava, she had just left Howard Duff:

> Our love affair lasted three, maybe four months. A magical little interlude. We hurt no one because no one knew – only Reenie on my side, and no one on his. I've never forgotten those few hidden months. I made two more films with Bob, *Ride, Vaquero!* and *Knights of the Round Table*, where he played Sir Lancelot (of course!), but we never renewed our romance.[2]

In late 1948 Ava was again working with Robert Siodmak, the director who three years previously had directed her in *The Killers*. Among this American director's films, *The Great Sinner* (his only production for MGM) was definitely not one of his more important works. Indeed, after Dore Shary decided to have Mervyn Leroy shoot additional scenes and re-cut the film, Siodmak himself disowned it completely.

Nevertheless, since at this point in Ava's career (1946-1949) her roles consisted mainly of only low-budget B-movie parts, *The Great Sinner* seemed like a lesser evil. It was motivated by undeniable artistic ambition, in part due to its story. The original story was inspired by the work of a great writer, a gambler himself, who played for his life and gained immortality.

Though the result did not live up to its worthy intentions, many elements bore the stamp of director Robert Siodmak. Behind the mutilated final cut there was evidence of the irreproachable casting, the excellent directing, the masterful control at least certain scenes. The film gave Ava a good role as Pauline, a Russian general's daughter. Ava got the chance to do some real acting and to play opposite Gregory Peck, as a writer destroyed by gambling.

Shattered and repentant, Pauline appears at her lover Dostoyevsky's deathbed as he lies delirious. She gathers the pages of a manuscript scattered by the wind in the tiny room under the roof and begins reading his work, *Confessions of a Sinner...* As soon as Dostoyevsky arrives in this town

Ava Gardner and Gregory Peck (Dostoyevsky) form an unforgettable couple in Robert Siodmak's *The Great Sinner* (1948).

The Great Sinner, an ambitious film on gambling fever. Standing behind Ethel Barrymore, are Ava Gardner, Walter Huston and Gregory Peck.

located "in a peaceful and playful Europe," he realizes that the casino and its gamblers are the material for a new book. Among the gamblers there is a Russian general and his daughter. They are on the verge of complete ruin and live in the desperate hope of soon being saved by an imminent inheritance. In the meantime they are at the complete mercy of the casino manager who agrees to cover their losses in exchange for marrying Pauline. Dostoyevsky, however, falls in love with Pauline and ruins the casino manager's plans by offering to pay back Pauline's debts.

Robert Siodmak uses admirable measure in his depiction of the gambling fever that gradually grips the writer. Dostoyevsky becomes consumed by the vice just as Pauline frees herself from the inferno of the casino's temptations. *The Great Sinner* shows the opposing development of the two lovers' lives. The couple are blessed with one fleeting moment of peace as they sit dreamily in each other's arms before a fireplace. They still believe at that point that they are free and have a happy future

ahead of them. And this decor has remained the ideal classic setting for uniting screen sweethearts in films ever since.

One of the merits of *The Great Sinner* was that it defined a future element of the "Ava Gardnerian" character. It laid the foundations of a theme which formed the heart of *Pandora and the Flying Dutchman*: that is, redemption through love. Love was first rejected, then accepted as a deliverance. Pauline is transformed, to the great displeasure of the casino manager. "You've turned into a woman because of a weakling," he tells her scornfully.

Ava Gardner's acting seemed much more professional than in her previous films. *The Great Sinner* indisputably marked a step towards a much more complex type of cinema that offered her serious roles. Her performance was memorable in the train compartment scene. Wearing fur coat and cap, she spends the entire journey engrossed in a game of cards, completely overcome with the desire to win. Her indifference to her

Ava Gardner acts in a Romantic costume drama for the first time. Directed by Robert Siodmak, the theme is one of redemption.

traveling companion is magnificent as she palys the enigmatic beauty par excellence.

East Side, West Side, made right after *The Great Sinner*, seemed to be somewhat of a stumbling block along Ava's career, now at its height. Her presence in only three sequences was nevertheless enough to spark Jessie's (Barbara Stanwyck's) fears for her marriage and Brandon's (James Mason's) enchantment when Isabel (Ava Gardner) suddenly comes back into his life.

Ava Gardner was one of those women who in life, just as in her films, instantly set hearts aflame. Just one of her looks, one word, or even just the memory of her, could trigger a burning romance, even in her absence. Obviously such a situation so early in the plot was impossible. And indeed, on-the-screen, Isabel played out her role as the bewitching charmer, superior and haughty beyond all tolerable limits. Though there were no swaying hips, she had a way of moving that seemed more like gliding (her

steps hidden by long gowns). Ava resembled the royal queens of animated films or a creature fabricated by optical illusion. This wondrous quality made Ava even more otherworldly in this film than in *Singapore* or *One Touch of Venus*.

As a modern drama, *East Side, West Side* left little room for poetic suggestion. Ava Gardner descended upon New York's high society with the ease and supremacy of a woman totally aware of her magnificence. Produced right before the fifties, *East Side, West Side* offered absolutely no cinematic innovation. However, it did propose a new look for Ava who, for the first time, wore a short hairstyle created by her faithful hairdresser Sydney Guilaroff. Her new hairdo made her look much more "womanly" and was very different from the thick flowing locks of the vamp in *The Killers*. Nor was it anything like the very young woman in *The Bribe*, whose hair is drawn innocently back at the nape of her neck. This cut brought out the features of Ava's face, just as her strapless dress exposed her back, revealing a beautiful harmony of curves: a very long neck, spared of any jewelry, and the most delicate shoulders.

Masterfully in control of her new image, Ava Gardner assailed James Mason, Britain's prestigious actor, challenged Barbara Stanwyck, at the peak of her own glory, and confirmed, even despite herself, her reputation as a femme fatale. Ava gave the bosses at MGM a thrashing, those who had refused to recognize her talent for comedy after *One Touch of Venus*. Before these two screen giants, Ava Gardner, who detested "these miserable women's roles," no longer had the slightest need to develop her talent any further. The mechanism of her two scenes with James Mason were very similar. They both revolved around Ava's insistent presence and the almost complete irresistibility of her husky voice which by now had become one of her most important attributes.

The intensity of these two scenes gave Albert Lewin the idea of prolonging the aura of the screen duo in another film, though he took them out of high society. In the meantime, Ava made *My Forbidden Past* (a.k.a. *Carriage Entrance*) for Howard Hughes, then head of RKO. Hughes had been trying to win Ava over for almost six years. She had always refused him. She found his total lack of humor, his look of a poor devil and his eternally worn suits unattractive, not to mention the questionable way he did things, too. Howard Hughes seemed to confuse the management of his business with that of his emotions. He had young women in all parts

In Mervyn Leroy's *East Side, West Side* (1949) Isabel Lorrison (Ava Gardner) is Jessie's (Barbara Stanwyck's) rival; Jessie is Brandon Bourne's wife (James Mason). The role of an irresistible woman has repercussions on Ava Gardner's private life and she is now considered the "ultimate" rival.

of the world who lived at his beck and call. Yet he tracked Ava's every move and each and every event of her life. He reappeared after each of her divorces, ready to satisfy her slightest whim. Ava took advantage of it. Did she feel like going out for a drink in Mexico? A plane was waiting for her. Did she want a huge tub of ice cream? There it was.

This was Ava's way of showing the absurdity of the sort of behavior and the values of a man who thought money could buy anything. She dangerously fed Hughes' hopes by accepting all of his gifts and pushed him to the limit. Finally, on a trip to San Francisco, he lost control. Bappie was there when Hughes turned on her sister. She tried as usual to reason with Ava. But Ava was adamant. The shy and innocent young girl of her earlier years in Hollywood was now a thing of the past. Was there an element of cruelty in her behavior? Was she getting revenge on all the men who had ever made her suffer? Was she anticipating the heroine in *Pandora and the Flying Dutchman*? A point of no return of rare violence was finally reached one night at a private gala. After one too many drinks, Ava almost murdered the richest man in the world.

My Forbidden Past was the story of Barbara who, just as in Ava's image, was trying to free herself of a man's control over her. The action was set in New Orleans at the end of the nineteenth century. As an orphan, Barbara had been brought up first by her grandmother and later by a cruel aunt. As a young woman she is intent upon

With Melvyn Douglas in Robert Stevenson's *My Forbidden Past (Carriage Entrance)*, 1949.

In 1949 Ava Gardner worked for RKO just for the making of a short-lived film entitled *My Forbidden Past (Carriage Entrance)*. Her partner is Robert Mitchum. Here and *opposite*: two stills from the film.

winning back Mark Lucas (Robert Mitchum), who has been discouraged by the ruses of Barbara's ill-intentioned cousin. The cousin torments Barbara and tries to take advantage of both her beauty and an inheritance of whose existence the heroine is unaware.

According to Robert Mitchum, the screenplay was probably the worst imaginable, a badly disguised imitation of *Saratoga Trunk* that had starred Gary Cooper and Ingrid Bergman. Yet Mitchum needed the money. He was facing serious legal problems after being found in possession of illegal drugs when his home had been searched. On the set, between takes, Mitchum tried to introduce his co-star Ava to marijuana, but she remained faithful to her own favorites, that is, tobacco and alcohol. They accompanied her all through life.

Ava was the heart and soul of *My Forbidden Past*. Her long gowns with matching feathered hats and little veils, white gloves, parasols and tiny handbags suited her perfectly, and *Newsweek* found Ava "superb but stiff in the role of Barbara Beaurevel." By the time the film was released a year and a half later in the United States (RKO had hesitated and delayed its distribution), Ava could already boast of her performance in a rare film, *Pandora and the Flying Dutchman*, as well as the triumph of *Show Boat*. *My Forbidden Past*, however, was a tremendous flop in the U.S. and did not fare any better in Europe where it was released in 1952. It would have fallen into complete oblivion except for a recent reprint which has reminded film buffs of its existence at all.

Ava had never hidden her weakness for singers, which even surpassed her well-known love for bullfighters. When she first met Frank Sinatra, Ava was married to Mickey Rooney. Frankie, with his devastating smile, had gone up to her saying: "Hey, why didn't I meet you before Mickey? Then I could have married you myself."[2]

In early 1949 Ava rented a house in the desert, in Palm Springs, a favorite spot for the Hollywood set. There was non-stop partying there and it was at one of these parties that Ava met Sinatra.

A lot of silly stories have been written about what happened to us in Palm Springs, but the truth is both more and less exciting. We drank, we laughed, we talked, and we fell in love. Frank gave me a lift back to our rented house. We did not kiss or make dates, but we knew, and I think it must have frightened both of us.[2]

"The measure of love is what one is willing to give up for it." Stephen (Nigel Patrick) has plunged his race car over a cliff in exchange for Pandora's promise to marry him.

Radiance: 1950-1958

The key events that skyrocketed Ava Gardner to international stardom occurred over this eight-year period, during which she matured, both physically as well as professionally. Indeed, this was when some of her most famous films were made. And everything converged to make 1950 a turning point in Ava's life. There was her appearance in a film as highly original as *Pandora and the Flying Dutchman*, backed by British capital. It was her first film in color. She had just signed an exciting new contract. Her affair with Frank Sinatra was now public. And Ava had discovered Spain, an experience that would change the course of her life.

Some bitter disappointments, however, were also brewing: her marriage with Frank Sinatra, which was so quickly celebrated, ended just as quickly. And her screen career, which seemed to almost systematically alternate mediocre films with good ones: *Lone Star* after *Show Boat*, *Ride, Vaquero!* after *The Snows of Kilimanjaro*, *Knights of the Round Table* after *Mogambo*.

Apart from *Bhowani Junction*, Ava Gardner's most convincing successes were independent productions or productions by competitor studios. The two Hemingway adaptations (*The Snows of Kilimanjaro* and *The Sun Also Rises*) were produced by Fox. *Pandora and the Flying Dutchman* was made in England. *The Barefoot Contessa* was produced in Italy by Mankiewicz who turned to United Artists for distribution. This masterpiece, which is more representative of Ava than any other film, together with *Bhowani Junction*, truly represented the height of her career (1954-1955), in terms of her beauty and her mastery of the acting craft.

Ava was at her zenith when she also began divorce proceedings for the third time. Following the distressing *Little Hut*, she plunged heart and soul into the pathetic yet charming role of Lady Brett Ashley, a woman adrift and quite the image of the actress herself. Yet what Ava lacked in fulfillment, *The Naked Maja* at least brought her in freedom. She saw her MGM contract finally become a thing of the past. By the end of 1958, Ava Gardner was no longer bound by any further obligations and was free to manage her own career as an independent artist. What did the future have in store for her?

January 1950. Ava was preparing to travel outside the United States for the first time in her life. Her sister Bappie was going with her. In fact her sister would accompany her on almost every trip when work called Ava away. Their destination: Spain, the little port of Tossa del Mar on the Costa Brava, for the shooting of a strange and enigmatic movie, *Pandora and the Flying Dutchman*. Ava considered this film important:

> … it wouldn't be an exaggeration to say that making it changed my life forever. Because *Pandora* got me outside

the United States for the first time and introduced me to the two countries, England and Spain, where I was to spend much of the rest of my life. One trip abroad, honey, and I almost never looked back. [2]

MGM did not expect to get anything out of this film, an independent production by Albert Lewin, who loved European culture. The Studio could only hope for a return perhaps on the film's US distribution. The strangeness of Albert Lewin's cinematic universe, so out of line with Hollywood's fare, promised respectable

Two other scenes from Albert Lewin's *Pandora and the Flying Dutchman* (1950) with James Mason.

recognition at best. Nevertheless, the Studio was overjoyed at the prospect of Ava being sent on location to Europe, since this would temporarily take her away from Frank Sinatra. Eddie Mannix, advertising head at the Studio, was getting nervous about the bad publicity being created by the couple's adulterous affair. The secret had been revealed to the world after a little "slip" by Ava.

Ava immediately took advantage of a delay in the shooting (James Mason was held up on the set of *One-Way Street*). She ignored the Studio's veto and went to join Frank, who was performing at the Shamrock Hotel in Houston. "Neither Metro nor the newspapers, nor anyone else is going to run my life," she declared then to Bappie.[17]

That was perhaps her first act of rebellion against MGM, and Louis B. Mayer was worried about a scandal. Sinatra had even gotten into a fight with Edward

Schisser of the *Houston Post* and hit him. The photographer had gone up to the couple's table to take the first shot of them together in public. Schisser gave up his photo, but not the pleasure of a scoop that blew the secret of Frank and Ava's affair. In less than twenty-four hours, 'people' columnists everywhere had their stories ready for their gossip hungry readers. It was a juicy piece of news that had been kept secret for over eighteen months. Yet, as Ava admitted, "As much in love as we were, Frank and I didn't really care if, sooner or later, people found out about us."[2]

America was still riding high on its post-war triumph and staunchly upheld the family values that had built the nation. Frank Sinatra was a Catholic and a married man with three children and a model wife, Nancy. They were a perfect example of the American way of life. In this idyllic and reassuring picture, Ava showed her true face –

full page at that – to America's puritan public. Her beauty, so greatly admired, suddenly became an insult to the American housewife. Ava was unfair competition on the market of the heart. Thanks to the formidable weapon bestowed upon her by nature, Ava Gardner undermined the foundations of a couple in an attempt to build her own happiness. But would she be successful?

Was there any difference between Ava Gardner and Isabel Morrison of *East Side, West Side*, who whispered to James Mason, husband of the severe and icy Barbara Stanwyck, "Is that what you've been missing?" None whatsoever. Ava *was* the malevolent creature of *The Killers*. A vamp. Irresistible. Paralyzing. No need for her to demonstrate an array of acting talents, all she had to do was play on her own natural gifts. Ava proved she was the woman in her films: the ultimate rival.

Her screen partners' wives thought it always wise to be on the set too: Pamela Mason was with James when he went to Spain for the *Flying Dutchman*; Barbara Stanwyck confessed she feared[10] Ava would try to lure Robert Taylor back while on the set of *Quo Vadis?* in Rome. Lauren Bacall joined Bogart in Italy as soon as shooting began for *The Barefoot Contessa*. In 1958 Shelley Winters would not let Anthony Franciosa out of her sight while he played Ava's passionate lover in *The Naked Maja*. All of these women wanted to spare their husbands a fatal weakness, as if it were inevitable that their husbands would fall prey to Ava the man-eater. The press loved these female duels, often entirely made up just to fuel their columns.

In *Whistle Stop*, George Raft melted when Ava wrapped her sinuous arms around him and let her lips linger on his. The framed picture of his fiancée, already forgotten, slips from his grasp. The highly symbolic image of breaking glass made Ava into a veritable wrecker of marriages, an immoral woman born to test the weaknesses of men.

From left to right, Sheila Sim, Harold Warrender, and Nigel Patrick.

Of course, in the tons of mail the actress received, there were not only letters from fans:

One correspondent addressed me as "bitch-Jezebel-Gardner", the Legion of Decency threatened to ban my movies, Catholic priests found the time to write me accusatory letters. I even read that the Sisters of Mary and Joseph asked their students at St. Paul the Apostle School in Los Angeles to pray for Frank's poor wife.[2]

In this real-life scenario, Nancy Sinatra was the "good guy", the faithful, devastated wife and mother. Her defenders wept in unison. Of course, Frank Sinatra was an infamous skirt chaser and was not at his first slip, far from it. The couple had often been shaken. Yet Ava Gardner represented an exceptional danger. All of benevolent America's heart went out to Nancy on Valentine's Day when she wrenchingly announced to the press:

Unfortunately, my married life with Frank has become most unhappy and almost unbearable. We are therefore separated. I have requested my attorney to attempt to work out a property settlement, but I do not contemplate divorce proceedings in the foreseeable future.[17]

Frank Sinatra had hit rock bottom. He was so shaken by his professional and family problems that he cancelled several Copacabana dates that were meant to launch his comeback. Broken, it was even rumored that he suffered from hysterical aphonia, an affliction that paralyzes the vocal chords. Ava made a stop over in New York on her way to London for costume fittings for *Pandora*. The illicit couple gave the press a chance of a lifetime when the two took a suite together at Hampshire House.

Though Ava and Frankie were not yet married, they were in fact already on their way to a break up. At the heart of all their fights, famous even to this day, was jealousy, a kind of romantic jealousy that was "primitive, passionate, bitter, acrimonious, elemental, red-fanged."[2] These are only a selection of the adjectives Ava Gardner used in her memoirs. If one pretty woman (and there were hordes) happened to simply rest her gaze on the crooner, that was enough to throw Ava into a flying rage. It became the classic scene of their romance.

There was the incident in a restaurant in Manhattan one evening in March 1950. Ava brusquely leaves the table and goes to cry on Artie Shaw's shoulder. With a keen sense of drama, Ava sows clues all the way to his

house. As in a bad off-Broadway play, the lover tails his mistress, rings at the ex-husband's door and, when he opens it, tells him how much he has always despised him. Then, Sinatra goes back to Hampshire House and sets up a mock suicide.

Frank waited until Ava finally came back to shout at her from the room, "I can't stand it anymore. I'm going to kill myself – now!" Then, according to Ava, "there was this tremendous bang in my ear, I knew it was a revolver shot… I threw the phone down and raced across the living room…"[2] Sinatra had fired into the pillow and the bullet had gone straight through the mattress. With Bappie's help and one of Frankie's friends, they did away with the evidence. The shot had alerted the hotel staff. It was not long before two

On the deck of a schooner Pandora covers her body with a canvas and goes to see the captain.

Opposite page: Mason and Gardner.

policemen were standing at the door and Ava and Frankie were playing their sweet and innocent roles to perfection.

Ava was restless. It was time to escape to a new country and she would soon discover the lands of Europe. This cradle of culture was also home to those film directors and producers in exile who had revealed her volcanic temperament five years before in *Whistle Stop* and *The Killers*. She left for shooting on location in London, Paris, and Barcelona for a film that already appeared to be a declaration of all-consuming love. The make-believe events in the opening sequences of *Pandora and the Flying Dutchman* were not really so far from the true tragicomic episode that had occurred at Hampshire House in New York in Ava's real life.

Fans and suitors in a small club are gathered around Ava's character Pandora Reynolds, a singer whose nonchalant majestic beauty is a feast for all. One of her admirers, Reggie Demarest, is at her beck and call. He says he is a poet, a ruined poet, and is devastated because he is not in the latest edition of *Who's Who*. This was perhaps a wink at Frank Sinatra who, after having been ranked number one on the 1942 Best Singers list, was now next to last in the Top 50.

Pandora sits down at the piano and begins to play a misty tune. The shy Reggie asks her to marry him for the umpteenth time, though she has always refused. The accursed poet decides to take his life: he swallows a dose of lethal poison and collapses before the speechless crowd. Hardly fazed by the dramatic scene, Pandora pushes cruelty beyond all limits by proposing an extraordinary test of love. Stephen, another admirer, must drive his race car, a valuable prototype with which he intends to set a new speed record, over a cliff that overlooks the little port of Esperanza. Stephen accepts this sacrifice without a moment's hesitation in exchange for Pandora's promise to marry him.

Then Albert Lewin, noted for his extravagant excesses as screenwriter and director, opens the arena of passions to toreador Juan Montalvo. Back in Esperanza, the village where Juan Montalvo was born, the toreador makes plans to take Pandora to Madrid to marry him. His mother, an astute fortuneteller, warns her son that this could be fatal. As she reads her cards, the figure of Pan-

In the sophisticated *Pandora and the Flying Dutchman*, the frames, windows and other openings create "frame-in-a-frame" cinema. They offer perspectives that reflect the story-in-the-story principle. Here and on the *opposite page* with James Mason.

65

dora is inextricably linked to the image of death. Already Pandora's first suitor had succumbed to his immoderate love for the cold woman, and Montalvo would not survive either.

To play the role of the bullfighter, Albert Lewin cast the (very) unconvincing Mario Cabre who was an ex-bullfighter in real life. During the filming of *Pandora*, Mario Cabre seemed to confuse his screen role and what he imagined his role in real life to be – something that happens more often than might be imagined. He therefore convinced himself that Ava Gardner should fall in love with him. With the unfailing confidence of a true conquistador, he was certain that he could get the actress to forget Frank Sinatra.

Ava had been living in a state of intoxication ever since setting foot on the Costa Brava. Surrounded by its heady perfumes of intemperance, and far from America, the studios, and malicious gossip, she felt suddenly liberated. "I have to admit, I was fascinated by Spain from the first... It was all wonderful, and I went on all day and all night. I loved it,"[2] she later reminisced.

And it was in this burning exotic climate that Ava surrendered to her screen partner after an evening of one too many. This was all Mario Cabre needed (his charm had worked, but had he ever doubted it?) to call a press conference and declare with panache that Ava Gardner was the love of his life. And that if Sinatra dared set foot in Spain – he had announced his plans to visit Ava – the singer would not leave the country alive. With Sinatra on his way to Tossa del Mar, Albert Lewin cleverly changed shooting and had Mario Cabre go to Gerone for his bullfighting sequence. But the toreador plunged into writing feverish poems and declared to a journalist of the Associated Press, "She's the woman I love with all my soul. I believe this love and sympathy are both reciprocal and mutual."[17]

Sinatra's stop overs in New York, London, and Paris were plagued each time by questions from journalists. Sinatra later recalled:

I'm not that naive. But I'd not counted on that bullfighter. He was an added starter they ran in at the last minute. I never did meet him. I assume that what he said was just a publicity stunt.[17]

Mario Cabre, left, one of Pandora's many admirers in the film, is infatuated with Ava Gardner off screen. He declares his passion in poems dedicated to her. But Ava is in love with Frank Sinatra, whom she marries the following year. On the right, Nigel Patrick.

Was the role that Albert Lewin had in mind for Ava Gardner as Pandora once again that of a distant arrogant woman who was cold and destructive? Something she seemed to accomplish quite well and with equal talent in real life just as in pictures. No. As writer and director, Lewin was not content with this now classic side of Ava's image. In spite of the first pages of his script, in which he pretended to return to this profile in the character of Pandora, brushing her main features in broad strokes, Lewin rejected the idea of destructive beauty. He put the finishing touches on his Pandora by making her a sinful woman yet someone enriched by a spiritual dimension. Ava-Pandora becomes a woman who is eventually transformed by love, a love that is only fulfilled in death. And through Pandora, Lewin redeemed the public image of Ava Gardner.

One evening, under a full moon, Pandora answers a mysterious call and swims out to a sailboat docked in the bay of Esperanza. On board, she sees Henrich Van der Zee finishing the portrait of a mythological Pandora. The woman is seized with rage when she discovers that the woman in the painting, who bears her own name, looks just like her. Pandora slashes the canvas and mutilates the face that reflects an image of purity that she finds unbearable. Yet Pandora feels confused. Her usual cruelty in destroying men's works does not affect Henrich Van der Zee in the slightest. The Dutchman, having attained a state of wisdom and self-mastery, journeys in a timeless dimension.

Eventually, yearning to attain this inner beauty too, Pandora delivers the Dutchman from a terrible fate to which he has been condemned. Three centuries before, the captain of the vessel was condemned to a brutal sentence after murdering his innocent wife whom he had suspected of adultery. Van der Zee was made to sail the seas for eternity. He could only go ashore to find a woman whose love would be so great that, despite his crime, she would be willing to sacrifice herself for him.

Pandora, of course, seemed the most unlikely woman to fulfill such a wish. Yet she would in fact become this very person to redeem the Dutchman of his crime. The infinite distance that separates woman as an ordinary mortal and woman in the sublime grows faint. Pandora is the ideal woman, the quintessence of the most utopian dreams of men. And, most of all, of the film's director Lewin.

There is an identical relationship with art in *The Great Sinner*, Ava Gardner's most ambitious work (though perhaps not her best), before *Pandora*. In the previous film, the writer Dostoyevsky was inspired by Pauline, a woman consumed by her passion for gambling. The hero creates a character in his novel, based upon Pauline, and gives her a soul. In *Pandora,* the Dutchman, through his painting, creates the woman of his quest. The theme of redemption dominates both films. Pauline tries to achieve her own metamorphosis, that is, to become like Dostoyevsky's literary creation, just as Pandora identifies with the woman in the painting.

Though Pauline remained the embodiment of evil as she led the novelist to his ruin, as well as her own, Pandora succeeds where Pauline failed. She is, however, swallowed up in the spiral of death in a formidable act of self-abnegation. The bodies of the Dutchman and Pandora are later found by the Esperanza fishermen, their entwined bodies trapped in fishing nets after their boat sinks during a storm.

Pandora and the Flying Dutchman was a definite turning point for Ava's image. Albert Lewin was responsible for this new direction. That same year it was developed in *Show Boat*. The film *Pandora* crowned Ava's career and represented an achievement that reflected eight years of apprenticeship in the art of acting. It was such a consecration that subsequent directors always felt obliged to measure up to it.

Yet *Pandora* (and Ava Gardner) owed much to the actress' earlier films, even if often they had been considered mediocre. All of Ava's previous films prepared her for the making of *Pandora*. All of the femmes fatales, the comedy Venuses, the goddesses of love, served as references to Lewin as he forged his heroine. Far from denying Ava's movie history, Lewin magnified it. Ava would be the femme fatale in *Pandora* too, just as in *The Killers* and *East Side, West Side*. Yet her effect would be even more devastating as she precipitated her ever more numerous chosen victims over the edge into suicide, self-sacrifice, and even murder.

If she was beautiful before, she would be even more so now. Photographed in color by British cameraman Jack Cardiff, Ava had never appeared more radiant. New nuances in her bursting luminous beauty were revealed. Every one of her appearances was blindingly beautiful, enchanced by the most sophisticated dresses with their ever more plunging necklines. The most inventive and erotically charged image of her will always remain the thick, rough canvas, improvised into a kimono, that Pandora winds around her nude drenched body in an effort to be decent in front of Van der Zee.

Of course, as already mentioned, the role had enough to stand on its own even without any extravagance. Initially distant, disillusioned, and reckless, Pandora later becomes tender, loving, and submissive, even to the point of welcoming death. She was an angel of ice transformed by love. For Pandora, just as for Ava herself, the intensity of one instant of true happiness was worth more than all the security a banal existence could bring.

Pandora and the Flying Dutchman was the expression of the purest romantic spirit. It was the work of a director who was not well known. Yet he was a man with a reputation for refined taste, an aesthete who displayed his culture (all too much?). When Albert Lewin undertook *Pandora* he had only directed three films. Among them was *The Picture of Dorian Gray* (1947) which became equally famous. More importantly, however, he had an impressive background as film producer and art director. Lewin did not make many films during his career (he stopped directing in 1957), for he worked with tremendous painstaking preparation, filming slowly and with meticulous precision. This even prompted André Bazin to once remark severely, "A little less well-made and this film would be perfect."

Sixteen weeks of filming, an incredible number of takes: here because of the wrinkle in Ava's dress, there for a loose strand of hair. Ava, who was used to Hollywood's well-oiled machinery, had never worked with such a fussy director in her life. She once asked, "Al, do you think I could go to the bathroom after the eighty-first take?"[2] Critics at the time reproached Lewin his too obvious effort to be poetic:

> *Pandora* will certainly leave the general public indifferent, the audiences of popular neighborhood theatres, who will see in it merely an exercise in pretense and boredom, and will not let themselves be abused by its false atmosphere of a masterpiece.[19]

"Heavy inanities (in all ways)," added another reviewer,[20] "expensive – certainly. In color, unfortunately! As interminable as a rainy Sunday at the seaside, *Pandora* is a good demonstration of human pretense and

Ava Gardner, the beautiful half-caste woman in *Show Boat*.

the entanglement of some minds perverted by false poetry and the mindless use of cinema." The sequences which in fact give the film its true poetic meaning are perhaps the least expected. There is Juan Montalvo's bullfight, of course. Above all there is Stephen as he tries to break the speed record on a long stretch of beach at Esperanza. Ava Gardner's gaze as she watches these men risking their lives in the hope of winning her heart certainly must have helped.

It was a long while before *Pandora* was reviewed again in a new light (from "obscure film" it was eventually promoted to "classic"). This status was certainly not unanimously shared at the time, nor was it definitive. Even today, Jean-Pierre Coursodon and Bertrand Tavernier qualified their critical praise which "applied more to its intentions than to the final result."[16] It is true that *Pandora* was not spared bad taste. The decoration and furniture, particularly, suggested the Italian-Spanish B-movies of the time, inevitably set during the Inquisition. This impression was aggravated by the lighting which, from what can be judged from new prints today (and the film has now been released on DVD), had lost all nuance. It seemed to beat down violently on the decors, while the closeups of Ava, though produced in Technicolor, often did not match up with the long shots.

Yet it is precisely in the film's incongruous stylistic mixture, structural complexity and abusive references that *Pandora* finds its *raison d'être*. Perhaps the film should simply be accepted as the excessive and irrational film it is. In all its exaggeration, might it not be appreciated for its breath of magic, without attempting to dissect its defects? *Pandora* is a surreal vision. How else may the indigestible and sometimes rather involuntarily comical interweaving of De Chirico, Greco-Roman archeology, jazz, Dutch legend and Ava Gardner be explained?

Lewin's mastery was reflected in his ability to establish a relationship between the underlying concept of his screenplay's structure (*Pandora* is a series of flashbacks and a succession of dreams that take the viewer back to a remote past) and his mise-en-scène. The way his settings are composed means that his 'frames' integrate numerous openings, mirrors, windows (frames within a frame), as if they were just so many stories told within the story. When Pandora slips on her wedding dress, the oval mirror frames and reflects her with her fiancé Stephen's image. And the frame of the French window isolates the Dutchman's boat anchored in the bay in the distance. The depth of field of this static shot alludes to Pandora's perspective and thoughts. Reassuring marriage or risky

adventure? In Lewin's work, formal research was not necessarily gratuitous.

A sophisticated literary and cinematic enigma, *Pandora* focuses on the myth of Ava Gardner and makes it larger than life. If Albert Lewin drew upon ancient tales and mythology, it was only to better establish the actress in *her* legend. "An ingenious idea" remarked Michel Pérez, "to link the destiny of a mythic woman forever... to a punished soul, condemned to eternally wander the vastness of the seas." [21] By refusing to limit the breadth of his inspiration by space or time, Albert Lewin thus made his film as legendary as his references, and Ava Gardner as mythic as Pandora.

From then on, all of Ava Gardner's roles stamped her with the indelible mark of tragedy. Her proposed incursion into musical comedy, MGM's favorite genre in the

Kathryn Grayson and Ava Gardner with Charles Rosher, Director of Photography of *Show Boat*.

George Sidney's *Show Boat* (1950) is an important turning point in Ava Gardner's career. The dramatic role of Julie La Verne gains her recognition from the industry.

early 50s, thus seemed all the more improbable. And undoubtedly it would have remained so had it not been for director George Sidney who felt, contrary to the Studio's new boss Dore Shary, that Ava was perfect for the part of Julie La Verne. As he recalled:

> Everyone thought I was crazy to buy *Show Boat*. And even crazier when they heard I was going to cast Ava as Julie, the tragic half-caste that Helen Morgan played originally. "Ava?" they kept saying. "She's nobody! Why cast her, of all people?" The Studio top brass were dead against it. But I *knew* she would be Julie.[9]

George Sidney entrusted his protégée Ava to his wife Lillian Burns, MGM's official acting coach. Quite ironically, they now had to work on Ava's Southern accent since by now she had completely lost her original drawl. *Show Boat* was set in late nineteenth-century Louisiana and Julie La Verne was a pretty young woman of mixed race persecuted by the discriminatory laws in force.

For the first time, Ava had a role that had a place in the tormented course of history. After this film there came roles in *Bhowani Junction*, *The Naked Maja*, *The Angel Wore Red*, and *55 Days at Peking* whose contexts also enhanced the importance of Ava's performances. The tone of *Show Boat*, a musical melodrama, was a far cry from the unbridled fantasy of *On the Town* starring Frank Sinatra and Gene Kelly. MGM's publicity department nevertheless boasted that the film's sumptuous Technicolor would put the other two previous screen versions to shame. There had been the 1929 version made at the dawn of the talkies, with a little sound; and the 1936 film directed by James Whale in black and white. The film's dazzling opening (as the Show Boat docks and artists joyfully parade), remains famous. Ava Gardner, alias Julie La Verne, splendid in a shimmering costume, contributed to the exuberant tones, colors and music.

Nevertheless the story very soon turns to tragedy. A law forbids non-white artists from performing in stage shows. Julie, whose mother was black, has to leave the show when she is reported to local authorities by someone in the crew. When we find her again, a few years later, Julie is a woman adrift. Make-up more strongly accentuates her mixed blood, perhaps to show why her fate has become more difficult. Having been left by her boyfriend Stephen, she is now an alcoholic and a very different Julie from the woman of those carefree happy days.

Once again Ava Gardner played a supporting role. The starring couple was Katherine Grayson (Magnolia) and Howard Keel (Gaylord). It is their torturous love story that *Show Boat* relates. Ava Gardner's part was nevertheless a key role in every way. Julie is instrumental to this couple's reconciliation. She gives up her job as a singer so that Magnolia can be hired in the nightclub. She awakens Gaylord's paternal feelings by revealing to him that he has a little girl, Kim. Whereas Pandora sacrificed her own posthumous happiness for the redemption of her soul and that of the Dutchman's, Julie La Verne, the heroine of *Show Boat*, sacrifices herself for the happiness of a another couple.

Ava Gardner was no longer the torturer of men's hearts. The woman who for so many years had symbolized the desired, lusted after, loved female was now a wounded, rejected woman sacrificed on the altar of oblivion. In the final scene, the Show Boat leaves the bank, with a reunited family aboard that reflects a conventional idea of happiness. Julie is left excluded and abandoned.

These images of solitude and suffering were nevertheless unsuccessful in supplanting the imposing female image firmly fixed in collective memory. That is, of a woman who made others suffer rather than being the sufferer herself. *Show Boat* was thus often left out when citing Ava's best films. Most likely too, interest in the film died out over the years. The old-fashioned tearjerkers in the great tradition of the embittered novels of the late nineteenth century were tremendously boring, despite the dynamic and lighthearted performances by Marge and Gower Champion. Nevertheless, it was thanks to *Show Boat* that the industry began to consider Ava Gardner as an actress in her own right.

Ava insisted on singing her character's two songs herself (*Bill* and *Can't Help Loving That Man*), though she had always been dubbed in films from *The Killers* to *Pandora*. Ava liked to think she had a gift for singing. Of course, she never claimed to rival the greats such as Howard Keel or William Warfield, who had the difficult task of singing the famous *Old Man River*, but Ava

was determined to convince producer Arthur Freed to let her sing. She managed a very honorable recording, gushing with emotion, on the borderline between singing and reciting. But Arthur Freed was adamant. Though he could not refuse the songs from being released on the original soundtrack album, he refused to use them in the film.

Though George Sidney was for it, Frank Sinatra was far less generous: "Now listen, Ava, you can't sing and you're among professional singers."[2] And this cutting

The bitter fate of a rejected woman (in *Show Boat*).

Burke (Clark Garble) works for the triumph of his cause and tries to win the beautiful Marta Ronda's heart. (Vincent Sherman's *Lone Star*, 1951).

uncompromising comment wounded her deeply. On 17 September 1951 Ava attended the premiere of *Show Boat* in Hollywood with Frank Sinatra who had just publicly announced his intention to marry her. Ava severely criticized the contrast between the acted and sung sequences. Yet, as valid as her opinion might have been, it did not keep the film from being a hit. Ava, however, never forgot the incident: "... the success aside, my anger about how callously Metro had treated me intensified the fury I'd been feeling toward them throughout my career."[2]

The film she made in the spring of that year, *Lone Star,* gave Ava yet another occasion to express her bitterness against MGM. This film treated a famous episode in American history, the joining of Texas to the Confederation. It would therefore have been expected that *Lone Star* be an important addition to the filmography of a by now confirmed star. Unfortunately, it was a bland and unimaginative production in black and white, despite the

heroic efforts of Clark Gable, Ava Gardner, Lionel Barrymore and Broderick Crawford.

Ava's only film in 1951, *Lone Star* shattered any high hopes sparked by the contract she had renewed in October of the previous year. The contract had increased her annual salary to 50,000 dollars and stipulated (as was customary), that she could not refuse any role. Ava therefore resigned herself to making the film, as did director Vincent Sherman, who hated the script as much as she did. Ava consoled herself with the prospect of at least being with Clark Gable again.

In Hollywood's inflexible world, directors such as Albert Lewin were few and far between. That is, there were not many filmmakers who managed to impose their own vision within the dictatorial domination of the studios. The director was considered a mere executor, just one more technician among the other crew. The producer was all-powerful and had the right to the final cut. To be a director under contract usually implied working on whatever was assigned. To be an actor or actress under contract meant the chance of working in a few prestigious productions (such as *Show Boat*), but more often in an infinite number of mediocre films. These were made with a well-oiled cast and crew and were ruled only by the financial considerations of assembly line production. And *Lone Star* belonged to this category.

Apart from the great historical event that serves as its backdrop, the heroine of *Lone Star,* Martha Ronda, portrayed by Ava Gardner, was at the center of a quaint sentimental story. Clark Gable supports Texas becoming part of the United States. Broderick Crawford, his rival and opponent, supports agreements with Mexico. They struggle for the triumph of their convictions as well as their love for Martha Ronda. The young woman is involved in the political debate as editor of the local newspaper of the small town of Austin.

This position of responsibility was a screenplay ploy to hide the inconsistency of the role that Ava Gardner had to make work. Her role was limited, and it was useless trying to associate it with any of her previous portrayals. There were very few scenes that gave her the chance of demonstrating her character or talent, which were by now widely recognized. Nor was Ava totally convincing. Her sporadic appearances seemed to be justified solely by the need for a seductive presence in a popular film.

Despite the earnest debates on why Texas should become part of the the United States, *Lone Star* had nothing to distinguish itself from the ordinary western, with its

In this costume film Ava demonstrates her goddess-like presence but does not have the chance to use all of her acting ability.

Ava rehearses the song performed on playback of *Lovers Were Meant to Cry* for Vincent Sherman, director of *Lone Star.*

dose of stampedes, shoot outs and attacking Indians, moonlight rides and dusty fist fights. Ava of course was absent from all of these action scenes. She only reappeared in the last reel to say that she preferred Clark Gable, just as audiences expected. More astounding was the patriotic happy ending that brought together the mortal enemies of the day before. They ride off side by side towards a common destiny against the American flag which now bears another star. A turnaround as improbable as it was audacious for the partisans of Texan independence.

For a year the Hollywood studios had been undergoing tremendous upheaval. The Anti-Trust law had dismantled their powerful hold by separating production and distribution. Dore Shary was appointed head of MGM to replace old lion Louis B. Mayer. But the world's leading studio that ranked before Universal, Fox, Columbia and RKO, was now living on a splendor completely estranged from

this new reality. The Studio reacted slowly to the winds of change and particularly to the growing, ever more pressing competition from television.

Dore Shary tried to be reassuring. In the future no more *Lone Stars,* no more of these films from another era which were inadmissible after *Pandora* and *Show Boat*. Empty promises. Ava's mood swings became more and more marked and seemed to express a deeper resentment. MGM was unable to control her excesses. Increasingly the profile of a betrayed and unfulfilled woman began to emerge. The true bitterness, however, would come later, exploding sometimes violently. Not only did Ava have to cope with a chaotic career, but also with an unhappy love life. Jo-Carroll Silvers evoked Ava's second husband Artie Shaw, whom she considered a monster and intellectual snob: "He just destroyed her, as he did many other beautiful women. As a result, I think Ava, who was

Artie's fourth wife, spent the rest of her life trying to get back at men."[17] Ava took refuge in an appropriate lifestyle of drink after drink, lover after husband, and wild night after wild night. "... In those days I did whatever went through my mind, and my decisions were often not all that sensible,"[2] she admitted.

There was only one hope for Ava: to experience Pandora's spiritual metamorphosis herself, to learn from the character she had portrayed and who had declared, "I've changed so since I've known you. I'm not cruel and hateful like I used to be, hurting people because I was so unhappy myself. I know now what distrust comes from. It's a lack of love."

Indeed, Ava still wanted to believe in a happy love life. For the moment the man in her life was Frank Sinatra. But Sinatra was going through a crisis himself. He was suffering from severe depression and his contract with MGM had been terminated. He was even afraid of not being able to pay for his divorce. And then the investigating committee on organized crime led by Senator Estes Kefauver was looking into allegations that the singer was associated with the mafia. The eight photos taken during his trip to Cuba in 1947 which showed him with Lucky Luciano on the balcony of the Hotel Nacional in Havana, did not help. The sessions were broadcast on television and his attorney just barely managed to spare him an appearance before the public. Frank continued his suicide blackmail. At Lake Tahoe he took an overdose of barbiturates, though he was careful not to take the lethal dose. The incident made all the headlines, but he denied them. Ava Gardner later wrote:

> I know now that Frank's mock suicidal dramas – his desperate love signals to get me back to his side – were, at root, cries for help. He was down, way down. His contracts were cancelled. His wife's lawyers were intent on screwing every possible dollar out of him, something that caused him to force a laugh and say, "Ava, I won't have enough bucks to buy you a pair of nylons once they're through with me." For Christ's sake, he was a human being like the rest of us. He'd been the idol of millions and now he was being taunted as a washed-up has-been.[2]

The press was holding its breath for the marriage everyone expected. The couple's escapade to Mexico City and Acapulco in August of 1951 did not go unnoticed by reporters. The couple's return to Los Angeles was marked by a new incident. Sinatra was accused of running into journalist William Eccles with his black Cadillac. Ava claimed that the photographer had deliberately thrown himself onto the hood to try to get a shot of them. The incident only aggravated the tension between Sinatra and the press. Ava realized that she had to help Frank. With the success of *Show Boat* she could now demand 100,000 dollars a film. She fought to have her contract changed to stipulate: "We agree that she be assigned to do this picture, and we further agree that we will employ Frank Sinatra to appear..."[17] Though Ava and Frank never did make a picture together, they did become man and wife on 7 November 1951 in Philadelphia.

After the chore of making *Lone Star*, Ava Gardner was happy to be approached by 20th Century Fox. For a

Ava Gardner, 8 December 1951 in London, with her husband of one month, Frank Sinatra. They perform a piano and vocal duet at Washington Hotel before a "Midnight Matinee" show at the London Coliseum.

number of years they had been considering making a screen adaptation of Hemingway's *The Snows of Kilimanjaro*. Film directors and producers found this work by the novelist an exceptional source, rich in visual and story potential. A number of the writer's other works had been brought to the screen: *Farewell to Arms* in 1932; *For Whom the Bell Tolls* and *To Have and to Have Not* in 1944; *The Killers* in 1945; *The Macomber Affair* in 1947; *Under My Skin* in 1950. The writer had not liked any of these films except for *The Killers*. Aldous Huxley once aptly remarked: "What Hemingway has to say is in the white spaces between the lines." The novel, just as the film, opened with an enigma in the form of an allegory:

> Kilimanjaro is a snow-covered mountain 19,710 feet high and is said to be the highest mountain in Africa. Close to the western summit, called *Masai Ngaga Ngai,* the house of God, there is the dried and frozen carcass of a leopard. No one has explained what the leopard was seeking at that altitude.

The hero, Harry Street (Gregory Peck), a writer and adventurer, is plagued by this riddle as he lies dying of a leg wound in his encampment at the foot of Kilimanjaro. The riddle is the only legacy his old uncle Bill has left him to help face a period of deep self-questioning. Just as the leopard, Harry has lost himself along paths that have diverted the ambitious young writer from his ideals, and led him to choose a career of easy success.

Though the hidden meaning of the work was seductive, that is, the anguish and doubts of an artist – even Hemingway's own – it was certainly not one to encourage action. As writer Harry Street sees the important moments of his life go by, the film becomes a lifelong voyage from Paris, to Spain, to the French Riviera, which prompted Hemingway to complain, "I only sold one novel to Fox, not my complete works!"

There was only one actress who found grace in Hemingway's eyes and that was Ava Gardner in *The Killers*. And it was Ava whom Hemingway wanted as Cynthia in *The Snows of Kilimanjaro*. He wanted her to portray this woman who permeates the senses of his hero. Producer Zanuck was not at all for the idea. He did not think Ava was a good actress, though he did admit that her performance in *Show Boat* had revealed a certain talent. He wanted Anne Francis for the part.

Cynthia is a night reveler who wanders through pre-war bohemian Paris in search of the happiness that has always eluded her. She meets Harry in a bistro and their love story is sparked in the smoky dimness of an artist's studio. The flame of a match casts the glimmer of a fleeting hope. Cynthia is a mysterious woman, devastatingly beautiful, who "drinks too much and smokes too much", an aimless wanderer who spends long evenings drinking with young artists biding their time until success comes their way.

Harry: Well everybody is trying to do something here. At least trying to try. What are you trying to do? Paint?
Cynthia: No, I'm not trying to paint.
Harry: Sculpt then.

Even more than *One Touch of Venus*, which despite its sparkle was nothing more than a fantasy; even more than *Pandora and the Flying Dutchman*, which borrowed too much from legend and aspired too much to myth, *The Snows of Kilimanjaro* drew a portrait of Ava Gardner which Mankiewicz did not take long to immortalize. A well-to-do American woman who comes to France to make arrangements for her war victim father's ashes, lives from one casual love affair to another, occasionally modeling for painters. Cynthia Green (Ava Gardner) clings, as if to a rock, to Harry Street (a Hemingway hero à la Gregory Peck !). Who would deny that Cynthia Green, a sketch of Maria d'Amata and Lady Brett Ashley (whom the screenwriter, a man of culture, was very obviously marking down), was not already extremely " Ava-Gardnerian "? Among other things, this could be seen in her fascination with Spain (the actress herself had discovered the country a year before the movie and had since escaped to Madrid, where she had become passionately keen on bullfighting); the taste for the statuary (she posed nude sometimes); her dissatisfaction in love, which was in no way an obstacle to her fleeting affairs (since her only ambition was to " simply be happy " while waiting for the right man, just as her greatest desire was to bear a child for "Mr. Right"); the "disaster " of her life lived with the man she loved and who loved her; her desire to save face – out of modesty of course and not out of hypocrisy (being above her fellowmen, she was, as Quinlan in *Touch of Evil*, above their laws) – just as those picadors' horses, whose caparisons conceal their wounds from spectators. What was now essential was that her *freedom* – and what a strange and cruel paradox was it not! – was her *prison*, and her triumph, her crushing defeat. Since, though for almost everyone what was important was to be loved (more than to love, which is always easier), what was important to her was, in fact, less to be loved or to love, but rather to find the one who *deserved* her love. Just as Ava Gardner, Cynthia Green breaks out of her chains only to find herself bound by others.

(*Portrait d'Ava Gardner*. Claude Gauteur. *Les Cahiers du Cinéma* n° 88, October 1958).

Cynthia: No, I'm not trying to sculpt.
Harry: Well then, you must be trying to write, too.
Cynthia: No, I'm only trying to be happy.

A supremely luminous Ava Gardner whispers rather than speaks her lines, words that echo her own real life. Who other than Ava Gardner could truly feel this scene? "I had written the part of Cynthia, that lost twenties girl, for Ava,"[9] admitted screenwriter Casey Robinson. Cynthia later blossoms under the warm rays of spring that brightly fill the Place de la Contrescarpe as Harry tells her the good news that his first novel is going to be published. Cynthia Green has become Cynthia Street. Harry is restless. He is one of those writers who draws his inspiration from experience, who feeds on the cries, sounds and tastes of the countries of his travels. Harry is attentive to everything, except to

his wife, and does not even realize how weary she is. When they make a trip to Africa, Cynthia longs to just settle down:

Cynthia: Harry darling, couldn't we just go home?
Harry: Home? Where's that?

She even decides to sacrifice the child she is expecting so as not to be an obstacle to her husband's career. She then accompanies him to Spain and there they separate. Cynthia is plagued by remorse, Harry fired by his ambition. The scene, as they sit in a restaurant, is like a formal condemnation of their couple. Cynthia finds a rival to their love in the vigorous new desire of a Flamenco dancer who cannot tear his eyes from her.
She reproaches Harry for having accepted to do one more news coverage, this time on the riots in Damas-

The final break up, filmed in one sequence shot, in a Madrid restaurant. *The Snows of Kilimanjaro*, adapted from a Hemingway novel, skyrocketed Ava to international stardom.

Fatally wounded, Cynthia is embraced by Harry for the last time before their love comes to a tragic end (*The Snows of Kilimanjaro*).

cus. This scene, filmed in one static shot that lasts three minutes and twenty seconds (an intense performance by Ava), also expressed the essence of what was being questioned in the couple Sinatra-Gardner. What should take precedence, personal fulfillment or a successful career? How much should each partner be willing to sacrifice? In refusing the Damascus job, Harry was affirming the underlying idea in *Pandora* that "the measure of love is what one is willing to give up for it".

Frank was against Ava doing the film and asked her to refuse. His own career was still at a standstill in those early months of 1952, and the press and the puritan leagues continued to harass him. His voice was shaky and the agents were finding it hard to get him booked into the most popular clubs. Sinatra opposed the film project mainly because he was singing in a small club in New York and wanted Ava to be by his side. It was out of the question for her to refuse to do *The Snows of Kilimanjaro*. This was, in fact, the first

time Ava had ever shown interest in a film since her debut in 1941:

> Of all the parts I've played, Cynthia was probably the first one I understood and felt comfortable with, the first role I truly wanted to play... This wasn't at all like some of those other slinky-black-dress parts I'd had. This girl wasn't a tramp or a bitch or a real smart cookie. She was a good average girl with normal impulses. I didn't have to pretend.[2]

Roland Flamini [22] reported this exchange which summed it all up:

> *Ava:* It's a perfect part for me.
> *Frank:* The perfect part for you is being my wife.

To appease her imperious husband's demands – though one wonders had he been in her place, would he have reacted in the same way? – Ava asked director Henry King to shoot all of her scenes in ten days.

*R*ide, Vaquero! (1953). Ava in a scene with Howard Keel.

From left to right, Anthony Quinn, Ava Gardner, Howard Keel, and Robert Taylor in *Ride, Vaquero!*

There were a dozen in all, mainly early in the film. This was quite feasible, in fact, since they were not shooting on location. They were to begin in the early months of 1952, and Kenya was going to be brought to Hollywood, reconstructed on Fox's Lot 8. Ava's request would nevertheless impose a grueling pace. It would also mean shooting at night at much greater cost.

The final day of shooting was devoted to the end of Harry and Cynthia's story. Though the couple has separated and Harry has had an affair with Countess Liz (Hildegarde Neff), he is still searching for Cynthia. He imagines seeing her on the Place Vendôme, but this turns out to be a woman named Helen (Susan Hayward), who later becomes his wife. Cynthia is in fact in Spain, where she has volunteered as a nurse in the Civil War. Harry joins the Republican factions, less out of conviction than out of personal interest.

On the battlefield, as fighting rages against the Falangists and explosions tear up the earth, an ambu-lance overturns after being hit by a grenade. Harry rushes to the vehicle and in one of those miracles that occur only in the minds of screenwriters, he finds Cynthia trapped beneath the van. She is dying and there is a brusque, desperate and tragic ending to the scene which Ava described not only as one of death, but also a love scene.[2]

In New York, Frank Sinatra was getting ready for his unimpressive engagement and his calls about the film's progress became more and more pressing. Henry King had underestimated the work needed for the sequence which called for the directing of 500 extras and many special effects. As screenwriter Casey Robinson recalled:

> We decided to go over the ten days and break the agreement. When King and I told Ava all hell broke loose. She became hysterical. She called New York and Frank was furious with her. God knows how we got through that last day.[9]

Cordelia's arrival at the ranch. Here they put the last touches to her costume before shooting.

Fortunately Ava was playing opposite her ex-partner and lover in *The Bribe*, Robert Taylor. Nevertheless the idyll was soon over and to rescue her from sheer boredom (they were shooting on location deep in the heart of Utah), Frank went to keep her company for a few weeks.

In *Vaquero*, Anthony Quinn played the role of José Esqueda with exemplary boorishness. His character was a lowdown criminal and virtuoso in the art of mistreating women. Cordelia Cameron (Ava Gardner) falls prey to him when the story sends her into the outlaw's hideout. She pleads him to stop persecuting her husband Tom, a hardworking pioneer armed only with good intentions. When Cordelia even threatens the brigand with a weapon, he merely scoffs. Cordelia returns to her role as model wife at the homestead, a dream ranch that the brute Esqueda keeps trying to burn down.

Tom makes a big mistake. He lets Rio, the handsome Robert Taylor, come to his ranch and entrusts his wife to him. As a character, Cordelia was a good example of the dilemmas of women during the time the film was produced. Though she was a woman of virtue, could she resist temptation? When Cordelia returns shaken from her confrontation with Esqueda and needs comforting, Rio is there ready to love her.

Yet Rio is also a righteous man and a person who keeps his word. He cannot betray his friend's trust. Just the kind of moral the people at MGM liked serving up. Any depth of character for Cordelia was virtually inexistent except for being rounded out by Ava Gardner's lovely forms which at least made the role's vacuousness more appealing. *Variety* euphemistically commented, "Miss Gardner provides physical beauty to a character that is not as well stated as it could have been." [23]

Ava Gardner was finished with shooting just one day late and was free of any commitments. She refused to act in *Sombrero*, an inane story set in a Mexican village (the role went to Yvonne De Carlo). Most likely she now thought she deserved roles at least equal to the one she had just played for Fox. The Studio threatened to suspend her and to block her salary. Ava quickly had second thoughts about her high standards (when it came to money she was quite level-headed). She accepted to appear in *Vaquero* in June 1952, a western still sometimes shown today on television to fill dull Sunday afternoons.

Ava hated everything about it, the film and the director, John Farrow, an Australian whom she found extremely uncouth. She considered it all just one more ordeal with bad shooting conditions to make it worse.

Shooting completed, Ava turned to the premiere of *The Snows of Kilimanjaro* in New York in September 1952. The publicity department's promotion had referred to the burning desire a Montparnasse model ignites in a man whom only the snows of Kilimanjaro can soothe. Ava's name was billed third, after Gregory Peck's and Susan Hayward's. When Ava did not hesitate to point this out to screenwriter Casey Robinson, he replied:

Miss Gardner, don't tell me you're a page counter. It's true you have less pages than the other woman. But believe me, Cynthia is the female star. Because she's the very heart of the picture, she's the very heart of the story of the hero. [9]

He was right. The film brought more glory to her

than any film until then. Despite reluctant distributors who complained about an unpronounceable title, and critics' bad reviews, *The Snows of Kilimanjaro* was a tremendous box office hit and grossed some 6,550,000 dollars for Fox.[24] Director Henry King later declared about Ava's performance:

> No one else could have given it the sensitivity, the bruised quality, that Ava imparted to it... she disciplined herself rigorously for the part – and she believed in Cynthia. Sometimes she'd come grumbling in the morning – she hated to get up early and drive to the Studio. But once she was actually on the floor she worked with a kind of desperate involvement and intensity that amazed me.[9]

While Ava was basking in the glory of *The Snows of Kilimanjaro*, which skyrocketed her into the echelons of inter-

national stardom, Frank Sinatra was deep in crisis. Though the public had turned against him, he never stopped believing in his talent. Ava, on the other hand, considered herself a horrible actress, despite the fact that publicity was now mailing out more than three thousand photos a week to all her fans, stamped with her signature. On 22 May 1952 she was among the stars who left their prints in the fresh cement of the Grauman's Chinese Theatre. Sinatra was not invited.

Ava had a cameo role in *The Band Wagon*. She is met by a horde of journalists as she gets off the train, striking up poses and smiling for photographers. She exchanges a few friendly words with Fred Astaire, an artist in a slump (like Sinatra), who for a moment had thought he was the reason for all the commotion.

Fred Astaire as Tony Hunter, a star on the decline, with Ava Gardner at the peak of her career in a cameo role. In Vincente Minnelli's *The Band Wagon* (1953).

Screen rivals Grace Kelly and Ava Gardner become real-life friends during the making of John Ford's *Mogambo* (1953).

Nevertheless, Ava was still a fervent admirer of her husband as an artist. She decided to be the architect of his comeback and help rebuild his career. Columbia was planning a screen adaptation of the James Jones best-seller *From Here to Eternity*. It treated the lives of five men in a military camp and was set in Hawaii at the eve of Pearl Harbor. Among the roles to be cast, there was an Italian from New Jersey. Frank Sinatra immediately identified with the character of Angelo Maggio. He had been dreaming for a long time of acting in a true dramatic role, unlike most singers who had forged their reputations in MGM musicals. His chances of getting the part were practically zero, though he was ready to accept anything, even to work for the pittance of a thousand dollars a week.

Ava Gardner secretly went to see Joan Cohn, the wife of the big boss at Columbia, to see if Joan could not plead Sinatra's case to her husband, Harry Cohn. Ava even offered to appear in the film for free in exchange for a simple screen test for Frank. But Harry Cohn was absolutely against casting Sinatra, whom he had once even referred to as "nothing but a fucking hoofer"[17] to the singer's face. And director Fred Zinneman already had an actor from the theatre in mind for the part: Eli Wallach.

MGM had a new super-production in the offing to be directed by John Ford: *Mogambo*. The word got around to Stewart Granger who wanted to prolong the success of *King Salomon's Mines*. This *Mogambo* was a remake of *Red Dust* and was shifted to Africa. Stewart Granger very much wanted the role that had originally been played by Clark Gable. Ava was cast as Eloise Kelly and Grace Kelly as Mrs. Nordley. Just a few weeks before shooting began, however, Clark Gable announced that he wanted to be in the film. Dore Shary realized that the King's career needed a boost and gave in to his demands, ignoring Stewart Granger's protests.

November 1952. While waiting for a most improbable acceptance from Columbia, Frank escorted his wife to Nairobi. September and October had been filled with incidents later cited as examples of how violent the couple's intimate relations had become. The period was punctuated with countless break-ups and reconciliations which were vented in private and public. The first of these infamous fights took place at Fort Lee in New Jersey after one of Sinatra's tours when Ava accused him of having heavily eyed actress Marilyn Maxwell. A second one, in their home in Palm Springs, broke out in the presence of Lana Turner. The couple's tumultuous relationship seemed to now be completely out of control. Nevertheless, on 7 November 1952, Ava Gardner and Frank Sinatra, slaves to their devastating passion, celebrated their first wedding anniversary at the foot of Mount Kenya, all to the rhythms of some fifty African singers and dancers. This was truly an event for Ava, whose two previous marriages had not even lasted a year.

In *The Snows of Kilimanjaro* there is a memorable scene in which Cynthia learns that she is pregnant by the man she loves more than anyone in the world. She realizes, though, that it is simply not the right time for them to have a child. On the set of *Mogambo* this was exactly the situation Ava was experiencing. As if inspired by the screenwriters, she had actually become one of their characters. Ava admitted that this had been the hardest decision of her life:

Ava Gardner with Clark Gable in *Mogambo*, a remake of *Red Dust*.

In *Mogambo* Ava Gardner perfectly embodies Eloise Kelly, a young seductive and liberated widow. (Here with Donald Sinden and Philip Sainton).

And that situation brought to the surface all my old doubts about having the right to produce a child unless you had a sane, solid lifestyle in which he or she could be brought up. Frank and I had no such thing. We didn't even possess the ability to live together like any normal married couple. Frank would arrive home at about 4 am after a singing engagement at a nightclub or concert. And I would have to leave the house at 6:30 am or earlier to get to the Studio on time. Not really much of a home life there.[2]

Robert Surtees, first cameraman for *Mogambo*, recalled:

Ava hated Frank so intensely by this stage she couldn't stand the idea of having his baby. She went to London to have an abortion. I know, because my wife went to London to be by her side all the time through the operation and afterward.[9]

The official story for the benefit of the press was that she had come down with a tropical infection, with serious anemia, which would justify her hasty departure from the set. Frank Sinatra had been called to Columbia for a screen test for the part of Angelo Maggio. When he returned at Christmas, he was kept from knowing the truth. He got the role that he had so ardently desired, and it brought him an Oscar, which also definitively relaunched his career. Sinatra's casting in the film was also in part thanks to the fact that Eli Wallach had pulled out for another role on the stage. A few weeks later Ava discovered she was pregnant again. She took advantage of being in London for the *Knights of the Round Table* to have another abortion only a few months after the first one.

But clearly someone told him about what I was doing, because as long as I live I'll never forget waking up after the operation and seeing Frank sitting next to the bed with tears in his eyes. But I think I was right. I still think I was right.[2]

Here again, it is impossible not to recall Gregory Peck (Harry) at Cynthia's bedside when he learns that she has had an abortion:

Harry: You did it deliberately.
Cynthia: It was an accident.
Harry: Just because of what I said.
Cynthia: It was an accident. I stumbled.
Harry: You didn't have any right to do it! It was my child too.
Cynthia: Don't darling.
Harry: Oh Cyn—-! My darliing, stupid little idiot.
Cynthia: And now we can go to the bullfights.

The shooting of *Mogambo* got off to a bad start. The leopard sequence was not turning out as hoped. Gable's and Ava's performances were not working and in her memoirs she evoked an incident:

As I got off the bed I said, quite casually I thought, "Oh, boy, that was a real fuck up. We goofed everything." Not the most politic thing to say, especially on a Jack Ford set. Because Jack thought the remark was directed at him. He decided I had to be put firmly in my place. "Oh, you're a director now," he said scornfully. "You know so fucking much about directing. You're a lousy actress, but now you're a director. Well, why don't you direct something? You go sit in my chair and I'll go and play your scene." All this was said in a loud voice in front of the cast and the crew and everybody.[2]

The jungle in the film *Mogambo* looks so inviting, with that fortuitous shower that is so deliciously exotic, that it is hard to imagine how difficult the conditions of the shoot really were. There was the risk of being attacked by tigers, sanitation problems, terrible accidents that eventually caused the death of two young Africans and the English assistant director, not to mention the personality clashes between Ava and John Ford. As Ava wrote:

It turned out that Ford hadn't wanted me at all. He wanted Maureen O'Hara, and he wasn't shy about letting that be known. He adored Gracie, but he was very cold to me. He called me in to see him before shooting began and he didn't even look at me. All he said was, "You're going to be overdressed." That was all. So I went back to my room and talked it over with Frank. I told him, "I'm going to talk to Ford." Then I stomped in and I said, "I'm just as Irish and mean as you are. I'm not going to take this. I'm sorry if you don't like me – I'll go home." He just looked at me as if he didn't know what I was talking about and said, "I don't know what you mean. Who's been rude to you?"[2]

Mogambo belongs to the category of films that enjoy mythic titles.[25] Those that the public savors with a pleasure most likely very distant from the titles' original impact. Nevertheless, we cannot be expected to see through the eyes of viewers of a half a century ago. Instead, we are compensated with the fun of watching these popular movies for what they were. Indeed, the hippopotamus hunt in *The Snows of Kilimanjaro*, filmed in the studio with a back projection, is a good example. It is rather difficult to be convinced of the dangers faced by our intrepid hunters, watered down by prop men and shaken in a boat by a hardworking crew.

MGM continued its series of remakes of films from the silent movie era in an effort to satisfy an increasingly demanding public. Yet sound, introduced in 1928, and Technicolor in 1934, already no longer impressed the public. Fox had recently launched wide screen viewing in Cinemascope with the release of *The Robe*. MGM decided to move its cast and crew to the actual places where the adventures of *Mogambo* take place. They hoped that dispatching some one hundred and seventy-five British and American crew and cast members, a number of planes, and at least a hundred motor vehicles to the spot might guarantee both illusion and success.

Provocative Ava Gardner, in *Mogambo* as Eloise Kelly, received the only Oscar nomination of her career. Here with Grace Kelly, Donald Sinden, Eric Polhmann, Philip Sainton, and Clark Gable.

Mogambo paradoxically had a studio recreated in the midst of a jungle location.

A production team scouted out the best locations in the Belgian Congo, Kenya, Tanganyika, and collaborated with British authorities, the Masai, and the Samburu. Yet, in the end, the authenticity obtained was only slightly greater than what could be achieved in the States shooting on good sets. The charm of *Mogambo* lies precisely in this paradox. The spectacle of the film's treacherous tropical forests and seas was far from being the main attraction of *Mogambo*. However, seeing Ava Gardner arrive in the heart of the African jungle with three suitcases, or watching her feed wild animals with the carelessness of any woman who has seen them only in picture books or at the zoo, is a delight only John Ford's film can boast. This already delighted audiences of the time, if we read what one reviewer wrote:

> Without going as far as the half-dozen negligees in satin and crêpe de Chine which Marlene Dietrich once walked around in across the sands of the Sahara, this pretty person suddenly appears out of the brush as impeccably made-up, manicured and coiffured as if she were just coming out of a beauty institute on 5th Avenue, and we

see her parading in front of the natives in hats that would be more appropriate in the grandstands of Longchamps on the day of the Grand Prix.[26]

Elegance graciously enveloped the fragility of the character. Eloise Kelly took up her place as a direct extension of Cynthia in *The Snows of Kilimanjaro*. Eloise is a young widow marked by a cruel fate (her husband was killed in a plane crash three weeks after their marriage). She is lonely and in search of love. Her rough language and quick sarcasm, however, make her character less tragic. Though in the film the confrontations with wild gorillas are rather disappointing (not once do wild animals and hunters appear in the same shot), the struggle between Eloise Kelly and Mrs. Nordley, the wife of a young ethnologist, that is, Ava Gardner and Grace Kelly, is absolutely convincing in its virulence. For at stake there is Vick, that is, Clark Gable.

A surly, wary and inveterate misogynist who just naturally equates problems with petticoats, Clark Gable tries his best to act as referee between the two women. They are opposites in every way: one is blond, shy and timid, high-strung, and a prisoner of her conventional and proper morals; the other is a street-smart brunette with a viper's tongue, whose jealousy and unfulfillment make her aggressiveness even more stinging. Promotion for the film alluringly played on this clash as it announced, "They tore each other apart like two panthers!... The sudden hostility of two women in love, or how the jungle reduces two civilized young women to their most primitive instincts." In actual fact nothing could have been further from the truth. Ava Gardner and Grace Kelly became the closest of friends. The princess-to-be would always symbolize for Ava a serene happiness that seemed forever inaccessible.

Joan Cohn remembered a little party thrown at the end of the shooting of *From Here to Eternity*:

> I still remember Frank sitting there telling everyone that in sixteen more hours he would be with Ava. "She's the most beautiful woman in the world."... He was desperately in love with her. It was kind of sad because all the

rest of us knew that the marriage was held together by mere threads at that point.[17]

The shooting of *Mogambo* wound up in London with some very clever studio work on the lighting and the scenery, yet *Mogambo* disappointed John Ford's admirers. They quite rightly judged this studio commissioned film by a director more at ease working with men than with women, as an unworthy successor to his pre-war productions such as *Bite the Bullet*, *Fort Apache*, or *She Wore a Yellow Ribbon*. The film was disturbingly conformist, and the action was predictable one reel in advance, so frequent were its allusions to *Miss Sadie Thompson* and *The Naked Jungle*. Nevertheless, there were some inspired scenes.

Among Ava Gardner's films, *Mogambo* is still considered an important picture of that period. It confirmed and strengthened the idea of how increasingly difficult it was becoming to distinguish between the actress's real life and the lives of her characters. The

89

Ava Gardner, here with Mel Ferrer as King Arthur, is Queen Guinevere in Richard Thorpe's *Knights of the Round Table* (1953).

A very boring role which leaves Ava a lot of free time!

iated in his life. The noise was so great he stopped singing. The orchestra stopped playing. Frank walked off. I got up, left the theatre, and went back to the hotel.[2]

In May 1953, Ava Gardner and Frank Sinatra put the finishing touches on the agitated screenplay of their private lives with a flourish. Ava was back from London after playing Guinevere in *Knights of the Round Table*. The manager of the hotel threatened to kick out both celebrities as they flung themselves into the final exasperated scenes of their marriage.

Knights of the Round Table, in dazzling Technicolor, was the first MGM film shot in Cinemascope. Based on the famous legend of Excalibur, it brought to the screen the legendary characters of King Arthur, Lancelot and Perceval, yet reduced Ava Gardner to a deluxe extra. Queen Guinevere was not Queen Christine and, whereas Greta Garbo had burst forth twenty years before in the starring role, Ava Gardner was relegated to a bit part. She only appeared a half an hour into the film after the "legendary heroes", intent on putting feudal England to right, established a new chivalric order. When it came time for a truce and amusements, Ava appeared. Just as Anne Crawford (the fairy Morgane), who had nothing medieval about her, Ava exuded a Hollywood look as if "the queens of the sixth century were, it seemed, trained to be top models".[27]

Ava Gardner's elegant gestures, graceful movements, heavily made-up lips, and finely manicured hands all participated in this idealization. Ava seemed to have devoted little to the role. She was distant, content to maintain a regal silence and give the occasional condescending smile with the reserve befitting of her rank. The action scenes were filmed with great brio by Richard Thorpe. He did not miss any traveling shot that would give us the enjoyment of speeding as fast as those horses across the green plains of England. The brilliant colors of the knights' costumes against the countryside were splendid. Everything was impeccable, gleaming, from the contrast of garish tones to the shining swords. Though Hollywood excelled in describing the eternal sentiments of love, adultery, jealousy, betrayal, and hunger for power, it shied away from representing the spiritual element, an aspect that was at the heart of the quest for the Holy Grail. The appearance of the luminescent vessel on the castle wall was a demonstration of this dimension.

A big-budget production, *Knights of the Round Table* was a Christmas box-office triumph (released in the U.S.

role of Eloise Kelly brought Ava her first and only Oscar nomination. It was Audrey Hepburn, the leading actress in *Roman Holiday*, who walked away with the statuette that year.

Ava managed to get away for three weeks to Spain, a country that fascinated her more and more. Ignoring the costume fittings and riding lessons prescribed by MGM in preparation for *Knights of the Round Table*, she went to join Frank Sinatra on his European tour. Sinatra still had difficulty filling the theatres in Milan and Rome. In Naples, in the middle of the concert, a spotlight suddenly beamed down on Ava, who was sitting incognito in the audience, and the crowd deliriously began chanting her name.

I don't think Frank has ever been more publicly humilin 1953). It grossed some 4,864,000 dollars,[24] which beat even the box office of *Ivanhoe* the previous year. The latter had also been made with the same people (same director, producer, director of photography and composer), and in the same castle!

On her divorce with Frank Sinatra, Ava commented:

I don't think I ever sat down and made a conscious decision about leaving Frank; as usual I simply acted on impulse and allowed events to sweep me along. But I remember exactly when I made the decision to seek a divorce. It was the day the phone rang and Frank was on the other end, announcing that he was in bed with another woman. And he made it plain that if he was going to be constantly accused of infidelity when he was innocent, there had to come a time when he'd decide he might as well be guilty. But for me, it was a chilling moment. I was deeply hurt. I knew then that we had reached a crossroads. Not because we had fallen out of love, but because our love had so battered and bruised us that we couldn't stand it anymore.[2]

Ava Gardner was back in the U.S. but thought it better not to let her husband know. On 23 October 1953 Howard Strickling, head of MGM public relations, officially announced the couple's separation. He added that Miss Gardner was beginning divorce proceedings:

I think the main reason my marriages failed is that I always loved too well, but never wisely. I'm terribly possessive about the people I love and I probably smother them with love.[2]

No other woman in Sinatra's life ever succeeded in healing the wounds left by Ava's decision. Actor Shecky Greene commented:

He always told me one of the things that fascinated him about Ava was that there was no conquest. He couldn't conquer her. That is where the respect comes. He never got her. He couldn't control her or dominate her. He'd get drinking and tell me how she always called him a goddamned hoodlum and a gangster. He'd never take that from anyone else but Ava. She was always a challenge to him, and he needs that. It's a definite part of his personality.[17]

Though they were perhaps unaware of it at the time, however, by freeing themselves from the bondage of their marriage, Ava and Frank actually tied themselves together forever. They remained close friends for the rest of their lives.

Our phone bills were astronomical, and when I found the letters Frank wrote me the other day, the total could fill a suitcase. Every single day during our relationship, no matter where in the world I was, I'd get a telegram from Frank saying he loved me and missed me.[2]

When Ava Gardner, breathless and exhausted, was admitted in September 1986 for a check up at Saint John's Hospital in Los Angeles, Frank Sinatra was by her side and offered not only moral support, but also financial help as well. They were no longer that glamorous, insolent couple of days gone by. Frank Sinatra was now sixty-six and Ava was a woman worn by her excesses. Their feelings for each other, however, were as fresh as the first day. And leaning on his arm, Ava took her first steps again after a three-week convalescence. In January 1988, Frank Sinatra was in Australia when he was told that Ava had had a relapse. Cancelling all his concerts, he took the first flight out to be by her side. Despite her age and condition, it was said that Ava still aroused the jealousy of Barbara Marx, then Sinatra's fourth wife. Upon Ava's death two years later, a wreath of flowers signed "Francis" read, "*With all my love*".

In 1953 Ava Gardner was firmly established in the pantheon of film greats. Yet curiously her fame surpassed that of any of her films. Of course, *The Killers* remained a classic of the noir genre. *Mogambo*, though very popular, was not a runaway success. *Pandora and the Flying Dutchman* managed only a meager box office and only owed its much later recognition to film buffs. Of course, no one had forgotten the haunting woman of *The Snows of Kilimanjaro*, nor the Julie La Verne of *Show Boat*, yet this record of achievements did not live up to what could be expected of a star now recognized as a serious actress.

Ava Gardner had never considered her career a priority. She never had the burning passion nor incommensurable drive to succeed at all costs. She lacked the confidence and the determination and admitted quite honestly, "Basically, I'm lazy". A rebel and a marginal, Ava Gardner never sought the support of a producer, husband or mentor, and became the muse of just one director: Albert Lewin. Yet their collaboration went no further than *Pandora* and the prospect of creating a body of work modeled after the creations of Josef von Sternberg and Marlène Dietrich never saw the light. Ava was not in love with Lewin. Ava used to say in moments of introspection, "I've never really worked hard at it because I didn't seem to have to. It all came so easily."[28]

And yet her encounter with what must be considered the "role of her life" was the result of her own determination and that of film director Joseph L. Mankiewicz.

After her separation from Frank Sinatra, Ava hopes to work in Europe. Joseph L. Manckiewicz gives her the chance thanks to *The Barefoot Contessa*, shot in Italy and on the French Riviera.

Opposite page: An artist makes a statue of the Contessa.

The Barefoot Contessa was a major work that forced her to reflect upon herself, her craft as an actress, and her condition as a star. Joseph Mankiewicz was a strong personality in Hollywood at the time and enjoyed a special sort of status: he worked within the system yet without bending to it. He made films both for Fox and MGM. The esteem from his fellow directors and the unheard of privileges he enjoyed were due not only to Mankiewicz's repeated box office successes. He also had an impressive track record of awards: an Oscar for Best Screenplay and Best Director for *A Letter to Three Wives* (1949), the Golden Globe for Best Screenplay and an Oscar for Best Director for *Eve* (1950).

Mankiewicz sought complete and unconditional freedom for directors. In the face of the growing failure of

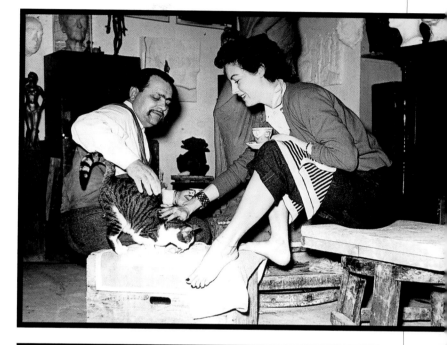

Cinderella of the outskirts

The story of Maria Vargas begins at the end, just like *Citizen Kane*, in an Italian cemetery, under the pouring rain, as the Contessa Torlato-Favrini is being buried. A few people who knew her during her lifetime tell the story of her destiny through their memories. At least, what they could seize along the way. The subjective point of view is always missing: that is, the Contessa's. Yet nothing surprising in that, since she is dead. Above her grave, her enigmatic statue keeps her memory's lips twice sealed over the mystery.

When Maria Vargas came into the life of film director Harry Dawes, he was in Madrid with producer Kirk Edwards. Maria was a dancer in a nightclub and Kirk wanted to cast her in his new movie. She refused haughtily to even talk to the producer. Harry, who was ordered to bring her back or lose his job, searches for the dancer backstage and surprises her in the arms of a handsome gypsy who then vanishes into the night. And what's more, Harry finds Maria Vargas barefoot. And barefoot he takes her back to her miserable home and then to the plane waiting to whisk her off to America. Indeed, that evening, Harry Dawes discovered the essence of Maria Vargas' secret in the passageway of that slum where Maria's family lived in all their conflict, cries, and hatred. She left for glory, carrying her shoes, the "Cinderella of the outskirts" who would never accept the glass slipper.

Le Mythe de la Femme dans le Cinéma Américain.
Jacques Siclier. Editions du Cerf. 1956.

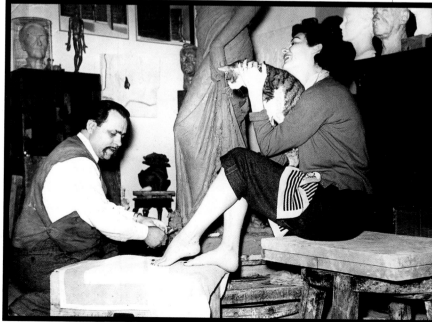

the studio system, he supported the still innovative idea of co-produced films shot in Europe (such as *Pandora*) to access new markets. He created his own company, Figaro Inc., to produce *Barefoot Contessa* in Italy, a film he both wrote and directed.

Mankiewicz was a godsend to actresses, who were always magnificently served with his intelligent directing and witty dialogues. All of the greatest actresses of the time dreamed of making a film with him. He so aptly understood their concerns and could pave the way to their consecration. Thanks to him, Bette Davis enjoyed her final triumph in the role of Margo Channing, an aging stage actress confronted with her young rival. This portrayal earned Bette Davis an Oscar nomination and the the Best Actress award at Cannes. The actresses who aspired to the title role of *Contessa*, barefoot or not, were many: Rita Hayworth, Yvonne de Carlo, Paulette Goddard, Elizabeth Taylor and, above all, Jennifer Jones, whose agent harassed Mankiewicz relentlessly.

In some ways *The Barefoot Contessa* was a film that ran parallel to *Eve*. As Maria Vargas, a flamenco dancer, performs one night in a seedy club in Madrid, she is discovered by a producer, press agent and director who are scouting for an actress to star in their next film. Maria is the victim of a poverty-stricken childhood and the traumas of the Spanish Civil War. She lets herself be swept off on this Hollywood adventure. Yet her success leaves her indifferent. The endless social rounds of this vacuous world bore her. She is not interested in the wealthy men she meets and instead seeks fleeting passion with casual encounters with her gypsy friends who evoke her origins.

She remains a simple girl who prefers the company of ordinary people. It is too late when Maria begins to seri-

Hollywood Decomposed

From the memories that unfold and interweave as the burial service continues under the pouring rain, the portrait of an extremely complex woman emerges, one which we feel has shattered all men's attempts to understand her. Only Harry Dawes realizes that Maria Vargas was not made for the world she let herself be led into. He understands why she is eventually swept away by the obscure gypsy wandering that had always plagued her throughout her life. In the most terrifying depiction of Hollywood that an American director had ever dared to make, Harry Dawes, portrayed by Bogart with his face marked by the blows of an aging *noir* hero, is the only character who deserves to be called a man. Though he is only a simple onlooker of Maria's destiny, he is the one who truly loves her. Certainly this is a very rare emotion for Hollywood. Harry Dawes is Maria Vargas's only true friend; he helps her avoid all the traps of the evil Kirk Edwards, who represents the producer-type rather than this or that particular person. An image through which the entire system is condemned. Despotic, sexually obsessed, Kirk Edwards shows a puritanical horror of the flesh and ceases to desire the magnificent woman who arrogantly refuses to surrender to him. Kirk Edwards creates Maria, but she is never his creature. And Harry Dawes, who directs Maria's first film, withdraws, thus helping her preserve her freedom. Maria Vargas is unquestionably a myth for Mankiewicz in her refusal to abandon herself to men. What her roles were in the films we do not see: vamp, femme fatale, pin-up? Perhaps a bit of each? Little does it matter. Maria forbids her legend to be created. The spokesman for Hollywood, Kirk Edward's servile and shrewd press agent, gives us the point of view of those in show biz. At the premiere of her film, the star comes alone, devoid of any mystery: she refuses to play the game. Though she wears the most elegant shoes, spiritually she continues to go barefoot. The lightning race, through a decomposed Hollywood, of the woman who, in complete disdain for scandal (this scandal could only be publicity), leaves, at the height of her glory, to testify against her mother in a court in Spain and gain the acquittal of her oppressed father. There are attempts, with sexual innuendos, to explain away her indifference to Kirk Edwards and the South American multimillionaire Bravano, revealing how our times have lost all sense of purity. Maria's moments of recklessness are not the caprices of a nymphomaniac nor the lapses of a frigid woman. The myth of the woman ("the most beautiful in the world") does not surrender to men, since they are undeserving. Maria Vargas is the ideal woman who is aware that after Garbo comes Blanche Dubois. A myth that refuses to be created so that it cannot be defamed. From this point of view, Mankiewicz's film is the moral condemnation of Hollywood. If we see a complicity with people of the poorer classes reflected in Maria's life, this should not be interpreted as perversion. By her desire to be close to nature and the *healthy*, by touching the earth with her bare feet, Maria Vargas desires to be nothing more than simply a woman. Free to love, free to choose whom she likes. The New World will not destroy her; it is no match for her greatness.

Le Mythe de la Femme dans le Cinéma Américain. Jacques Siclier. Editions du Cerf. 1956.

95

Influenced by Harry Dawes, Maria Vargas agrees to try her fortune in Hollywood (with Humphrey Bogart in *The Barefoot Contessa*).

ously reflect upon her incredible destiny. She pays with her own life for the socially unacceptable decision to bear the child of another man. Nevertheless, Maria does this to give her impotent husband an heir, though he does not realize the greatness of her act.

The screenplay of *The Barefoot Contessa* was brilliant, incisive, and inventive. It used the flashback in a new way, by developing the narrative principle with four voices (in voiceovers), whose different points of view then interweave. It freed itself of "backstage" conventions by dispensing with the usual rehearsal, make-up and shooting scenes typical of such films as Cukor's *A Star Is Born*, made in the same year.

Instead, Mankiewicz cultivated the "art of frustration" and implied more than he showed. He delayed Maria's appearance to the absolute limit and pushed this audaciousness to the point of depriving us of her stage show. The camera lingers heavily on the specta-

tors and their petty concerns. The off-screens are more important to Mankiewicz. The lover Maria hides in a cabin in the garden is never shown. His presence is only expressed by the chords he strums on a guitar. Mankiewicz erases the image to retain only the essential: the film text. And then, finally, he delays solving the mystery of Maria's death. He heightens the enigma surrounding the heroine and keeps us in suspense right up to the end. Mankiewicz was convinced that Ava Gardner was ideal to portray Maria Vargas, a young woman from a poor background suddenly plunged into the world of the rich and powerful.

David Hanna, the director's new publicity agent, shared the view of many in the industry that Ava Gardner was nothing more than fodder for gossip columns. The rare bursts of a possibly blossoming career were crushed beneath the sheer weight of copy on the star's private life. Hanna, however, did recall with some fondness *Whistle*

As a contessa, Maria wants to believe in her new happiness. She shares her joy with her former director and friend. With Humphrey Bogart in Joseph L. Mankiewicz's *The Barefoot Contessa* (1954).

Opposite page: The drawing by Cerruti that appeared on the posters promoting the film *The Barefoot Contessa*.

Stop and *One Touch of Venus*. He had detected a much greater acting ability than had been recognized in Ava at the time. He found her rather cold beauty, magnetism and feline qualities well suited to those roles.[28]

The fact that Ava was still under exclusive contract with MGM posed a problem. Mankiewicz was not on good terms with the major after publicly protesting against the poor screening conditions of his last film *Julius Caesar*. The film had been presented in New York in a cut version without wide screen or stereo sound. Bert Allenberg, one of the most influential agents in the industry, was given the task of handling the long and difficult negotiations.

As for Ava Gardner, she felt less and less affinity with Hollywood. The actress had hoped to make a film in Europe for a long time. Her separation from Frank Sinatra had been officially announced and she was also undoubtedly anxious to put some distance between the two of them. Her heart was now throbbing for the world famous bullfighter Luis Miguel Dominguin. She had met the toreador at a party in

Madrid right after the shooting of *Knights of the Round Table*. Ava read Mankiewicz's script and strongly supported Bert Allenberg's efforts with the Studio. She definitely wanted to make the film.

Of course, it was only a question of money. MGM finally ended up agreeing to loan Ava to Figaro Inc. (it was always more profitable when she worked for other studios) for the exorbitant sum of 200,000 dollars. Ava was to receive 60,000 dollars of the payment. Humphrey Bogart and Edmond O'Brien had already signed to do the film. Bogart, as Harry Dawes, Maria Vargas' director as well as friend and confidant; O'Brien in the role of the busy press agent. Filming was to start at the latest by January 1954, since Bogart was working on another film. His salary was 100,000 dollars.

David Hanna related[28] how the meeting with Ava and director Joseph Mankiewicz went:

Mankiewicz: I don't suppose you read the script?
Ava: No, I didn't, but I read the outline. Anyhow, I just have to play it. Hell Joe, I'm not an actress, but I think I understand this girl. She's a lot like me.
Mankiewicz: That's why I wanted you. But the main

thing is that you're here. How did you manage it?
Ava: Bert kept calling, but all they gave him was a run
around. And there wasn't anything ready for me, not one
damned script. And you know, I always do better outside
the Studio anyhow. I went to everybody: Dore Shary,
Eddie Mannix, Harry Rapf and finally Benny Thau. He
always liked me. Joe, I raised the roof. I told him what I
thought, that I'd always been the good girl of the Company, doing every lousy part in every lousy damned picture Metro ever made. I never complained, never took a
suspension, nothing. I told him I just had to get out of
Hollywood now – right now – or I'd blow my top. I
guess that scared him. So he said yes and that's all there
was to it. He called Bert and here I am.

Ava Gardner returned to Italy a year and a half after
the famous incident in Naples when an adoring audience
had chanted her name instead of Sinatra's during the
singer's own concert. Ava's popularity in Italy, as an
American movie star who looked so Latin, was a phenomenon that called for skillful handling by David
Hanna. Journalists and photographers were greedy for
details about her separation from Frank Sinatra. They
were only vaguely interested in the film.

Ava gave a press conference as soon as she arrived in
Rome. To every question about her private life she
laconically responded: "No comment." The press was
not even told the name of her new flame, Luis Miguel
Dominguin, with whom Ava had spent Christmas in
Madrid. Frank Sinatra had preferred to ignore their
affair. Back in Rome, Ava told David Hanna confiden-
tially that there was no hope of a reconciliation. She
rented an apartment in a dark, massive building adorned
with statues on Corso d'Italia and settled in with Bappie,
who was always by her side. Luis Miguel Dominguin
often came to visit her.

> We were good friends as well as good lovers, and we
> didn't demand too much of each other. Luis Miguel
> was great fun and I loved having him around. Quite
> frankly, I was intrigued by the fact that he didn't seem
> to need me and he certainly wasn't looking for publi-
> city like so many of the European men who came my
> way. I guess I loved the easy going way we could just
> hang out together after all the fuss I'd aroused with
> Frank.[2]

The filming of *The Barefoot Contessa* began with interiors
shot in Rome's Cinecittà studios. Though Bogart's film
character was attentive, friendly, and warm, the actor
behaved exactly the opposite on the set when not in front
of the camera. As a legendary figure of American cinema,

Humphrey Bogart stares in disbelief at the lifeless body of the Contessa in Rossano Brazzi's arms.

Opposite page: Stewart Granger in George Cukor's *Bhowani Junction* (1955).

Bogart had little esteem for Ava Gardner and reproached her movie star airs, and as Ava remembered, "He was always needling me, calling me the Grabtown gypsy and complaining that he needed a running start toward the set if he wasn't going to be trampled by my entourage."[2]

Bogart savored the gossip about Ava. He had particularly relished an article in *The American Weekly* that drew an extremely unflattering portrait of her as a woman plagued by psychological problems. He himself judged her to be lacking in dramatic expression and felt that her only talent was her natural ease in front of the camera. "She gives me nothing. I have to lift her everytime,"[28] he complained. And Ava recognized this without bitterness:

> He certainly knew a lot more acting tricks than I did, and he didn't hesitate to use them. But I have to admit he probably forced me into a better performance than I could have managed without him.[2]

In one of their first scenes together, Maria Vargas asks:

Maria: Mr. Dawes. do you think really that I could be a movie star?

Harry: That's a question I always avoid like the plague because it never worked out. But with you, I think it would. You couldn't miss.

Maria: I think that I'm pretty enough, but I wouldn't be that kind of star... If I could act a little, would you help me to become really a good actress?

Maria's lines sounded rather like a lament and seemed to express Ava Gardner's own doubts as to whether or not she was a true actress herself. The honest and convincing way she acted the scene, however, proved how unfounded Ava's doubts were and demonstrated her mastery. Another important theme in *Barefoot Contessa* was the questioning of a way of life that was imposed rather than chosen, and this was also a concern in Ava's personal life:

Maria: I think I should go back to Madrid and stay there. I should stay where I belong.
Harry: Where is that?
Maria: In the dirt of the streets.

Harry: You think you'll stay there?
Maria: Probably not. I would not belong there anymore than where I am.
Harry: Where are you, Maria?
Maria: Half in the dirt and half out.

Mankiewicz brilliantly expressed Maria's uncertainties through his mise-en-scene, by tracking (or suggesting) her movements: from cabaret to dressing room, from her family house to the passageway; from the sumptuous villa to its outbuildings, the casino to its gardens, the Torlato-Favrini castle to its surrounding grounds. Each element of the setting reflects another, a main space its annex, its interior an exterior. The passageway, where everything is decided for Maria, in front of her parents' miserable house, is a path to freedom. Once launched, however, Maria discovers that gilt prisons also exist. Exclusive places, where she must wear shoes, with their microcosms: the Hollywood fauna, high society, nobility. Maria does not feel any more at ease there. "I feel afraid in shoes and I feel safe with my feet in the dirt," she confesses to Harry.

Maria's secret self catches up with her. She will always prefer the dusty ground to a castle's waxed parquet; going barefoot to wearing elegant pumps. She likes her dressing room or the cabin deep in the garden, private hidden spots that shelter lovers, suggest makeshift solutions, or promise sensuous adventure. The casino's balcony overlooks the gardens where a furtive gypsy's figure appears. Maria helps him with the millionaire Bravano's money. Outside in the park, the castle's domestics celebrate her wedding with music and dancing. Maria grudgingly abides by the elite's social conventions, yet regrets she can no longer join the party outside where the common people are having so much fun.

With Maria's shifts between places she detests and places she desires, Mankiewicz created dynamics in his film's structure. This he divided into a few painstakingly developed

Favrini "*Que sara sara...*", Ava Gardner knew it was much too late to turn back now to her origins in North Carolina. Just as Maria, and Pandora before her, Ava Gardner's fate was inexorably written into the course her life was taking.

Although in the credits Humphrey Bogart's name appeared before Ava Gardner's, *The Barefoot Contessa* was definitely not a "Bogart" film, that is, in the way films such as *To Have and Have Not*, *The Big Sleep*, or *African Queen* were. Ava Gardner's personality completely permeated *The Barefoot Contessa*, which was under the spell of her noble presence. Mankiewicz received an Oscar nomination for Best Screenplay and Best Director. Edmond O'Brien, as the press agent, won an Oscar for Best Supporting Actor, the only Oscar that the film received. Ava Gardner did not receive any recognition for her performance, widely regarded as one of the finest of her career.

To those who believed that Ava Gardner was never more convincing than when she portrayed herself on the screen, *Bhowani Junction* demonstrated her ability to act a dramatic role that was not a reflec-

Victoria as a half-caste Anglo-Indian must face difficult choices (Bhowani Junction, 1955).

and dialogued scenes. He showed his character's inability to become part of the worlds in which she lived. The last image of Maria that Harry, her director and friend, remembers is her anxious look and the door which makes her a prisoner forever.

David Hanna, who later became Ava Gardner's agent, related how melancholic she had been during the making of the film. Though the story more closely resembled the life of Rita Hayworth, the subject of *The Barefoot Contessa* came close to the heart of Ava's own anxieties and must certainly have driven her to deep introspection. Completely consumed by her role, and with regained serenity now that she was finally separated from Frank Sinatra, Ava nevertheless remained distant from the others on the set. Perhaps Ava was secretly cursing the day in 1941, so heavy with consequences, when her brother-in-law Larry Tarr had had the idea of putting her photo in his shop window for passersby to admire. Just as Maria, condemned to live out the tragic story of the Torlato-

tion of her personal life. Victoria Jones is an Anglo-Indian woman whose destiny is deeply bound to the history of India at the end of colonial rule in 1947. Victoria returns to India after having served for four years in the British army. She is requisitioned by Colonel Savage (Stewart Granger), who must protect the country's railways, a target of extremist attacks and also of the passive resistance actions of Gandhi's followers.

The dramatic action pivots around the marshalling station, the Bhowani Junction of the film's title. Indeed, its switchings and tracks seem to symbolize a network of human consciences. For Victoria, the decision is painful. Which direction should she choose? Patrick Taylor, of mixed race like herself, who is pro-British, the English Colonel Savage, or Ranjit, an Indian? Victoria must try to distinguish between her feelings of love and her political beliefs. Ava Gardner approached this role with rare force and conviction and her progress was impressive when compared to the actress' modest performance in *Ghosts on the Loose* just twelve years before. What was more, Ava never thought it necessary to actually prepare for her roles. In London, where interiors were being shot, she never went to the diction lessons intended to familiarize her with the British accent. "I don't have to waste time on that junk. Hell, I'll pick up the accent the minute I get to London,"[28] she retorted.

Ava now seemed to assimilate her roles with astonishing ease. She did not burden herself with acting theories. All she had to do was put on the costume for the scene, get made-up, and she became her character. Indeed, the "English" Victoria discovers her "Indian" self by changing from uniform into sari. The elderly Indian mother, so desirous of a traditional wedding for her son Ranjit, brings the final touch by modestly covering Victoria's head with part of her sari. The metamorphosis is disturbing: when Victoria gazes into the mirror, she discovers a part of herself that she has ignored for far too long. The prospect of acting this scene, so essential for her character, did not faze Ava. She simply relied on her instincts and acting experience gained with other directors.

Though there were these quiet moments, there was another Victoria of *Bhowani Junction*, a woman who gave vent to her ardent nature. The icy Ava Gardner had often been known for her regal bearing (*East Side, West Side*), but never had any of her earlier films made her fiery. George Cukor was the first director, even before John Huston, to scratch beneath the surface of the affectations with which MGM customarily enveloped its stars.

Victoria contrasted with the frozen woman of Ava's mythic image (*Pandora*) and with the elegant mask of intimate tragedy (*The Barefoot Contessa*). George Cukor undermined the images immortalized by these two films, burning the Dutchman's manuscript, shattering the marble statue of Maria Vargas, to create Victoria Jones. She was a searing character, lost in the labyrinth of her own self-questioning and struggling against the certitudes of an entire people.

With Cukor directing, the days when actresses were kept crisp and spotless with a laundry service on the set were a thing of the past. Cukor filmed where the action was.[29] Yet, unlike *Mogambo*, he created a real link between characters and events. In *Bhowani Junction*, Ava falls from a motorcycle or pulls herself onto a steam locomotive. She is blackened by the smoke of coal and spattered with mud as she rushes to help the wounded after a railway disaster. Her clothes are violently torn as she resists Lieutenant McDaniel (Lionel Jeffries), whom

A va Gardner? She is extremely intelligent. She is tremendously fascinating, but she is haunted by despair. She is a woman dominated by fate. She doesn't have a very good relationship with herself and, among other things, she considers herself a bad actress. It is really unfortunate. In *Bhowani Junction* (1956), she acted some wonderful erotic scenes... She brushed her teeth with whisky, which was very vulgar and exciting. But all of that was cut by the censors.

Paraphrased from a quote by George Cukor.
Film Culture n° 34. Autumn 1964.

Victoria at a turning point in her life with Colonel Savage (Stewart Granger) in *Bhowani Junction*.

With Bill Travers
in the same film.

she finally murders. The filming was extremely physical, something Ava was not used to, and this rape scene deeply marked her.

I left that scene without speaking and went immediately back to my trailer. Trembling and shaking, I swallowed an enormous whiskey. At that moment, I felt sick with fright, as if I'd been literally fighting for my life. I'd known Lionel for weeks now; he was a sweet man and I adored him, but I knew that if I didn't see him *quickly*, that scene was going to stick in my mind forever and I'd hate his guts. George knocked and came in to see if I was alright. "George," I said, "for God's sake, please get Lionel over here *now*! Because unless I see him and give him a big hug, I'll never speak to him as long as I live." Of course Lionel hurried over, I gave him my hug, and things were alright between us. No film scene had ever affected me so deeply before, had left me with such a nightmare sense of terror, and nothing would ever do so again.[2]

The cinematography of *Bhowani Junction* was one of the most beautiful of any of Ava Gardner's films. Freddie Young, an exceptional artist, took advantage of the new technical possibilities of Eastman-Color, which were soon to replace Technicolor. This process offered a much richer spectrum of nuances and Young used this to highlight the plot's subtleties. As director of photography, he focused the light on Victoria's face in the first part of the film. Her fair skin contrasted with her jet-black hair and underscored her English origins. Later, when she rallies to the Indian cause for independence, the light becomes softer and her make-up deeper.

Costumes and hairstyles were not created just to make Ava look good. They also corresponded to the heroine Victoria's changes in social and political commitment. She wears a severe chignon that accentuates her British uniform and a sari that softens her face. Her hair falls loosely over her white dress in an English garden, or it is a red outfit that the extremist Davay tells her to put on when she is taken hostage. Freddie Young created a refined composition: the red dress, the white scarf that Victoria waves, and the locomotive's headlight are transformed into stains of color in the night. The red dress and scarf are signs to the driver of the convoy to stop. They also arouse the suspicion of the railway worker on duty, who sounds the alarm. The costumes, accessories, make-up and lights all fuel the dramatic action and accompany the character's psychological development.

The screenplay, however, did not burden itself with the same formal concerns. The plot of *Bhowani Junction*

held no surprises and the conflict between the British and the Indian nationalists remained schematic. Cukor's directing was intended to be innovative, but a screen preview caused the film to be taken out of his hands and completely re-cut to adhere to conventions of traditional cinema. Cukor was not Lewin or Mankiewicz, directors who had understood the need to free themselves from the studios to make their own films. Cukor was working within the strict limitations of MGM and enjoyed very little creative freedom. Some brazen scenes that he had risked that made Victoria into a torrid woman whose erotic charge bordered on vulgarity (Ava Gardner brushing her teeth with whiskey), were cut from the beginning and replaced by a voiceover which overloaded the dialogue to the point of absurdity.

Nevertheless *Bhowani Junction*, which had the biggest production budget of 1955, surpassed anything Ava Gardner had ever done since her film debut under the aegis of MGM. Her name dominated all billing and, for the first time, she came before the leading actor (Stewart Granger)

The scene of the Indian wedding, with Francis Matthews, in *Bhowani Junction*.

104

Ava and David Niven in the prologue, filmed in London, of Mark Robson's *The Little Hut* (1956).

in the credits. Just as Mankiewicz, George Cukor was known to be an actress' director. He gave Ava Gardner, who had been somewhat deified by previous directors, the role she needed to detach herself from her movie star myth. As Ava commented:

> Actually, though you'd never know it from all that, *Bhowani Junction* was one of my more serious films, one that allowed me to get more emotionally involved in a part than I usually did. Partly that's because George Cukor was the director. I'd known George socially for years and had an enormous amount of respect for his ability... He was attentive to detail, he really cared, and he knew how to pull the kind of performance he wanted out of me.[2]

Ava was breathtakingly beautiful in *Bhowani Junction*. Electric, gentle, and violent, she was swept through the film

by exalting images of the uprising of an entire impassioned people against backdrops of burning and vibrant color.

Nor was Ava's perspective now completely American. She spent most of her time traveling, partially for the demands of her career, but many times simply as an attempt to escape to another world. Most of 1954 was devoted to her world tour for the promotion of *The Barefoot Contessa* (South America, the Far East, Europe). Exteriors for *Bhowani Junction* were shot in Lahore, interiors in London. *The Little Hut* was shot in Rome and she later made films in Mexico, Australia, Great Britain and France. Ava Gardner had not made a film in the United States since *Vaquero* in 1952, and her true return to Hollywood did not come until 1974 in *Earthquake*.

Since first visiting Spain in 1950, Ava had such a passion for this country that she eventually even fell in love with one of the country's symbols, bullfighter Luis Miguel Dominguin. In December 1955, just shortly before her thirty-third birthday, much to general skepticism, Ava announced that she had decided to move to Spain permanently.

> Why did I go? For one thing, for as long as I lived there, I'd never liked Hollywood. It wasn't my favorite place to put it mildly; I found it provincial and superficial by turns. I just didn't fit in with the way things were done in the movie capital, and it was becoming more and more impossible to have any privacy there. I couldn't walk my dog, go to an airport or a restaurant, I couldn't even go to the ladies' restroom without somebody around watching me, reporting on me, spying on me. I felt imprisoned by the lifestyle of a movie star and I just couldn't live with that anymore.[2]

Though Ava represented the kind of woman that was unacceptable to the traditional Catholic morals prevailing in Franco's Spain (she was a movie star and divorced three times), the country nevertheless gave her a warm welcome. She immediately set about learning Castilian, "a language," she had said, "so pure and musical for the ear, especially when you understand it, that it is a delight to the senses." She bought a ranch-style house in La Moraleja, on the outskirts of Madrid. The house got its name from a little figure of a sorceress (*"La Bruja"*) placed like a weathercock on her roof. Ava settled in with her trusted companion, Reenie: "I filled *La Bruja* with books and records and, for the first time since I'd left North Carolina, I felt I was *home*."[2]

Ava Gardner was definitely no homebody and Spain was the ideal place for her passion for parties and nightlife. It was quite obvious she would never be able to fulfill Luis Miguel Dominguin's great desire to have a

studios. As for the pre-Titanic maritime disaster, it was replaced with a model ship in a tub spinning on a simulated wave. The screen adaptation added a prologue and epilogue shot in London. Nevertheless, most of the action took place on a set in front of back projections, painted canvas horizons, and potted palms.

The love triangle of author André Roussin's play was inevitably at odds with the puritanical morals of American society at the time. Loose living generally was condemned and adultery shown in films was not tolerated. In the screen adaptation of the story, Susan is therefore a neglected wife intent on rekindling the interest of her busy husband Sir Philip (Stewart Granger). Though in the play Henry (David Niven) is her lover, in the film he simply becomes a long-time admirer whom Susan uses to arouse the jealousy of her husband. The English adaptation retained a healthy ambiguity concerning their adulterous relationship. French critics, however, reproached the sweetening up of the menage-à-trois theme in the screen version.

Of all of Ava's films, *The Little Hut* is by far the "best" of her flops. This adaptation of André Roussin's play has the strange power, despite its incredible idiocies, to transform our indignation into pleasure. Much of the film's comedy is based on the English phlegm of these shipwrecked survivors on a desert island, who still adhere to all the social conventions despite their desperate situation. They continue to dine by candlelight just as if they were in one of the best restaurants in London.

"By definition we can say," wrote Claude de Givray[30], "that Ava Gardner validates any film. It is certain that without her participation, this film would have been devoid of interest. For an hour and a half she declares, with her lovesick expressions, all the disdain she feels for movies of this kind. And she has all our sympathy." Indeed, Ava detested the film:

> I hated it, that's all. Every minute of it. It was a lousy story. I shouldn't have done it. The director was awful. It's not going to be much but what could I do? If I took another suspension they would keep me at Metro the rest of my life.[28]

The Little Hut did not enjoy the same success as the play, which ran for five consecutive seasons in Paris. Nevertheless, it was a chance to demonstrate the little explored talent of Ava Gardner for comedy. The closing shot of Ava in her cozy country house knitting a layette for a baby is as heartening as it was improbable.

The Sun Also Rises, directed by Henry King in January

Ava's performance in *The Little Hut* showed that her talent for comedy was underestimated.

family. Shortly after their separation (after Ava had returned from Pakistan), he married actress Lucia Bosè. She was in fact Walter Chiari's ex-mistress, and Chiari very soon entered Ava's life.

Ava Gardner had Walter Chiari cast in *The Little Hut* as Mario, the cook on Sir Philip's yacht. He disguises himself as a native on their shipwrecked island and makes Susan, or Ava, his hostage. In June 1956, when Ava was in Paris for the costume fittings, popular playwright André Roussin, author of the play, expressed his perplexity. Indeed, he counted no fewer than fourteen creations designed by Christian Dior for a story that took place on a desert island with three shipwrecked men and a bedraggled woman. The film's budget could rival any American super-production. Was the film to be shot on an island in the Pacific? Would the sinking yacht be the high point of the film? No. *The Little Hut* was to be shot almost entirely in Rome's Cinecittà

With Stewart Granger. *The Little Hut* remains the most pleasant of our "bad memories".

1957, was the very premature closing – Ava was just thirty-five years of age – of the period when her beauty and career were at their peak. It seemed as though Ava had been preparing all her life to be Lady Brett Ashley, again a Hemingway heroine: a rash and unstable woman who wastes her exceptional energy in a chaotic search for happiness. The combined devices of make-up and lighting still successfully concealed (but not always) an obvious change in Ava's physiognomy. During fleeting moments, her face grew slack and betrayed a weary, haggard look. With dark rings under her eyes, Ava Gardner had already lost the fresh looks of that face of just the year before in *The Little Hut*. Yet what did it matter? As R.-M. Arlaud commented, "Her slightly waning beauty makes her all the more moving." [31]

And indeed Ava's waning legendary beauty magnificently served her and her screen role. Lady Brett Ashley was slowly killing herself by her dissolute life, an endless frenzy of partying, champagne breakfasts and intoxicating bullfights in San Sebastian:

> When Henry King, who'd directed me in *The Snows of Kilimanjaro*, sent me the treatment, I felt an immediate kinship with Lady Brett who papa wrote was "as charming when she's drunk as when she's sober". I always felt close to papa's women.[2]

Nevertheless, Ava had hesitations about being Lady Ashley. Indeed here again was a heroine who falls hopelessly in love with a man who is impotent. The film's hero, Jake Barnes (Tyrone Power), had been wounded during World War I. Ava was afraid that the comparison with another of her screen loves, Count Torlato-Favrini in *The Barefoot Contessa*, would create in the public's mind the image of a woman who rendered her lovers impotent. In the film, Lady Ashley is having an affair with a penniless Scottish aristocrat, a hopeless adventurer and alcoholic (Errol Flynn), whom she feels forced to marry. An American intellectual (Mel Ferrer) on holiday in Paris, however, woos her with his attentions.

After the story has been set in Paris between the two World Wars, passions are then unleashed under the blazing sun of Pamplona, a town exalted for its feverish bullfighting. Lady Brett loses herself in an all-consuming, hopeless new love affair with the young Pedro, but must face the reality of a cruel destiny: her love for Jake. The story's tragic impact was heightened by a cast of aging actors. Errol Flynn was almost unrecognizable. There was no trace of the bounding svelte hero of Michael Curtiz's films. And though Tyrone Power was only 45, he was to die suddenly, only a year after the film was made, in 1959. He made only one other film after *The Sun Also Rises*. Errol Flynn's death

followed a few months later. As for Ava Gardner, she was living the final years of her great Hollywood epoch. Indeed the making of some films seem to become one with the lives of their stars (John Huston's *The Misfits* comes to mind, the last film of Marilyn Monroe and Clark Gable, and Montgomery Clift who was to die soon after).

Unlike the performances of the film's leading actors, the supporting actors were not as convincing. Besides Marcel Dalio, who successfully repeated his bistro role of *The Snows of Kilimanjaro*, Juliette Gréco's vulgar prostitute was not particularly accomplished, and Robert Evans bordered on the ridiculous in his role as a bullfighter. Ava Gardner tried to get her lover Walter Chiari cast in a role, as she had done in *The Little Hut*, but he had not been considered good enough for the part. Chiari nevertheless went to join Ava on location in Mexico. She was staying in a rambling villa with Bap-

Five years after *The Snows of Kilimanjaro*, Henry King directs Ava Gardner and Tyrone Power in a new Ernest Hemingway adaptation, *The Sun Also Rises*.

A scene from Darryl F. Zanuck's *The Sun Also Rises.*

Studio photo for the promotion of *The Sun Also Rises.* Ava is Hemingway's heroine, Lady Brett Ashley.

pie and Nicole Fontana. As creator of the sumptuous costumes of *The Barefoot Contessa*, Nicole continued to design Ava's personal wardrobe for many years.

Though a series of eight post WWI costumes were created for Ava for *The Sun Also Rises*, with an occasional bell hat or Charleston-style dress to recall the period, basically the costumes reflected contemporary styles. Italian fashion was already looking to the sixties and was setting those trends long before other creators. Whether Ava wore a seductive polo with matching black beret pushed back bohemian-style, or severe suits with the inevitable accessories of pearl necklaces, gloves and purses, Lady Brett Ashley was definitely modeling the Spring-Summer 1957 collections.

The Sun Also Rises was a production made in the wake of *The Snows of Kilimanjaro* and intended to repeat its success. The film was based on a work by the same author (Hemingway), it had the same producer (Zanuck for Fox), and the same director (Henry King). King and Fox beat all records for the length of their collaboration, which lasted some twenty-five years. They both had the same points of view and the two films shared the "Fox spirit." Tyrone Power had been discovered by King and was his favorite actor. Together they made ten films after their first, which was *Lloyds of London* in 1936.

When Hemingway saw the film he found his story unrecognizable. The shattering experience of the novelist's visit to an Italian hospital had inspired the story, and particularly the life of its hero Jake, who represented an entire sacrificed generation. The night of the premiere Hemingway was said to have commented that he had been betrayed even by the bulls, and that "Mr. Zanuck has shown a cheap Cook cruise through European bars, bullfights and more bars. All of that is very disappointing and I'm being polite."

Nor was the French press any more enthusiastic. The critics, always eager to draw comparisons between books and their film adaptations, denounced the fate to which the screen adaptation had condemned Hemingway's novel. Ava Gardner was praised as the guiding light of the film and her acting as the best ever. The noted critic Jean de Baroncelli wrote: "Thanks to Ava Gardner, who infused the heroine with her beauty, mystery and the enigmatic nostalgia of a woman adrift, a little of the book's substance does manage to emerge in the film."[32]

109

Here with Robert Evans who portrays a bullfighter.

Ava Gardner and
Tyrone Power in
The Sun Also Rises.

Hemingway also agreed. He associated his physicality and way of life to that of his heroes. *The Sun Also Rises* was indisputably a much better film than *The Snows of Kilimanjaro,* and shooting on location in Morelia, Mexico (instead of Pamplona, which was then under snow), brought an untouched authenticity to the film. The performances of Huston and Hawks were perhaps not their finest. Nevertheless, the vacuity of these broken lives devastated by war is cruelly felt. The feelings of futility, failure and despair wend their way from one café to another. It is a suffocating climate of compulsive drinking that Peter Viertel developed *ad nauseum.* Indeed, he had been called to the rescue by Hemingway to re-write a first version of the screenplay, which the author considered unacceptable. The sun at the beginning and at the end of the film encircles the heroes in a total absence of perspective.

The Sun Also Rises remains a film unjustly forgotten, most likely because it is rarely screened in theatres or on television. Yet it is a film essential to understanding Ava Gardner's relationship to her characters. When the film was released in the United States in August 1957, her divorce with Frank Sinatra had just been made final by a Mexican court. Ava Gardner's life was faltering just as Lady Brett's was, though Walter Chiari in Ava's real life was a devoted and attentive lover:

> Walter was amusing, good looking, even-tempered, highly intelligent, and a delightful companion. He followed me all over Europe, all over the world in fact. Our association lasted a long time and we even lived together on many occasions. And, yes, Walter often asked me to marry him, but I couldn't and I didn't. The distance that separates liking from love is as wide as the Pacific as far as I'm concerned. And that was always the bottom line between me and Walter Chiari.[2]

Ava Gardner had wanted MGM to undertake the adaptation of Hemingway's works and the three films based on his novels: *The Killers, The Snows of Kilimanjaro* and *The Sun Also Rises,* held some of her best memories. Ava became closely involved in a project on the life of Conchita

111

Goya paints the "Naked Maja" for which the Duchess of Alba poses, in Henry Koster's *The Naked Maja* (1958).

Cintron, a female bullfighter. She was looking forward to this in October 1957, but the film was never to be made. Carried away by her enthusiasm, the effects of the heat and "solasombra," a mixture of absinthe and cognac, Ava decided to test some young bulls at Angelo Peralta's ranch. Ava's horse reared just as she was about to drive the banderilla into the bull. She was thrown off. The accident was soon forgotten. Gypsies came from all around, the wine flowed generously, and Ava danced until dawn. Only in the first rays of morning did she discover the injury on her cheek. Ava immediately flew to London to consult Archie McIndoe, one of the world's best plastic surgeons. His diagnosis was simple, it was a hematoma to be treated with heat and massages. Fortunately, the shooting for Ava's next film, *The Naked Maja*, was running late by several months.

Everything about the project of *The Naked Maja* seemed to point to Ava Gardner as its ideal heroine, so close were its themes to her own heart. *The Naked Maja* recounted the love between the painter Goya and Maria Cateyana, the Duchess of Alba, who also posed as his model. It was set in Spain during the Inquisition.

Maria is a dissident in the court of King Charles IV. Her political activism has gained her the popular support of the people. Not only does she struggle alongside them, but she also spends her time in the popular dives in endless nights of drinking and flamenco. She is an independent woman and with her progressive ideas, she cannot accept the persecution suffered by free-thinkers and artists. She finds it intolerable that artists whose works do not reflect the official established order should be censored. Condemned into exile by the queen, Maria poses nude for a painting by Goya, *The Naked Maja*. The painter is imprisoned. To protect Goya from being compromised any further, Maria denies that she is in love with the painter and intervenes personally before the king to plead for his release. Military chief Godoy supports Maria in the vain hope of winning her favors, and she dies poisoned by Godoy after she refuses him.

In the film, Maria Cateyana is a widow who has adopted

a little girl from Africa. The character also contained a bit of Julie La Verne from *Show Boat*, another woman who is rejected for her differences; a bit of Pandora with her sense of sacrifice; a bit of the barefoot Contessa, living on the fringes of society and destined to a tragic fate; a bit of Lady Brett Ashley, as a frenetic night reveler. And there was much of the real Ava Gardner, too. Perhaps too much: Spain, which recalled above all the actress' passion for her adopted country; a beauty who is rebellious and proud; Ava's own unfailingly devastating effect on men (three in Ava's case); a private life deemed disgraceful; and a gift for the art of provocation honed to perfection. It is pleasant to imagine that with the many qualities Ava Gardner and the Duchess of Alba had in common; had Ava lived during that period in history, she could perhaps have been the Duchess herself. Nevertheless, this time it was the star who seemed to serve as the model for the screen character and not vice versa.

In actual fact, Ava Gardner was allowed to be the Duchess of Alba because conditions for a co-production were perfect. MGM, as distributor of the film, would not be involved in its production. MGM's contribution would be the equivalent of Ava's salary for a film in 1958. Artistic decisions were entirely left up to Titanus.

Apart from Sydney Guilaroff, Ava's faithful hairdresser, close friend, and soon-to-be lover, the film had an all-Italian cast and crew. Though the corporate studio system had never given her the chance to participate beyond the strict limits of what she was paid to do, that is to act, Ava Gardner thought this time she would have a say in other aspects of the making of the film. She offered her experience to the European production, and brought to it her interpretation of the character. This was all the more justified, since shooting had been delayed by some of the screenplay's seemingly unresolvable problems.

The project was ambitious and the budget generous (3 million dollars). The story, based on artistic endeavor and political struggle, was worthy. Yet the galaxy of screenwriters working on the project were having problems giving substance to the story. Ava Gardner deplored that the most European of all the filmmakers who had ever directed her had been kept from participating in the writing. He was the only person in her eyes capable of improving the script: Albert Lewin, her director in *Pandora and the Flying Dutchman*. Producer Goffredo Lombardo made several trips to Madrid to ask Ava Gardner's opinion. Nevertheless, she kept rejecting the many

The Duchess of Alba, an ally of the Spanish popular movement, spends her nights in city dives. If Ava had lived during the time, she would have been this woman rebel. (*The Naked Maja*, 1958).

Opposite page: After a bad fall from a horse, Ava Gardner is afraid of going before the camera. She uses a fan to conceal the injury on her cheek.

She put all her hopes in a promising new talent, young director of photography Giuseppe Rotunno, to restore her beauty. He accomplished this so successfully that Ava asked for him again for the next film. There was one scene, however, in which a closeup revealed her wound: when Goya draws near to Maria's face. No lighting or make-up could conceal the mark on her right cheek, a little dimple in addition to the one on her chin.

The accident at the ranch triggered a new anxiety which began to obsess Ava. The wound became a fixation and her fears gradually increased over the months. Ava, who had always taken her body for granted and who seemed not to care in the least if her beauty were not eternal, suddenly began to realize what an important part of her capital it was. Already this capital was eroded by her abuses, alcohol and tobacco. Of course, Ava still had the same impact on the screen, her regal and elegant way of moving were inimitable. Yet *The Naked Maja* revealed a face that, rather than being made-up, was covered up. A thick foundation was used, her eyes heavily circled with black liner, and her eyelids darkened. This was all accentuated as the years went by. Jean Douchet wrote of the film[33] that its only real interest was that it happened to be Ava Gardner's last great film before her decline. Her eyes weary and expressionless, she exhibits her haughty beauty with a sort of indifference that somehow makes her suddenly endearing. She is no longer a goddess, but a woman.

The making of *The Naked Maja* was complicated. Ava acted in English to actors who responded in Italian. As was customary in Italy, dialogues were synchronized during post-production. There were serious production problems: scenes with dialogue came to her as they were shot, and there was no rehearsal

The role of the Duchess of Alba, a tireless night owl, outsider and rebel, reflects many of Ava's personality traits as a star.

versions, saying that the Duchess sounded like someone born in the Bronx. In the meantime, the descendants of the Duchess of Alba, who were opposed to the project, put pressure on Franco's government to refuse permission to shoot *The Naked Maja* in Spain. It was therefore in Rome, in July, that Henry Koster finally began filming after a six-month delay.

Ava Gardner approached the shooting of this film with terrible apprehension because the hematoma on her cheek was still visible. Photographers were tracking her even more relentlessly. Her fall from the horse had been caught by a professional photographer, and a series of photos had been sold and released for 75,000 dollars. How a photographer had just happened to be present on the isolated ranch in Andalusia, made Ava believe she had been the victim of a plot in which Walter Chiari might have been accomplice. In Hollywood it was rumored that Ava was disfigured and her career jeopardized. She was receiving countless calls and letters from worried friends.

planned even for her dance scene. Ava was surprised that there were no assistants to dress her when she was expected to wear as many as sixteen costumes during the film, all in thick heavy silk. On the set she virtually took over as associate producer. Taking advantage of her position, she demanded that her agent David Hanna negotiate a night shoot with production. Her involvement was such that Goffredo Lombardo, who was always eager to cater to the caprices of his stars, agreed to her request. It was never known, however, whether her screen partners acquiesced with a smile to this regime, nor to what extent the budget was exceeded because of the decision.

Nothing distinguished *The Naked Maja,* which was a French-Italian co-production, from a standard Hollywood movie. Poorly developed, historical truth gave way to tasteful lyricism and cinematic clichés. During the period in which the story's events take place, Goya had in fact not yet painted *The Naked Maja.* He was 50 years of age, married, and suffered from deafness. None of these elements, however, are mentioned in the film. Indeed, in the late fifties, with the movie industry in crisis, it was thought unnecessary to unduly discourage spectators from the outset. Ava Gardner and Anthony Franciosa, as Goya, were represented in a way that pleased people's aesthetic sense and romanticism.

The film sweetened up Maria's political activism: the true nature of her involvement in the struggle against the regime is never made quite clear. Her request that Goya carry a note to people vaguely referred to as "our friends" is barely hinted at in the film. There are no other details about the contents of the message, the dangers faced in the mission, or what is at stake. The story served simply as a backdrop for characters based on standard models. The Duchess of Alba, an expansive woman madly in love with Goya, is a night reveler and talk of the town. She lives her life just as she pleases, to the rhythm of her passions. Despite precautions, the filming nevertheless turned into a formidable fiasco.

In the role of the Duchess of Alba, Ava Gardner appears in all her rebellious beauty. She is superb, intelligent, voluptuous and sensitive. To find a partner who could equal this marvel was admittedly not easy, and that was precisely where the film ran into problems. How could anyone believe that Goya even distantly resembled awkward Anthony Franciosa? That would have been just too sad, wrote Jacqueline Michel.[34]

Anthony Franciosa had been discovered by Elia Kazan

the year before. He had won the Best Actor award at the Venice Film Festival. Trained at the Actors Studio, he belonged to the family of actors who had studied under Lee Strasberg according to principles based on the Stanislavsky method. Indeed, a new type of actor was emerging in the United States, creating an approach to acting that rejected Hollywood conventions. Marlon Brando and James Dean were the children of this school. The sixties and seventies produced Pacino, De Niro and Hoffman who worked their roles by drawing from the depths of their inner selves.

Perhaps *The Naked Maja* was already a film of a bygone era. "The Method" made Ava smile, and it seemed doubtful that Anthony Franciosa had truly assimilated it in any case. He overacted to such a degree that in the final scene, at Maria's deathbed, director Henry Koster decided against a closeup. Instead he filmed Franciosa over the shoulder to spare viewers his contorted expressions of pain. What saves the film from mediocrity is Ava Gardner's incomparable performance as the overpowering and disturbing Duchess of Alba and her passion for Anthony Franciosa. The actor's portrayal of Goya resembled the performances of those players at the Odeon in *Britannicus*, who rolled their eyes and growled from the throat.[35]

Ava Gardner did not believe in The Method, which was based on the principle of total identification with the character. Describing her screen partner, she related, not without some humor, that before each scene "he'd be standing off to the side, carrying on as if he were choking to death and nearly vomiting before he would come on."[2] Ava Gardner's affinity to her characters and what she brought to the great roles of her lifetime are undeniable. Yet she accomplished this in a purely instinctive way, without intellectualizing or theorizing about her work. Ava was from another school, and soon from another generation; she had learned to act "on the spot", in front of the camera, with directors who helped her to progress step by step. Ava obeyed only one principle, and that was to always listen to the director.

During the shooting of *Bhowani Junction*, George Cukor had made her relive all the anger she had felt towards an indiscreet journalist just to help her act a difficult scene of fury and rage. She did not realize that what she was doing was nothing more than applying the Lee Strasberg method. Ava Gardner had acquired the ease of the "greats" who had no need for a technical method, since they had already assimilated acting so completely. "There is the Ava Gardner phenomenon," remarked Louis Chauvet, "and the shock that her hypnotic beauty always creates, and also that special way of being, so typical of this actress. Two hours with someone like Maria Cayetana, closer to the ideal Duchess of Alba than the true figure upon which she is based, is enough to excuse all the weaknesses and defects of the film in which Ava Gardner stars."[36]

As for Maurice Lantheme, he wrote:

Finally and above all there is Ava Gardner. There is Ava, Ava sublime in her grace and freedom, with Koster's gaze upon her, loving, lucid, inflamed, passionate. There is the hope of seeing Ava's smile; there is a movement of Ava's hand; a palpitation of her chest, a profile that looks away. There is Ava whom we are not too certain is the Duchess of Alba, or if the Duchess of Alba is Ava. And so, in the end, the world and time stop, subjecting us to this delicious torture which is the burning contemplation of beauty in the pure state. [37]

The Naked Maja marked the end of Ava's seventeen years under contract with MGM. Failures and obligations of all kinds had transformed these years into a prison. Ava shared her joy with a journalist from the *New York Times* when she declared that the only decent thing about the film was that it was her last one under contract. She was to be free of MGM in September.[38]

When shooting finished on *The Naked Maja* there was a big party and Ava, now completely freed of any obligations, invited all the crew to join. Indeed, she had just signed a brilliant contract with Stanley Kramer's production company to star in the director's new film *On the Beach*. Ava was determined that from then on, all the money that had contributed to making MGM rich would be paid to her. To achieve this, Ava would have to assimilate new rules of filmmaking, since nothing would ever be the same again.

Ava Gardner as the Duchess of Alba in *The Naked Maja,* her last film for MGM.

Waning: 1959-1968

Ava Gardner was finally released from her bondage under MGM and was free to manage her own career. The entire film industry, however, was undergoing tremendous transformation. The Nouvelle Vague had been born in France and, in the United States, an entire new generation of independent directors and producers was emerging. The big studios, which sometimes even faced the risk of bankruptcy, were not renewing actors' exclusive contracts. To be an actor now meant being independently employed and represented by an agent. In this new world could Ava, a star from a vanished golden age, still come out on top? Could she still attract the directors and producers? The answer was yes.

And *On the Beach* proved it. This was a bleak movie whose story was set in the not too distant future, in the aftermath of an atomic explosion. The protagonist Moira Davidson was an an extension of some of the most powerful characters created for Ava Gardner (such as Lady Brett Ashley). Directed by Stanley Kramer, who represented the new trend in filmmaking, *On the Beach* did not resemble any film that Ava had ever made. Yet though this new direction promised a fine future, any bright hopes were short-lived. That same year, the ambitious but disastrous experience of *The Angel Wore Red,* with its meager box office, caused Ava's first absence from the screen which lasted two and a half years. During that time, the press seemed to be interested in the solitary diva only to record the wounds of time and scrutinize any traces of aging.

Ava returned to the screen in 1962, in a classic super-production directed by Samuel Bronston, *55 Days at Peking* (whose failure was as resounding as it was undeserved). This was followed by an excellent, yet all too small part, in *Seven Days in May*, directed by John Frankenheimer. John Huston, an enthusiastic admirer of the actress, offered Ava her last great role in *The Night of the Iguana.* Though at the time Ava declared that this was her last film, three years later she accepted a part in *Mayerling,* and left Spain forever.

It seemed as though at least a quarter of a century of film history had elapsed between *The Naked Maja* and *On the Beach*. Indeed, these two films, made within six months of each other, could not have been more dissimilar. Not only because of their screenplays, but also because of their degree of director's involvement, means of production, and mise-en scène. Ava too was quite another person. In *The Naked Maja*, Technicolor helped to maintain the illusion of Ava's bloom of youth, though in fact it was already fading quickly. The apocalyptic *On the Beach*, starkly shot in black and white, revealed how she had aged.

The Naked Maja was dated even before it was released and reflected a style of filmmaking that soon fell into total oblivion. However, *On the Beach,* made at the dawn of the sixties, promised a type of protest cinema committed to burning world issues. In this case it was the threat of nuclear war. It represented a radical cinematic break in content and form, despite some unfortunate studio link shots that ruined the credibility of a car race, or the inevitable lovers' embrace to the strains of violins.

Ava was on the set of *The Naked Maja* when she was offered the part in *On the Beach*. Her agent, David Hanna, encouraged her to say yes to director and producer Stanley Kramer. The film certainly seemed to be in line with the new direction Ava hoped for her career. It was a big risk though. Would her public like it? Would moviegoers accept to see the myth of their star destroyed? Those close to Ava were reticent.

The austerity of the story, not to say the sheer despair, was rooted in the anguish of the times. Its message was uncompromising, a warning to mankind of the risks of nuclear war. Ava hesitated. She had read the book by Nevil Shute, upon which the screenplay by John Paxton and James Lee Barrett was based. She found the story terrifying. Escapees on an American submarine disembark on the coast of Australia after an atomic bomb and radiation has annihilated the United States. The submarine is under the command of Captain Dwight Towers. As a wave of radioactivity slowly approaches Australia, the inhabitants of Melbourne await their inexorable death. Among them is Moira Davidson, a lonely woman and an alcoholic. Her per-

I worked with Ava over the years in three totally different movies: *The Great Sinner*, *The Snows of Kilimanjaro*, and *On the Beach*. Certainly Ava grew in experience and maturity with every one of them. I've always admired her as an actress and felt that she was underrated because people were deceived by her beauty and did not expect more from her. Also, she herself was not overly ambitious about becoming a great actress. Yes she did constantly improve and at her best I think she could certainly be counted among the better actresses on the screen...

... Stanley Kramer, who produced and directed *On the Beach*, is a filmmaker who, whether the subject is racial prejudice or the nuclear arms race, very much wants to say something about crucial matters of world importance. He seized on Nevil Shute's book and said, "I'm going to make a picture and perhaps I can have some effect on people's attitude, perhaps I can change their mindset about the dangers of nuclear build-up." I think we all became somewhat imbued with Stanley's mission, we all wanted to help him do it, including Ava. I believe that she felt good about being in that picture.

It did turn into quite an adventure, however. Terribly hot. There was a spell where the temperature was over one hundred degrees. Ava and I, our characters having become lovers, were trying to play a lighthearted romantic scene on the beach. But the air was so thick with flies that they almost blackened the skies. There would be thousands of flies crawling on Ava's forehead and in her hair, and the effects men would rush in with a smoke gun and blow smoke in our faces. That would get rid of the flies for a minute or two for all of us to say a few lines before they settled in again.

I have worked with a few actresses, who will remain nameless, who would just not work under those conditions. But Ava was never, never the kind of actress who would complain about her working conditions. She took it like a trooper and we just kept plugging away despite everything until we got the scene.

In Nevil Shute's novel, my character determined that since he was going to die, he would die faithful and true to the wife whom he loved. This in spite of being terribly attracted to Ava's character and it being obvious that they were meant to be lovers. But he resisted the temptation, and she understood that. So when they parted, when his submarine steamed out of Melbourne harbor and she stood on the point waving to him, it was a love that had not been consummated. That's what Nevil Shute wrote.

Stanley Kramer, however, decided that the audience just wouldn't accept that a man like me would be able to resist a beautiful, willing woman who was in love with him. "We have to give them some sex," he said. "This is a serious picture, it's about the death of the world, and we have to give them some romance and sex." I told Stanley he was wrong, that he was corrupting my character and Ava's character, that self-denial on a matter of principle was romantic. But he didn't agree. And Nevil Shute always hated that scene.

By the time we did *On the Beach*, Ava had a wonderful style. There were certain things she did that I think no one could equal. She was perfect for *On the Beach*, and I don't know of anyone who could match her performance in the *Snows of Kilimanjaro*. She had this poignancy and her feelings ran very deep. To my mind she developed into a fine actress. I've been telling her that for years and she always waves it off.

(Gregory Peck. *Ava, My Story*. 1990)

In 1959 Ava Gardner is again at a turning point in her career, as many other actresses whose contracts are not being renewed by the major studios. She risks launching into independent film and is directed by Stanley Kramer, one of the new exponents of the young American cinema. Here, with Gregory Peck in *On the Beach* (1959).

Above:
A moment of relaxation between two takes.

kind of light for the story. "I began to produce lots of new filters from existing ones. I put a perfectly transparent lens in front of the objective, once the shot had been set, and the light was transformed into rays through a filter. It looked like the effects of atomic radiation and the sensation was overwhelming."[39]

Under this light, Ava was almost unrecognizable compared with the fresh, radiant woman who, only two years before, had graced the screen in *The Sun Also Rises*. Her slightly bloated face, lifeless hair, wrinkled neck and heavily made-up eyes seemed more accentuated with every passing year. In certain close-ups the wound on her cheek could still be glimpsed. Ava was well aware of how worn the camera made her look, yet accepted willingly since it so well suited her role. Stanley Kramer heightened the pathos by consciously choosing older actors for the other parts. He cast Fred Astaire who, at 57, had just filmed his last musical comedy, *Silk Stockings*. In the role of Julian Osborne, a scientist and car racing fan, this film

sonal despair clearly echoes the more general desperation. Stanley Kramer wanted Ava for this role. Gregory Peck had already signed to play Captain Dwight Towers, a man of integrity who has lost his wife and two children in the nuclear disaster.

When Ava received the script, she simply could not put it down. "I cried all night," she confessed to David Hanna, and asked him to begin negotiations. After a career spent making movies for a studio, Ava naturally raised her salary by half a million dollars, an astronomical sum at the time. Ingrid Bergman was also interested in the project and offered to make the film for a hundred thousand dollars less. Stanley Kramer was on his way to the Berlin Film Festival and made a stopover in Rome with a pile of Flamenco records for Ava. Much to the director's concern, however, their serious business discussions soon turned into a wild party. Yet by lunchtime the next day all the terms of the contract were set and Ava agreed to make the movie for 400,000 dollars.

Shooting began in Melbourne in early January 1959. One of the clauses of Ava Gardner's contract provided for the collaboration of cameraman Giuseppe Rotunno, who had so flatteringly filmed her in *The Naked Maja*. Rotunno, who was destined to become famous for his use of color in the films of Federico Fellini, reveled here in a style of black-and-white photography that completely revolutionized the Hollywood classicism of the forties and fifties.

In fact, the Italian cameraman had to invent a special

Below:
The only happy scene for an impossible couple in a film that is both lucid and despairing in its warning against the dangers of nuclear war. (*On the Beach*, 1959).

The last shot of *On the Beach*. Moira watches as the submarine carries away her true love, Captain Towers (Gregory Peck). This scene recalls the Show Boat's departure as it leaves a sorrowful Julie behind on the banks of the Mississippi. Both are characters condemned to solitude or death.

would mark the end of his career. Both Ava Gardner and Fred Astaire were now the vestiges of a bygone world. Kramer could do without the aging dancer's lightness and Ava's beauty. The end of the Hollywood era also happened to correspond to the end of the world announced in his film.

Moira (Ava Gardner) falls in love with Captain Dwight Towers (Gregory Peck) and is forced to compete with the memory of his dead wife. The usual wiles for winning the heart of a desired man had been no secret to Ava's characters for a long time. Yet these skills had no place here. Moira, to attract the captain, is even willing to "become" his late wife. Dwight seems to be the last chance for this unfulfilled middle-aged woman. Moira, in fact, chose to throw herself into a series of loveless affairs rather than pursue the chance of a happy marriage with Julian Osborne.

Ava seemed to regard this character as a reflection of her own deepest self and brought all her memories as a wounded woman to the role. Indeed, she had reached a point in her life when she now envied the happy marriages of many of her friends such as James Mason, Gregory Peck, Van Heflin, or Grace Kelly. These were the kinds of relationships she had never been capable of building. Aware of her fate, she threw herself heart and soul into this character. Never had Ava been so moving, desperate, tragic and pitiful. Her portrayal, driven by an immense despair, was also filled with all the foreboding of her own downfall. In his book, David Hanna described the change that gradually overcame Ava following the making of *The Barefoot Contessa*:

> There was a vast difference between the Ava of then and now... four years before, she had been a more disciplined, conscientious and stable person... I could not remember a period in the years I had known her that life had been so turbulent. Nothing satisfied her. Nothing gave her pleasure. Her new car, a Facel Vega, was a clinker; the servants were stealing eggs; I couldn't be reached when she wanted me. And on it went.[28]

Nightlife in Melbourne was virtually non-existent. Ava hated that city, where bars closed at 6:00 pm. "This is a film about the end of the world," she declared, "and this is the right place to make it." Walter Chiari, foreseeing this, arranged to join her. Ava had suspected for some time that he was only interested in being seen with her for the publicity. She tried to have his show in Melbourne cancelled, but the organizers refused. The show went on. When Walter Chiari began an imitation of Frank Sinatra during his performance, Ava got up and left. She finally broke off with the Italian actor altogether after one too many of his arrogant comments at a press conference.

Just as Moira in *On the Beach,* who knocks on her former lover's door, Ava began to retrace her romantic past. Frank Sinatra responded immediately to her appeal and accepted concerts in Sydney and Melbourne. Indeed, as Ava wrote in her memoirs:

> What's six thousand miles when you're still in love? …The truth was we wanted to talk, to look at each other, to be together. The press were, as usual, as thick as flies on the beach, but we had our ways and means of being private. And with only two nights, we didn't even have time to have a fight.[2]

On the Beach traveled around the globe like a shock wave. Stanley Kramer's film was released simultaneously on 18 December 1959 in seventeen world capitals. His work was a cry of alarm, a committed film calling for peace in the world. Its disturbing effect was magnified by the fact that the events were not set in some distant future or unknown galaxy, but right here and (almost) now, in 1964. Stanley Kramer refused to point a finger at any one country for being responsible for the cataclysm. Author Nevil Shute had suggested Albania was guilty. For Kramer, all of mankind was responsible. In the United States, the film was not well received. Kramer's apparent defeatism seemed inappropriate to an America that had not yet experienced the great traumas such as President Kennedy's assassination or Vietnam. Its response was just a forewarning to any director who put his art to the service of a threatening message. Even today, *On the Beach* arouses sharp criticism:

> An ambitious, thought provoking subject (the survivors of an atomic disaster), an all-star cast (Gregory Peck, Ava Gardner, Fred Astaire, Anthony Perkins), the latter disarming the former. It called for an ingenious, sublime director; Kramer, as usual, was serious and vaguely competent, and his effort ran aground.[16]

Though *On the Beach* was slightly didactic, its effectiveness was undeniable, and its analysis of human behavior in the face of imminent destruction is particularly successful. Viewers remain transfixed by this film, which Ava Gardner recalled with great admiration:

> As for my performance, the critics couldn't seem to decide what was more surprising: how well I acted or how unglamorous I looked. *Newsweek* was typical, deciding that "Miss Gardner has never looked worse or been more effective." Frankly, I didn't care what the hell they thought. I was proud of being part of this film, proud of what it said.[2]

Ava was in New York in September 1959 when she was contacted by Nunnally Johnson, a screenwriter who began directing late in his career. Ava had many reasons to accept the part of Soledad in his film *The Angel Wore Red.* Above all, Nunnally Johnson was a friend. Also, since the story was set in the torment of the Spanish war, it reminded her of one of her favorite films, *The Snows of Kilimanjaro.* The reference to Hemingway was only thinly disguised in the character of reporter Hawthorne (Joseph Cotten). Finally, the role of a prostitute who falls in love with a former priest (Dirk Bogarde) was unique and challenging.

Shooting began on 2 November in Italy soon after Ava accepted. Just as in the case of *The Naked Maja,* the Spanish authorities refused the production company Titanus permission to shoot in Spain. The cast and crew were a curious mixture of veterans from golden age Hollywood and new talent. Ava had brought back her faithful hairdresser Sydney Guilaroff for the picture, and director Nunnally Johnson, at 62, was now an old timer himself. One of the newcomers on the set was a deeply moving Dirk Bogarde as the dissident priest who nevertheless remains loyal to his own conscience. At Ava's request, Giuseppe Rotunno was again director of photography.

The Angel Wore Red was a dark film. Co-stars Ava Gardner and Dirk Bogarde made an unimaginably poignant couple. Their many scenes together drew the viewer into the story and helped to gloss over its defects. The distress which Ava emanated through Soledad, a woman who continues against odds to believe that happiness is possible, confirmed that Ava was no longer truly the same woman. As Nunnally Johnson remembered:

> She would cry a lot, she had no confidence in herself, she felt she couldn't act, she had no home, no base, no family, she missed them terribly, she felt she'd missed out in life. It was hard to believe her unhappiness.[9]

Opposite page : Ava with Dirk Bogarde in Nunnally Johnson's *The Angel Wore Red* (1959), which remains one of her least popular films.

A shot from *The Angel Wore Red.*

Nunnally Johnson undoubtedly understood better than anyone else the futility of trying to recreate the splendor of Ava at her peak. He opted for a neo-realist approach, in black and white, and had her appear without make-up. After the first week MGM, who had no sympathy for the auteur approach, however, forced the director to completely re-shoot the film in a more conventional way. A different wardrobe was designed for Ava by a famous high fashion couturier. Ava rediscovered the force of her earlier performances as a wrathful woman filled with desire. As war rages, she taunts a woman who has come for a confession, "Have you ever seen a priest with a girl in his arms?" The Studio's commercial efforts were in vain, however. Despite a poster which emphasized Ava's voluptuous curves, and a red dress which justified the title but hid the fact that the film was in black-and-white, journalists could still comment, "this woman trying to pass as Ava Gardner."[40]

The Angel Wore Red was a victim of its over simplification. The reasons for the war between the Republicans and Falangists were reduced to the quest for a relic which became a spiritual treasure hunt. The film received extremely bad reviews, worse than any film Ava had ever made. Disappointed by the film's failure (even today *The Angel Wore Red* remains one of her least popular films), Ava stopped working and devoted all of 1960 to traveling. In April she was in Palm Springs, and in May in Monaco to accept an invitation from Princess Grace Kelly. She decided to put La Bruja up for sale.

Living there made me feel too cut off from the center of things. It was Madrid I really loved. The damned place had *life*! The narrow streets were full of old bars with tapas on the counters and hams hanging from the rafters, places that rang with the sounds of guitars, castanets, and flamenco dancing. If you knew your way around, the nights went on forever.[2]

The following year Ava Gardner moved to Madrid, to the Richmond Hotel, and then to a duplex at 11 Calle Dr Arce. Her address soon became familiar to a small court of admirers always eager to party until dawn. It was rumored that her new lover was baseball player Roger Maris.

After two and a half years away from the set, Ava finally accepted a starring role in *55 Days at Peking*. She accepted for a number of reasons, firstly because once again the offer came from an old friend, this time Phil Yordan. The film would be shot nearby, about 25 kilometers from Madrid. And then, it was about time she got back to work (her financial situation could never have been worse, and the fee was almost 400,000 dollars). After two films filled with despair, Ava Gardner reappeared on the screen in this sumptuous production which recounts, even with some humor, the fall of the Manchu dynasty after a historic siege of 55 days.

The film remains the last work to be attributed to Nicholas Ray. It was made despite the dictatorial control of producer Samuel Bronston and an unfortunate heart attack which forced Ray to hand over the directing (perhaps even with relief) to Guy Green. Shot in 70 mm, *55 Days at Peking* returned to the great Hollywood tradition of an all-star billing with Charlton Heston, David

Niven and Ava Gardner. Released a few days before it was presented at the 1963 Cannes Film Festival, *55 Days at Peking* was received coolly. Critics accused Nicholas Ray, renowned for his unconventional films (*The Lusty Men*), of selling out to a deliberately commercial genre after *King of Kings*. Nevertheless, it was not a very fortunate venture since the film only grossed five million dollars and cost more than six. *55 Days at Peking* marked the end of producer Samuel Bronston's career and the name of Nicholas Ray disappeared definitively from the contemporary film scene.

Though the film was out of favor for years, *55 Days at Peking* had more merit than was acknowledged at the time. The first sequence, with its establishing shot over Peking, was a show of sheer virtuosity. Nicholas Ray put imposing national anthems against a rising flag to evoke the eleven delegations struggling for precedence over the capital. Blatantly biased attitudes fueled many sequences and sometimes created even madcap comic relief in this tale of the bloody struggle between China and the Western powers. At a reception given by Sir Robertson (David Niven) in honor of Major Matt Lewis (Charlton Heston), Chinese clarinetists in traditional dress and pig-

Ava Gardner and her co-stars in Nicholas Ray's *55 Days at Peking* (1963), Elizabeth Sellars, David Niven, Robert Helpmann, and Charlton Heston.

tails play the fox-trot with pontifical seriousness. This prompts not only a chuckle, but also a reflection on the surreal and incongruous effects of the cultural interweaving of the time.

It was believed that the decor for the city of Peking had come from a last-minute recycling of sets from *The Fall of the Roman Empire*, another of Bronston's productions at the time. Here and there a few columns too Roman to be Chinese could be noted. In actual fact, the anachronisms and aberrations in architecture and costumes expressed the intense confusion that reigned in Peking during those years. Haughty elegant ladies stroll arm in arm with their debonair husbands among the needy Chinese crowds as if they were going down the Grands Boulevards of Paris. The reconstruction of the Forbidden City under the rule of Empress Tzu Hsi, prince Tuan and Jung Lu was extravagant. The emblematic figures of ancient China were here parodies of three great names in British film: Flora Robson, Leo Genn, and Robert Helpmann.

Ava Gardner as Baroness Ivanoff was more convincing and her performance is always a joy to see. The radiant noblewoman, whose sumptuous jewels are the envy of all the dignitaries' wives, undergoes an impressive transformation. Who would have imagined that once the conflict exploded, this same woman would don a nurse's uniform, pawn her precious stones for opium to relieve the victims' suffering, and finally be killed in action? Without being absolutely indispensable, the completely fictitious story of the Baroness Ivanoff is an integral part of the siege of Peking.

Screenwriter Philip Yordan had met Ava in 1945 during the shooting of *Whistle Stop*, the film that launched her career. He drew an unhappy portrait of Ava at the time that confirmed David Hanna's comments on the set of *On the Beach*:

> Her manner had grown disdainful, bitter, superior, contemptuous. All through the picture she was constantly drunk. She would remain in her dressing room, terrified by thousands of extras, and her double appeared in endless over-the-shoulder shots. In many scenes when she was needed and when Heston begged her to join him in a scene, she again hid, and drunk, and sulked. The real reason was fear: she was terrified of the competition from the major British stars appearing in the film and terrified also of the mob.[9]

This was also reflected in her acting. Charlton Heston, her partner, accused Ava of being directly responsible for Nicholas Ray's heart attack. Niven, who tended to excuse and justify her behavior, declared that she had become nervous and negative after promises about the role had not been kept. In *55 Days at Peking* Ava once again plays the type of beauty who is able to conquer her counterpart, Major Lewis (Charlton Heston), at first sight. Yet the death scene of Natasha Ivanoff was a shock. The ravages of alcohol were obvious in Ava's eyes and bloated face. And her screen image, buoyed by sumptuous wardrobes and makeup, was clearly an illusion.

Seven Days in May was a movie along the lines of *On the Beach*, an independent production with a similar theme (relations between East and West), and it shared the same pacifist convictions. Ava supported these courageous initiatives in which actors and actresses were given the freedom to take a more active part in the creative process. Kirk Douglas, star and co-producer of *Seven Days in May*, invested in the project with John Frankenheimer by buying the rights to adapt the book by Fletcher Knebel and Charles Bailey. The actors and actresses were expressing a serious political commitment through their art. "The destruction of nuclear arms, peace in the world, human rights, these are what I believe in," declared Kirk Douglas at the time.

Just as Stanley Kramer, John Frankenheimer became the spokesman for a certain current of thinking on topical questions in America as he focused on social issues of international concern. With *Seven Days in May*, Frankenheimer created a political fiction genre that was flourishing during the sixties and seventies in France, in the films of Costa-Gavras, and in Italy, with Rosi. He gathered together a group of like-minded actors and friends who had all worked on his previous films. There was Burt Lancaster, of course, but also Whit Bissell, Martin Balsam and John Larkin. The star status Ava had always enjoyed was by now completely a thing of the past. Frankenheimer said:

> Ava Gardner was an after thought: we had nothing really in the budget to pay her salary so we said to Paramount and Seven Arts that we would like to have her, of course, but we didn't want to spend that much money. "Now if you want to have her, then you have to put up the extra money" we said, which they did. The part is a very important device, and I'm glad we had Ava Gardner. It surprised me that she was so good.[41]

The film's story, set during the cold war, relates the foiling of a military coup led by General Scott (Burt Lancaster) against the President of the United States, Jordan Lyman (Fredric March). The two men have opposing ideas concerning the Russian superpower. Lyman is for détente. Scott, who is still living with the trauma of Pearl Harbor, refuses to trust a country that does not respect the international agreements. He plots to transform a simple alert exercise into an offensive against the Communists.

Ava, as Eleonore Holbrock, acts with rare conviction in the film's only female role. She is a finished middle-aged woman and an alcoholic (this was a role in which by now it seemed easy to cast Ava). The woman is left disillusioned by a military officer who sacrifices love for his duty to the country. Kirk Douglas is ordered to recover General Scott's compromising letters. Ava misinterprets his visit, thinking he has come to see her. In this role Ava Gardner, whose slimness recalls her debut appearances, moves gracefully across the spacious apartment furnished in the taste of the times. As the sixties obliged, for a cocktail scene she wears her hair in the inevitable French twist created by her inseparable hairdresser, Sydney Guilaroff. She wears a black skirt and gray cardigan for her serious classical character. The pearl necklace she had insisted upon wearing ever since *Singapore* gives the subtle finishing touch to her discreet elegance.

Ava (with Kirk Douglas) with hairstyle and dress in vogue in the sixties. In *Seven Days in May* directed by John Frankenheimer.

Opposite page: after three years of absence from the screen, Ava makes her comeback in a Samuel Bronston super production. The film, shot in the outskirts of Madrid and directed by Nicolas Ray, was *55 Days at Peking* (1962).

It took all of John Huston's single-minded stubbornness to lure Ava Gardner from her Madrid retreat to relocate to a hilltop residence overlooking a Mexican bay. This was where the hotel run by Maxine Faulk was located; Maxine was the character he had in mind for Ava. As she recalled:

The Night of the Iguana started with a phone call. The year was 1963 and I was sitting around in Spain, getting up late, talking to my friends, dancing flamenco all night long. In short, I was enjoying life and minding my own business and I wanted to go on doing so. I did not want to be in a movie at all. And then the damn phone rang.[2]

John Huston ignored Ava's refusal to see him, convinced that she was just trying to play hard to get. He put his producer Ray Stark, "in the front line". As he later recounted:

The first night we went out, I left the scene around four in the morning. Ray stayed on with Ava. This went on for three or four days – through most of the night spots and flamenco dance groups in Madrid – and I started leaving at midnight. Ray became more haggard and gray faced. Ava blossomed. She was just pursuing her regular routine. When we left, poor Ray was a shattered wreck, but Ava had agreed to do the picture.[42]

The size of the check must definitely have helped her make up her mind: 500,000 dollars, the most Ava had ever been offered for a part in her career. Filming began in September 1963, on a desolate, almost inaccessible peninsula in Mexico. Huston had the set for the Costa Verde hotel built on a mountain plateau overlooking the sea. There was Ava Gardner, owner of the establishment; Richard Burton, prodigious in his role as a pastor torn by the temptations of the flesh; Deborah Kerr, a painter and rather mystic virgin; Cyril Delevanti, the world's oldest poet; and Sue Lyon, the new Lolita.

Elizabeth Taylor joined Richard Burton on the set, screenwriter Peter Viertel, one of Ava's former lovers, also came up, and Deborah Kerr arrived. Foreseeing a lively filming, cynical John Huston offered each potential protagonist of a tragic love story a Derringer and a gold plated bullet, each engraved with their names. The explosive mix of people stimulated the imagination of the press, which was on the alert for scandal, as it headlined: "*Burton and Ava under close surveillance, Liz watching.*" Liz and Ava, however, both pure products of MGM, were also longstanding friends and would never become rivals.

In the past Ava had all too frequently been put before back projections to which she was to add interest. Now,

thanks to John Huston, she became the living reflection of a rich exotic habitat. She was perfectly suited to this wild landscape and heightened its allure. Huston, as creator of *The Bible* a year before, added a free and elevated spirit to Ava's voluptuous sensuality. He completely disregarded Ava's past roles, even her greatest ones, and explained that he had been inspired to cast her after an incident which occurred in 1946:

I had met Ava when Tony Veiller and I were working on the script of Hemingway's *The Killers*. As I watched her on that set, I was intrigued. I sensed a basic, fundamental thing about her, an earthiness bordering on the roughneck, even though she was at pains to conceal it. Sometime later I met her again and tried to make a conquest. I was completely unsuccessful. No midnight swims, no weekend... no Huston... During our visit with her in Madrid – some eighteen years later – the impression I had had concerning Ava's fundamental character was reinforced. Before, she had been shy and hesitant in her delivery, having to overcome a Southern accent which prompted her to speak slowly and carefully; now she spoke freely – I might even say with abandon. This, combined with her beauty and her maturity, made her perfect for Maxine.[42]

Before Huston, only George Cukor in *Bhowani Junction* had been successful in freeing Ava from Hollywood's stranglehold. John Huston was a director who filmed his own fantasies and went beyond simple erotic suggestion. He showed Ava in a blind rage, deliciously furious. She is pursued down the beach by two young Mexican musicians, whose advances she has refused, after pushing the games of seduction just a little too far. Without makeup, vaporous diction, or hypnotic looks, she acted with a guttural voice, an honest though sometimes self-conscious laugh, and a dash of the healthy vulgarity of the decadent star.

Her wardrobe was reduced to its simplest expression: pedal pushers, a very wide-necked poncho which, now and then, depending on how she moved, exposed her right or left shoulder. To emphasize this free and easy look, her hair was piled up in a tousled nonchalant style by Sydney Guilaroff. He had been brought over especially from Hollywood to create the effect. Ava's eyes were heavily circled with black liner. She was adorned with only one touch, a remnant from the past, a pair of huge earrings that broadened her face and "Mexicanized" it. John Huston only conformed to her legend in one very important detail: her bare feet.

At 41, Ava's beauty in *The Night of the Iguana* was

raw and devoid of almost all embellishment. If she still had the famous high cheekbones, the charming dimple in her chin and her malicious look, her face and figure had grown heavy. Her broad shoulders gave the character Maxine all of the temperament of a woman consumed by jealousy. John Huston's stroke of genius was to have cast Ava Gardner for a role that perfectly corresponded, physically and emotionally, to what she was experiencing in her real life. Indeed the part had no equal in her entire career.

The screen adaptation of *The Night of the Iguana* was based on the play by Tennessee Williams staged on Broadway in 1961. "A writer who hates women should never give his stories to a film director who loves them," wrote Jean Collet.[43] This presumed incompatibility did not worry John Huston in the least. He bought the rights to the play, enriched it with an astonishing prologue (the sermon of the pastor Shannon under the

unbearable scrutiny of his accusing congregation), and with a "road movie" opening (the pastor's bus trip when he accompanies a group of elderly tourists). These additions were meant to broaden the scope of the story, which for the most part was set in a hotel. There were nevertheless long scenes that pitted Ava Gardner against Deborah Kerr, then Deborah Kerr against Richard Burton, and finally Richard Burton against Ava Gardner, which recalled the original play behind the film. It focused on issues dear to the heart of the author. Religion was denounced for the ravages it could wreak upon a man otherwise healthy in body and spirit.

Of course, Huston disagreed with the misogynist vein in Tennessee Williams. Bette Davis, who had portrayed Maxine on stage, had accentuated the bitterness and cruelty of the character. Ava Gardner, however, brought more warmth and humanity to the part. John Huston created a more positive outcome for Shannon's fall in

129

In 1963 in *The Night of the Iguana*, based on the Tennessee Williams' play, John Huston films an Ava Gardner free of the chains of Hollywood. Here with Fidehmar Durán and Roberto Leyva.

130

Ava Gardner, Richard Burton, and James "Skip" Ward in John Huston's *The Night of the Iguana* (1963).

The Night of the Iguana by finally bringing Maxine and the pastor together. Tennessee Williams did not like this ending. He had seen Maxine as a praying mantis born to destroy the male. Nevertheless, for John Huston, if religion could ruin a man's mental health, a woman such as Maxine could only be his salvation, particularly if she had the qualities of Ava Gardner. Even twenty years later, Tennessee Williams still reproached Huston for the film's ending.

This film, together with *On the Beach*, revealed an Ava Gardner completely freed of her own myth. *The Night of the Iguana* promised good acting to come. It was in fact the final spark offered by an enchanted director who was completely spellbound. Ava, who received an award for Best Actress at the San Sebastian Film Festival declared, "The director I trusted most of all was John Huston. Working with him gave me the only real joy I've ever had in movies."[2] Nevertheless,

John Huston had not seemed to take any special interest in directing Ava, whom he had more or less left on her own. It was as if her presence in itself was enough. Ava's tendency to sometimes overlook subtleties and overact scenes confirmed her objections when Huston had first offered her the part. "Why me? You need a powerful actress. You know I'm not a real actress," she had argued.

John Huston ignored Ava's critical self-assessment and continued to want Ava in his films. The following year he cast her as the biblical Sarah, despite producer Dino de Laurentiis' objections, who wanted Maria Callas for the role. In *The Bible*, Sarah is barren and suffers to see her husband Abraham childless. The slave Hagar is taken to give Abraham a son and Ishmael is born from their union. Sarah's inability to have children was shared by many of Ava's characters (and this was also true of Ava in real life).

Indeed, in *The Snows of Kilimanjaro*, Cynthia was forced to have an abortion; in *The Sun Also Rises* the man whom she loves is impotent; in *The Angel Wore Red* the man Ava desires is a priest. In *The Barefoot Contessa*, Maria Vargas is murdered by the impotent Count Torlato-Favrini when she becomes pregnant by another man in order to give the Count an heir. In Ava Gardner's films there was always love and passion, but rarely children. Apart from Susan in *The Little Hut*, who knits a layette for a future baby in the final scene, Ava never upholds the American "happy ending". She is only a surrogate mother in *On the Beach*, as she cradles her dead girlfriend's baby, or when she adopts a young African child in *The Naked Maja*. Respectful of the miraculous events in the book of Genesis, John Huston in *The Bible* finally offered Ava motherhood. Sarah gives birth at ninety years of age to the little Isaac, "the son of laughter". And in *Mayerling*, which Ava Gardner made at the end of 1967, Terence Young prolonged this joy, perhaps the only one empress Elisabeth would ever know.

Terence Young's *Mayerling* was the fourth version of the tragic story of Rudolph, the young heir and prince of Austria, and Maria Vetsera. The two lovers were fated to die in the little town of the film's title. Ava Gardner's appearances were limited. After two brief scenes with her son Rudolph, she only reappears much later in the film at a ball when she acts opposite James Mason (the emperor Franz-Joseph). It had been seventeen years since Ava first appeared with the great actor in *Pandora and the Flying Dutchman*. Mason was also a star in decline. Now all eyes were riveted to the film's leading couple Omar Sharif and Catherine Deneuve. Nevertheless, outside Ava's dressing room at the Boulogne Film Studios, where interiors were being shot, a horde of journalists waited in vain. She did not intend to do any promotion for the film and her contract

had dispensed her of it. Producer Robert Dorfmann related, not without some exaggeration, how he had mustered all his courage to ask Ava Gardner to play empress Elisabeth of Austria and how the budget of the film had been sorely depleted as a result.

The portrait that a disappointed suitor, the prince of Wales, draws of the empress, fully justified the director's decision to cast Ava in the part. She was described as a

Ava Gardner was aged for her role as Sarah in *The Bible* (1966).

Ava Gardner (the Empress Elisabeth of Austria) and Omar Sharif in 1967 in the fourth version of *Mayerling* by Terence Young. This recounts the tragic story of the heir Prince Rudolph.

woman who had always lived to the wild pace of her horses, the most capricious woman he had ever known. Elisabeth of Austria, "the wandering princess", spent most of her time traveling around the world fleeing her numerous admirers. Indeed, there was some of Ava Gardner in the historic figure who, with regal poise and haughty beauty, inquires if her dress is draped nicely over her horse. Just as the empress Elisabeth had fled the Vienna palace, Ava had freed herself from the oppression of Hollywood.

All of Ava Gardner's career had been marked by the roles of highly desired women who were nevertheless also rootless and rebellious outcasts. In *The Naked Maja*, Ava was a political activist condemned to exile; in *Show Boat*, she was a banished half-caste woman; she was torn between cultures in *Bhowani Junction*, and was a Russian baroness expelled for her pro-Chinese affinities in *55 Days at Peking*. All of these women were in transit, looking for themselves, fleeing a condition, a place, a memory, and they all appeared destined to wander forever. From Mary (*Whistle Stop*, 1945) to Lady Brett Ashley (*The Sun Also Rises*, 1956), all of these women dreamt of sharing a happy life with someone who usually turned out to be disappointment.

Mary returns to her hometown of Ashbury for Kenny (George Raft), her former sweetheart; Lady Brett arrives in Paris with a future husband, whom she soon leaves. In *East Side, West Side*, Isabel comes back from Europe to join Brandon (James Mason). Cynthia decides to stay in Paris (*The Snows of Kilimanjaro*) instead of going back to America. All of these women seem to be trying to multiply their chances for at least fleeting happiness through their many wanderings. None of them is destined to live conventional happiness in an everyday and (perhaps) banal reality.

If MGM never truly took an interest in Ava Gardner's career, might it also have been because she seemed destined to misfortune? Perhaps the sense of failure that she embodied had never been on the Studio's books. Was Ava Gardner perhaps a casting error that lasted an entire career? MGM desperately tried to reverse this fate. Thus in *Mogambo*, Eloise Kelly, a young widow who fills her life's emptiness by endless traveling, finds a happy anchoring point in Victor (Clark Gable). Yet in *Bhowani Junction* (produced by MGM), a departing train separates Ava from Stewart Granger, who is forced to return to England. Ava Gardner, refused to be the representative of an easy and artificial universe. Undoubtedly this explains why the tragedy of Ava's life could only find an echo in filmmakers and writers who were also outside Hollywood's mainstream.

Ava had been living in Spain for twelve years now. Totally integrated into Spanish life, she spoke the language fluently but regretted not having met anyone there. At the time, Spain was still a victim of the general turmoil. Ava was irritated by the thousands of little inconveniences of everyday life. Her neighbor on the same floor was none other than the Argentine dictator Juan Perón, who had been offered refuge by Franco's regime. From his balcony he harangued an imaginary crowd with empty speeches. For the actress who had been the favorite of author Hemingway, so committed to the Republican cause, this proximity to the dictator was embarrassing. Ava was not amused when the IRS knocked on her door one day and demanded a payment of one million dollars. Having paid her taxes every year, the impulsive Ava decided on the spot to leave Spain.

There are many places I could have lived. Italy. But those damned *paparazzi*! And then there is Honolulu: but they won't leave me alone there either. And Japan, I love Japan. But it seems there isn't a place on the globe where I can walk without being photographed, interviewed.[8]

London had become her favorite city after shooting the interiors for *Pandora*. She decided to move there. Britain's capital was to be her last and final destination, though she would still make little trips to many other places. In fact, the location of a shoot often determined whether she accepted one film rather than another.

Sunset: 1969-1986

Ava Gardner now lived a reclusive life in London. If she still accepted to act, on average once a year, it was out of necessity. Her indifference to film was becoming increasingly obvious and the rare successes of the period were a matter of sheer chance. Ava refused more offers than she accepted and notably rejected the part of Mrs. Robinson in *The Graduate*, which launched Dustin Hoffman.

Ava herself admitted that she did not always make the best choices and that she was mainly motivated by money or at times by her feelings for the people involved in a film. It was for her friend, actor Roddy McDowall, that she accepted to make *The Ballad of Tam Lin,* an unusual film. And then for John Huston that she accepted to embody her own myth in the tempestuous *The Life and Times of Judge Roy Bean*. It was for George Cukor that she became the allegorical "Lust" in the director's next to last film, *The Blue Bird*.

During the seventies Ava was swept up in a series of disaster films. These productions, with their colossal budgets, invited one or more guest stars to appear, as if in tribute to their overall careers. *Earthquake* thus brought Ava Gardner back to Hollywood. Now directors only cast Ava in roles that reinforced her symbolic image as a movie star. She overacted as she played herself to the point of derision in such films as *The Cassandra Crossing*, *City on Fire* and *The Sentinel*. These were all roles that paid a lot and demanded little.

Ava Gardner's screen career was drawn to a dignified close in 1980 with *Priest of Love*, a biography of the writer D.H. Lawrence directed by Christopher Miles. From 1982 to 1986 Ava worked for television. She appeared in the ambitious six-episode historical costume production, *A.D.*, and a few minor episodes of *Knots Landing*. Nevertheless, the only film of note was probably *Regina Roma*, a telefilm by Jean-Yves Prate, in which Ava Gardner gave a remarkable portrayal of an abusive mother.

At Heathrow Airport in June 1969 with her dog Carra. Back in London, Ava prepares to play in the modern adaptation of a Scottish legend, *The Ballad of Tam Lin (The Devil's Widow).*

Ava Gardner as a high priestess in Roddy McDowall's *The Ballad of Tam Lin* (1969).

orful, everyone's hair was long, and love was free and without constraints. The body was no longer considered shameful, but rather an object of celebration. Communal life was being experimented, one that rejected the bourgeois conception of the couple with its remnants of Victorian England.

It was therefore unsurprising that *The Ballad of Tam Lin*, directed by Roddy McDowall, exposed the nude bodies of Ava Gardner and her young lover Ian MacShane. If this might not seem surprisng today, it was an absolute first for Ava Gardner. American films of previous decades were far from allowing the daring scenes which European films could boast. In those days eroticism was only suggested, and carnal passion was never expressed in more than a kiss on firmly closed lips.

Legends were popular. Roddy McDowall, singing the praises of a return to nature, transposed a poem by Robert Burns into a filmic folk-pop ballad. In this experimental work, entirely given over to the fads of the period, Ava Gardner rediscovered a role that finally did justice to her talent. This was the character of Michaela, "Micky", a rich elderly widow who reigned over a group of hip young people from upper-class London. Among them there was the photographer Tom, her lover. They all get together on her great estate in Scotland and indulge in a favorite pastime: the occult sciences and fortune-telling (seances of spiritualism, card reading, blood pacts, etc.).

Roddy McDowall made Ava Gardner into a magnificent high priestess, at once protector and man-tamer, a mother and a muse, as well as a jealous and demanding lover. She is a domineering woman who turns sexuality into the fine art of life and death. By being with these young people, Micky thinks she can prolong her own youth, though the age difference between Tom and her is a torment:

Michaela: Where will you be when I'm older?
Tom: When you'll be old, I will be in the prime of my life.

Micky, vibrant with new sexuality, bursts out laughing. Tom then meets Janet, the innocent daughter of a pastor. Like Salomé, who demanded the head of John the Baptist on a silver plate, Micky orchestrates a macabre plan of vengeance that ends in a manhunt. Under the effects of a drug he has unwittingly taken, Tom flees a furious horde and mentally transforms himself into a snake and then a bear. *The Ballad of Tam Lin* has all the foibles of the filmic language of the sixties: deformed focuses, violent zooms that pull

When Ava Gardner moved to London in 1968, England was the world's exciting cradle of pop culture. Her first British film, *The Ballad of Tam Lin*, was strongly marked by the non-conformism of the late sixties, which owed much to oriental philosophy. The Beatles, under this influence, propagated Buddhist wisdom through their songs, and brought a message of peace and love. They created musical cross-fertilizations, mixing the strains of the sitar to the chords of electric guitars. Clothes and ideas were loose and col-

> T he highly irritating thing about Ava, of course, was that she had no regard for her intellectual capacity or her talent. She was a wonderful actress and she never believed it. If you told her that, or if you told her how beautiful she was, she'd get very uncomfortable and virtually begin to shake. She didn't know what to do with this information; it unnerved her...
>
> In 1969, we made a movie together: I directed her in the *The Ballad of Tam Lin*. She hadn't made a film in a couple of years, it was a very large part, and she was very nervous. It was not a successful movie, by any manner or means, but her performance is remarkable and dead-on.
>
> The film was based on a Scottish border ballad by Robert Burns that is about a beach goddess – who walks the earth in perpetuity, refurbishing her godhead with the sacrifices of young people. She takes them and she destroys their lives; she's a magnet for them and she sucks them dry. And the ultimate triumph in the piece is that a young man is saved by the true love of a pure young girl.
>
> In modern terms, the film was about this very rich, opulent, seductive, enchanting woman who at base was a killer of creativity and productivity. It's a piece that could only be played by a creature who, when coming on from wings, carried with her glamour, maturity, and mystery. Vivien Leigh could have played her, but she was dead. Probably Jeanne Moreau could have done it. But Ava was unique because she was an imperial creature with a great peasant's streak, which is a miraculous combination to find. Her ability to scrub the kitchen floor, you know, was always there. Hers was the most unpretentious elegance I ever knew.
>
> Ava was one of the most perfect screen actresses I've ever encountered because she had a childlike concentration, which is widely important. It's one of the major things that a film actor or actress should have, because immediacy is tremendously important to hold. I found that when you were working with her you should never really have more than three takes. Because she really *did* it.
>
> Watching her act was a fascinating thing to me – I was often stunned. There was one time when she had to take a dagger, stick it into a desk and say something like, "I will not die." And when she said it her eyes in that moment just filled with blood. It was incredible. She didn't have acting craft, but she had this immediate instinct. So in a sense perhaps the toll was larger for her than somebody who had craft at their fingertips. Because she had to really completely do it at that moment.
>
> **Roddy Mc Dowall. *Ava, My Story*. 1990.**

back, psychedelic subjective visions seen through colored glass. The musical score, half folk ballads in the Joan Baez style and half pop songs, also contributed to creating this special universe, though it was used heavily only as a filler for bucolic intervals. The fashion of the time did nothing for Ava Gardner, judging from her long dress with yellow and orange horizontal stripes created by Balmain.

For the first time in her career, Ava was working on a film that had no distributor. The production of *The Ballad of Tam Lin* was chaotic and plagued with mishaps. Shooting began in 1969 in Scotland and then continued at the Pinewood Studios in London under the title *Tam Lin*. The filming was soon interrupted, however, when Commonwealth United declared bankruptcy. Rights were then acquired by American International and the film was finally released in 1971 in the United States as *The Ballad of Tam Lin*. This version was not approved by McDowall, who managed to do a director's cut and reinsert certain scenes. Nevertheless, eight years later, when the film was finally released in

its country of origin, it seemed only a clumsy manifesto of a dated pop-art form and was never commercially circulated.

The quality of Ava Gardner's performance was recognized, however, and Eric Braun wrote:

> This is Gardner at the peak of her maturity, interpreting the part of a woman who combines compassion with ruthlessness – the face has a beauty far more interesting than the plastic loveliness of her early years, and physically she is, literally, in great form. She achieves here the considerable feat of suggesting the vulnerability of the woman within the goddess – the fear of growing old alone, the kindness, and, when crossed, the utter implacability.[44]

Ava also expressed implacability through the character Remy, Charlton Heston's jealous, bitter wife in *Earthquake*, in 1974. The film opens with an argument between a couple and the threat of one of them to commit suicide. Remy accuses her husband of having an

affair with a young actress (Geneviève Bujold). As Jean de Baroncelli indulgently remarked:

> The romantic or professional problems of these characters are of absolutely no interest to us. But we know we have to put up with them. Later, these characters will be the privileged witnesses of the disaster. [45]

The cataclysm this time was amplified by a technical innovation, "sensurround". Not only were the hearts of spectators shaken, but their very seats were too. The viewer could feel the quaking just as the people in the film, victims of the catastrophe that hit Los Angeles. Though it created a sensational effect, the process was not used again after *Roller Coaster* in 1977. As Robert Chazal wrote:

> The main feature of this type of super production is to put the stars in their place and shift their importance to the real forces of nature. There is more dramatic power in the water that threatens to flood a city after a dam breaks, or in the earth splitting open, than in the domestic squabbles between Charlton Heston and Ava Gardner. [46]

This could not have mattered less to Ava. She accepted the part since the film was being shot in Holly-

wood. London was freezing and with fuel rationed she much preferred to be in California. Ava also looked forward to seeing her sister Bappie.

Though it was not as great a hit as *Towering Inferno* or *Poseidon Adventure*, *Earthquake* was a box office triumph that grossed Universal and the Filmmakers Group 36,250,000 dollars. [24] This approximately equaled takings all combined from *The Snows of Kilimanjaro*, *Show Boat*, *55 Days at Peking*, *Knights of the Round Table*, *On the Beach* and *Mogambo*. Listed in chronological order, these were Ava Gardner's six greatest commercial successes.

Ava was now 52. The last years had been ruinous for her. Hard drinking had taken its toll. The fashions of the seventies, particularly the hairstyles, made her face look heavier. The characters she was asked to portray no longer attempted to dazzle, but rather imposed emotional tyranny, such as Michaela in *The Ballad of Tam Lin*. Ava decided to undergo a detoxification treatment at the Grayshott Hall health clinic. She wanted to be more appealing to Freddie Davis, a thirty-year-old Afro-American singer she had met. Ava told friends, "I'm not drinking anymore because I'm in love with Freddie. There was a time when I drank a lot, but I've drastically reduced the whiskey now." [22]

Ava Gardner made two other disaster movies, *The Cassandra Crossing* in 1976, and *City on Fire* in 1978. In the former, produced by Carlo Ponti, Ava seemed to have fun making her character, Nicole Dressler, into a caricature. This was a millionaire's wife whose traveling companion is a gigolo dealing in heroin and twenty years her junior. She steps ostentatiously off the train in Geneva in a broad-rimmed hat, and with a basset hound and countless suitcases in her wake. In *City on Fire*, inspired by *Towering Inferno*, Ava played the role of television journalist Maggie Grayson. The briefness of her appearance recalled films of her debut. Maggie is a reckless woman and hard drinker. When she collapses drunk in the studio, the director of the program gets her to pull herself together and go on the air. Not without first, however, drenching her in the shower fully dressed.

Another genre that flourished in the seventies was the political live-action film. Ava made two such pictures: *Permission to Kill* co-starring with her partner in *The Angel Wore Red*, Dirk Bogarde, and *The Kidnapping of the President*. Neither film went down in the annals of film history. As one journalist remarked about *Permission to Kill*:

In 1974 Ava Gardner returns to Hollywood and appears in a series of disaster films. Above: with Lorne Greene in Mark Robson's Earthquake (1974).

Opposite page: She tries to escape the earthquake that threatens to annihilate Los Angeles.

With Martin Sheen in George Pan Cosmatos' *The Cassandra Crossing* (1975).

With Dirk Bogarde in Cyril Frankel's *Permission to Kill* (1975).

It is not really me who should be giving this eulogy, though it is true that Ava Gardner and I met, talked, had fun, and though it is also true that we spent listless afternoons, sleepless nights and shared our little scandals, points of view and the giggles. In short, we were sort of accomplices for a month, a very long time ago, while she was making *Mayerling* with the exquisite Omar Sharif...

She was more beautiful than her rivals, more amoral and reckless, too. And she was more alone than any of them, too. She was like a very beautiful animal and very noble as such, and very foreign. To her lovers she offered no solution, no future, no explanation, since her beauty stressed the great abyss, not always clear in cinema, between sensuality and vulgarity.

And in the same way her career was an inexplicable paradox: neither a has-been nor a glorified deity, nor inclined to nude scenes really, nor truly recognized in her own circles, she was the actress whose beauty reigned supreme and was an evocation of herself only...

I saw her as she went on the set to film a tragic scene with a smile on her face, cocking her hat, throwing winks, I saw her fall asleep on the floor when the scene was too long (in fact, in these scenes, she was admirably beautiful and superbly elsewhere). I saw her much more concerned by a gypsy orchestra who played out of tune or by a despicable maître d'hôtel, or by a hypocritical company president: her irritation, I should say, was expressed in wrenched tablecloths, overturned tables, members of the board thrown out of taxis, or by her own interminable disappearances. I saw banquets given in her honor where she never turned up, I saw her walk the streets the whole night, I saw her take refuge in stormy silences, but these weren't the caprices of a star that I saw, far from it, they were the sudden bursts of a trapped animal that alcohol often relieved, of course, but not always though, not enough that is, when I recall the depth of her silent sorrow...

Who was she? The more I think of it, the less I remember, the less I know. I can only say that she was beautiful, and alone, and generous, and that she liked to laugh sometimes. I can say that she was one of those people who make your life a poetic landscape, yet you cannot help feeling she was but a bitter desert, akin to those primitive or decadent people whose destinations you do not know, and who probably don't truly know themselves, so bound are they by nature. And, in Ava Gardner's case, by her intrinsic beauty.

Ava Gardner par Françoise Sagan. Elle. n° 2301. February 12, 1990.

Political cinema is a noble genre, but when politics is used as a pretext for a series spy or adventure story it is a sad impostor. It is betrayal. It is no less sad to note that artists of the caliber of Dirk Bogarde (not to mention a sacrificed Ava Gardner) have compromised themselves in this unlikely and forced story. The Austrian landscapes are pretty. Not much of a compensation.[47]

The Kidnapping of the President was a suspense film marked by the obsession with presidential security after the assassination of J.F. Kennedy. The attempt to assassinate President Reagan in March 1981 preceded the American release of the film and made excellent publicity. Reality again surpassed fiction. Ava is the opportunistic wife of the Vice-President (Van Johnson). She gets her husband to take advantage of the situation (the kidnapping and demand for ransom) to be well placed for the succession. In her brief scenes, Ava recalls the volcanic temperament of Gena Rowlands.

Ever since the success of *The Exorcist*, the seventies also meant fantasy cinema. Ava's films were no exception, with *The Sentinel*, directed by Michael Winner, whose films were often merely vehicles for furthering Charles Bronson's career. There were six days of shooting in New York for this film (she no longer accepted longer periods). Ava was a real estate agent in charge of finding new tenants, victims who became "sentinels" against the forces of Evil.

Her scenes seemed badly paced and Samuel Lachize noted:

It is curious to see Ava Gardner come and go in the film with the expression of someone who has opened the wrong door and apologizes saying, "I saw a light and came up, but it wasn't what I was looking for".[48]

Yet it is true that her role was very far from horror. All of her scenes were shot under blinding sun-lights, as if she needed to give contrast to the reality of her sinister profession.

In a sequence of George Cukor's *The Blue Bird*, Ava Gardner embodies Lust and Debauchery. Here with Elizabeth Taylor.

Finally, during the seventies, there was *The Blue Bird*, directed by George Cukor. At seventy-six he was working again with his old buddy from *Bhowani Junction*, cameraman Freddie Young, and also Ava. *The Blue Bird* is the wondrous adventure of two children on a quest for a mythic bird that promises happiness on earth. A series of trials accompany their journey. The little boy Tyltyl meets the allegorical figure "Lust" played by Ava Gardner. Part witch, part teacher, part ambassadress of pleasures, she tries to lead the little boy astray.

In *The Blue Bird* here again a theme emerged which, ever since *East Side, West Side,* had run tirelessly throughout all of Ava Gardner's films and her own existence: the choice between a conventional life or one filled with risk and adventure. All of this unfolds in a light key as director Cukor and his star also seem to take malicious pleasure in the story. The moral fable celebrates the simple joys of the family rediscovered, and the "blue bird" turns out to be nothing but a lovely utopist vision. As a first American-Soviet co-production, though the film was not a box office success, it was still a very charming movie.

At the beginning of the twentieth century, if there was an author who, well before the sixties and seventies, symbolized the sexual revolution in England, it was D.H.

Lawrence. Indeed, he had even referred to himself as "the priest of love", in a letter dated 1914. It was in 1980 that director Christopher Miles, a great admirer of the writer, made a film on the last years of Lawrence's life from 1924 to 1930. The story opens as a hundred copies of Lawrence's recently published *The Rainbow* are burned in a public square in London at the request of the National Puritan League. Lawrence, proud, free and uncompromising, leaves reactionary England with his German-born wife Frieda.

The rebel couple have been invited to Mexico by Mabel Dodge Luhan, a benefactor who collects money, artists, and women's husbands. Christopher Miles cast Ava in the role of Mabel. Crossing the Mexican countryside seconded by her third, self-effacing husband (an Amerindian employed as her driver), and flaunting her sublime "roaring twenties" outfits, Ava Gardner is ravishing. This role, which suited her more than any other, was an extension of two previous characters. Just as Michaela in *The Ballad of Tam Lin,* and "Lust" in *The Blue Bird*, Mabel is a domineering and possessive character who wields tremendous power over her protégés. D.H. Lawrence, however, was not a person to be easily manipulated. Prisoner of a woman who demanded much and hoped for even more (no doubt a physical relationship), Lawrence cut his stay short and went to Italy where he published two of his most important works, *Women in Love* and *Lady Chatterley's Lover*. As *Variety* reviewed the film: "Supporting cast is well-chosen with Ava Gardner looking great and utterly convincing in her best role in years as the duo's free-spirited American connection."[49]

Ava Gardner did not appear in the best of American and European cinema of the seventies. When she was cast in *Priest of Love*, she knew that this experience and her performance would achieve a standard that she should always have set for herself. Her co-stars Ian McKellen and Janet Suzman, distinguished stage actors from the Royal Shakespeare Company, were excited to be playing opposite a Hollywood star. Certainly they did not realize that Ava had never rid herself of her complex before artists she considered real actors. *Priest of Love* was Ava Gardner's last feature.

Television offered new horizons for Ava two years later with *Regina Roma*, directed by Jean-Yves Prate. This was a telefilm shot at Cinecittà studios in Rome during the summer of 1982. Prate, a Frenchman who had emigrated to the United States, made a film of the oedipal drama by Pierre Rey. Against a minimalist decor, the director staged a mother's triumph over her son during a family gathering. Carry, a clumsy and inhibited man in his forties, has never broken free of his suffocating mother. His timid girlfriend Regina, who accompanies him on the visit, soon realizes she is an intruder. Carry's mother completely ignores Regina, who has no place in this tight family threesome.

Ava Gardner played the cruel and virulent mother who does everything to destroy her son's girlfriend and rival. Carry is his mother's whole life. A trapped woman frustrated by her husband's modest social position, she lives through Carry and his career prospects. The tension mounts to an ultimate confrontation when Carry announces his intention to marry Regina. His mother will hear nothing of it. Carry tries to go against his mother and impose his own will. The whole film was carried by Ava Gardner as she acted opposite Anthony Quinn, her weak husband. The aging couple has been torn for a long time; the trivialities of everyday life cover deep wounds. During the course of the evening these are also revealed. Years before the mother, after a casual affair, had found herself pregnant and was forced to have and abortion instead of an illegitimate child.

141

Above: Ava in *The Sentinel* (1976).

Left: Christopher Miles directs *Priest of Love* (1980), Ava's last feature film.

142

Though this episode is related by dialogue, in the American version it was evoked by insert shots. Most certainly the director did not agree to these scenes. Though they were intended to give relief to the confined atmosphere and create dynamics in the structure, they only contributed to breaking up the unity of time, place and action. The American cut imposed its inevitable happy ending and rejected the French version's more logical conclusion. That is, Carry goes back to his mother. As he cuddles in her arms, he takes up a foetal position, like a baby asking for love. Carry would never become a man.

Ava's role resembled no other, nor was *Regina Roma* like any film she had ever made. This is the film's unique quality. No one before director Jean-Yves Prate had ever dared show Ava Gardner in an ordinary domestic setting. Unlike her excessive carefree portrayals, here Ava was an ordinary woman preparing a meal in the kitchen for her son. Whatever

made Ava accept to participate in this project will remain a mystery. It was so unlike her. The film's budget was as modest as her playing against type was disconcerting and unexpected. Nevertheless, as this abusive suffocating woman, "mom Gardner" was tremendous. She was hateful yet moving, depressed yet full of rage, despicable and wounding, yet pathetic as she released all the smothered hate and frustration of a lifetime. Ava seemed to have completely forgotten the easy portrayals to which she had limited herself in the super-productions of the seventies.

She ignored the camera, in the past all too often intended to flatter her looks, and instead concentrated on her role, which was the longest of her career. As she plunged into the anguish of a hurt and disillusioned wife, a rare Ava paced the modest apartment of a normal family for an audience of television viewers. At sixty years of age, nothing remained of Ava Gardner the big star. Instead she was simply an actress confronting her character. In this production, Ava entered the eighties with a look that corresponded to the days of her youth. Sydney Guilaroff, her faithful friend and collaborator ever since her first steps in film in 1941, was there to style her hair again. *Regina Roma* was their last film together. The actors' fees probably absorbed most of the budget, leaving little for artistic expenses (sets and lighting). Apparently, little did it matter since these financial constraints were felt to correspond to the characters' own social condition.

Since *Regina Roma* was originally a play before being adapted for television, this could have been the ideal bridge to theatre for Ava. Nevertheless, she had never dared to appear on the stage, though it had been suggested many times. While making *The Great Sinner*, Gregory Peck had offered her a part. Bennie Thau, however, number two at MGM, had vetoed the idea of a minor part, demanding "a leading role or nothing". Ava had

often said that she preferred the stage to film. In 1986 she gave her last interview and remarked:

> I've never done a play. Never! If I'd started young enough, perhaps I would have the courage. It's something I would like to do. I'd love to do *Night of the Iguana* on stage. I was asked to do it last year, and I toyed with the idea for a long time, but finally concluded that I simply couldn't, because I know I would be terrified. I really like the idea of working on the stage under those lights for two or three hours a night.[50]

The following year a brief press release announced her much delayed stage debut in Los Angeles. Ava Gardner was to appear in the play *Sweet Birds of Youth* by Tennessee Williams. The project, however, never got off the ground. Ava had already had a first warning (in *Regina Roma* her hoarse voice signaled lung problems after years of heavy smoking). Her health

Paul Newman and the image of Ava in the film, *The Life and Times of Judge Roy Bean* (1972).

143

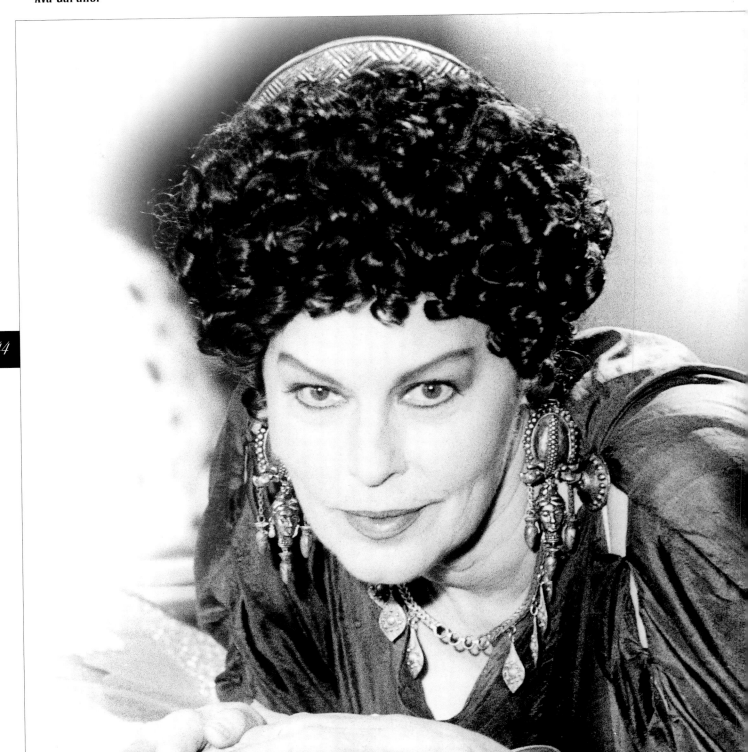

To capture the essence of this myth, John Huston had directed Ava Gardner as Lily Langtry in *The Life and Times of Judge Roy Bean* in 1972. Lily is a star idolized by the judge, and Huston played upon the elements of this myth. A blow up of an old poster that "even damaged, is worth all the women in flesh and blood in the world," Lily's photo excites the judge and fuels his hope and fantasies. John Huston, however, preserved the myth by keeping the judge from his so ardently desired meeting.

In the film, years after the judge's death, the heroine Lily makes a pilgrimage to the town of Langtry. The judge had the town named after the actress. Huston structured the final sequence of his film around the appearance of Lily. His camera tracks her face through the windows of the train. Ava-Lily visits the town's museum which pays tribute to her with a famous photo of the actress damaged by a real bullet shot through her heart. The person responsible for this infamous act was killed on the spot. A letter that was never mailed, signed by the judge, is waiting for the actress. It is a declaration of love and adoration for his idol.

This distance kept between the narrator and his object of worship guaranteed the existence of the myth. It was often prolonged by the narrative process of flashbacks or Hollywood's heartrending music and artistic blurs. The myth is set through the hero, in the very first minutes of *Singapore*, *The Bribe*, *The Great Sinner*, *The Barefoot Contessa*, and *Bhowani Junction*.

As time passes the myth grows stronger. Perhaps we are all much like those film heroes looking for an impalpable memory, that of an unattainable woman who has escaped us or who never existed. Like Judge Roy Bean. Or as in *Singapore*: "Is that really her?" wonders Fred MacMurray when he thinks he glimpses Linda on the dance floor. Does Gregory Peck really see Cynthia on the Place Vendôme? Is Pandora the mythic woman the Flying Dutchman has been seeking for centuries?

Frank Sinatra never forgot Ava Gardner. And she remained in the hearts of publics in Europe and America and around the world. The impact of her screen appearances largely surpassed the intrinsic value of any one of her films. Ava became an emotion preserved on film, the product of a total abstraction. And the power of Hollywood was in making us believe that the object of our attraction had become accessible, just when it had escaped those whose stories these films told.

Opposite page: In *Anno Domini* (1985), a television series in six parts shot in Monastir in Tunisia. Ava Gardner is Agrippina, Caligula's and Nero's mother, who plots for her sons to become Emperor. She is murdered by Nero.

This page: Ava appears in six episodes of the television series *Knots Landing* (1985).

forced her to give up the idea. The last four years of her career were devoted to minor productions for television. She appeared in six episodes of *Knots Landing* and had a small part in *The Long Hot Summer*. The ambitious historical colossal *A.D.* showed her as a physically worn Agrippina.

Finally, she appeared in *Harem*, the love story of a young Englishwoman, Jessica, betrothed to a British diplomat. The heroine falls in love with a Turkish rebel. Ava Gardner would have been Jessica if she had been young enough. She accepted the role of Kadin. Ava was hoping to recover soon enough to appear in the special *Hart to Hart* with Robert Wagner and Stephanie Powers, yet she never regained her strength. The end was near. With the announcement of her death, Ava Gardner's myth rose again intact.

Filmography

SHORT FILMS

FANCY ANSWERS
N°5: What's your I.Q.?

1941. USA 10'
Director: Basil Wrangell. *B/W. Screenplay:* Joe Ansen. *Voice:* Pete Smith. *Production and Distribution:* MGM.

"Number 5" of the series *Fancy Answers* was presented in a game show format, which gave viewers the chance to measure their IQs. Each question (such as "Who drank the first time in a glass?) had its respective experiment: a wine glass that burst at a certain frequency. Then there were 15 seconds to choose the right answer from the ones proposed without falling into any of Peter Smith's famous traps such as when he would ask, "In what year was the war of 1812 declared?"
Ava Gardner appeared during a recital.

WE DO IT BECAUSE

1942. USA 10'
Director: Basil Wrangell. *B/W. Screenwriters:* Harry Poppe Jr., Douglas Foster. *Production and Distribution:* MGM.

Cast (in alphabetical order): Mark Daniels, **Ava Gardner** (a girl at the party, as an extra not credited), Tom Herbert, Mitchell Lewis, Dorothy Morris and the voice of John Nesbitt.

Just as its title suggests, this short explains our habits and customs (Why do we kiss? Why do we shake hands?) and the origin of practices such as why ships are baptized.

OUR GANG
Mighty Lak a Goat

1942. USA 10'
Director: Herbert Glazer. *Screenplay:* Hal Law, Robert A. McGowan. *Director of Photography (B/W):* Jackson Rose A.S.C. *Art Director:* Richard Duce. *Editing:* Leon Bourgeau. *Production and Distribution:* MGM.

Cast: Robert Blake (Mickey), John Dilson (banker Stone), George B. French (movie theatre owner), Billy "Froggy" Laughlin (Froggy), George "Spanky" McFarland (Spanky), Robert Emmett O'Connor (detective King), Anne O'Neal (teacher), Lee Phelps (policeman), Charles Sullivan (bus passenger), William Tannen (bus driver), Billie "Buckwheat" Thomas (Buckwheat), Joe Yule, and **Ava Gardner** (box office cashier, role not credited).

A car splatters children on their way to school. One of them has his own special stain remover that gives off a horrible stench. When their teacher refuses to let them into class, the children decide to spend the afternoon at the movies. One by one the spectators who cannot bear the smell leave the theatre, except for one person, because he has a cold. The actors in the film suddenly materialize out of the screen into the theatre. The police intervene with gas masks and take away the kids, who have to bury their clothes.

FEATURE FILMS

H.M. PULHAM ESQUIRE

1941. USA 120'
Director: King Vidor. *Producer:* King Vidor (MGM). *Screenplay:* Elisabeth Hill, King Vidor, based on the novel by John P. Marquand. *First Assistant Director:* Walter Strohm. *Director of Photography:* Ray June. *Sound:* Douglas Shearer. *Art Directors:* Cedric Gibbons, Malcolm Brown. *Sets:* Edwin B. Willis. *Costumes (women):* Robert Kalloch. *Costumes (men):* Gile Steele. *Make-up:* Jack Dawn. *Music:* Bronislau Kaper. *Sound:* Julian Robeldo. *Music Director:* Lennie Hayton. *Editing:* Harold F. Kress. *Distribution (USA):* MGM.

Cast: Hedy Lamarr (Marvin Myles), Robert Young (Harry Pulham), Ruth Hussey (Cordelia "Kay" Motford Pulham), Charles Coburn (John Pulham), Van Heflin (Bill King), Fay Holden (Mrs. John Pulham), Bonita Granville (Mary Pulham), Douglas Wood (J.T. Bullard), Charles Halton (Walter Kaufman), Leif Erickson (Rodeney "Bo-Jo" Brown), David Clyde (Hugh), Sara Haden (Miss Rollo, Harry's Secretary), and **Ava Gardner** (a socialite, not credited).

USA release: 1941

Harry Pulham lives a boring conventional life, though he wishes for change. One day a pretty young woman enters his life and helps him to break loose.

JOE SMITH, AMERICAN

1941. USA 62'
Director: Richard Thorpe. Producer: Jack Chertok (MGM). Screenplay: Allen Rivkin, based on The Big Operator by Paul Gallico. Director of Photography (B/W): Charles Lawton Jr. Sound: Douglas Shearer. Art Directors: Cedric Gibbons, Paul Groesse. Sets: Edwin B. Willis. Make-up: Jack Dawn. Music: Daniele Amfitheatrof. Editing: Elmo Veron. Distribution (USA): MGM.

Cast: Robert Young (Joe Smith), Marsha Hunt (Mary Smith), Harvey Stephens (Freddie Dunhill), Darryl Hickman (Johnny Smith), Jonathan Hale (Black McKettrick), Noël Madison (Schricker), Don Costello (Mead), Joseph Anthony (Conway), William Forrest (Gus), Russell Hicks (Mr. Edgerton), William Tannen (Eddie), Mark Daniels (Pete), Frank Faylen (man in the waiting room), Robert Homans, Selmer Jackson and **Ava Gardner** (an extra).

USA release: 13 January 1942

Joe Smith, an employee in a defense factory, is kidnapped by Nazi spies. They torture him for information about a new type of bomber. Joe resists by following the advice a doctor once gave him when he had broken a leg. At the time, as a remedy against the pain, the doctor had suggested he conjure up all the happy moments in his life. Joe finally manages to escape. He turns over photos to the police that help them discover the Nazis' hide-out. Recovering in his hospital room, Joe is congratulated by his superior officers when he suddenly notices that one of them is wearing the very ring of his torturer. Thus the officer is unmasked as the leader of the spy ring.

WE WERE DANCING

1941. USA 94'
Director: Robert Z. Leonard. Producer: Robert Z. Leonard, Orville O. Dull (MGM). Screenplay: Claudine West, Hans Rameau, George Froeschel, partly based on Tonight at 8:30, by Noel Coward. Director of Photography (B/W): Robert Planck. Sound: Douglas Shearer. Art Directors: Cedric Gibbons, Daniel B. Cathcart. Sets: Edwin B. Willis. Hairstylist: Sydney Guilaroff. Costumes: Adrian. Dresses: Kalloch. Music: Bronislau Kaper. Editing: George Boemler. Distribution (USA): MGM.

Cast: Norma Shearer (Vicky Wilomirsky), Melvyn Douglas (Nicki Prax), Gail Patrick (Linda Wayne), Lee Bowman (Hubert Tyler), Marjorie Main (Judge Sidney Hawkes), Reginald Owen (Captain Tyler-Blane), Alan Mowbray (Grand-Duke Basil), Florence Bates (Mrs. Vanderlip), Heather Thatcher (Mrs. Tyler-Blane), Connie Gilchrist (Olive Ransone), Nella Walker (Mrs. Bentley), Florence Shirley (Mrs. Charteris), Russell Hicks (Mr. Bryce-Carrew), Norma Varden (Mrs. Bryce-Carrew), Sig Rumann (Baron Prax), Dennis Hoey (Prince Wilomirsky) and **Ava Gardner** (a guest at the party).

USA release: 5 February 1942

Vicky Wilomirsky, a penniless Polish princess, breaks off her engagement to Hubert Tyler to marry Nicki Prax, a Viennese baron. Nicki is a gambler and hates the idea of having to get a job. During a visit to his ex-girlfriend Linda Wayne, a decorator, he discovers his taste for the profession. Linda has him decorate an apartment which Vicky's ex-fiancé Hubert intends for her, since he still wants to win her back. Vicky and Nicki separate. Apparently there is now nothing to stand in the way of Vicky marrying Hubert. Nevertheless, on their engagement day, Vicky drops Hubert again, gliding off with Nicki to the rhythm of a waltz.

THIS TIME FOR KEEPS

1941. USA 105'
Director: Charles Riesner. Producer: Samuel Marx (MGM). Screenplay: Muriel Roy Bolton, Rian James, Harry Ruskin, based on characters conceived by Herman J. Mankiewicz. Director of Photography (Color): Charles Lawton Jr. Music: Lennie Hayton. Editing: Frederick Y. Smith. Distribution (USA): MGM.

Cast: Anne Rutherford (Katherine White), Robert Sterling (Lee White), Guy Kibbee (Harry Bryant), Virginia Weidler (Harriett Bryant), Irene Rich (Mrs. Bryant), Henry O'Neil (Arthur Freeman), Dorothy Morris (Edith Bryant), Richard Crane (Eustace Andrews), Connie Gilchrist (Miss Nichols), Joe Strauch Jr. (Milton), Tim Ryan (Professor Diz), John "Buddy" Williams (hunter), Ken Christy (driver), George Noisson (caddy), Robert Emmett Keane (Mr. Reiner), Frank Hagney (linesman), Doris Day (Freeman's secretary), Bess Flowers (saleswoman), Babe London (woman), Regina Wallace (Mrs. Lornow) and **Ava Gardner** (girl in a car).

USA release: 10 February 1942

Lee White is offered a job in an agency managed by his father-in-law, Harry Bryant, despite the little esteem the latter has for the younger generation. Katherine, Lee's wife, urges him to accept the offer. Lee however is against the idea of business and family. And indeed, the two men clash the day Harry refuses a deal that Lee has already closed. However, all's well that ends well.

KID GLOVE KILLER

1942. USA 74'
Director: Fred Zinnemann. Producer: Jack Chertok (MGM). Screenplay: Allen Rivkin, John Higgins, based on an original story by John C. Higgins. Director of Photography (B/W): Paul Vogel. Sound: Douglas Shearer. Art Director: Edwin B. Willis. Sets: Cedric Gibbons. Music: David Snell. Editing: Ralph Winters. Distribution (USA): MGM.

Cast: Van Heflin (Gordon McKay), Marsha Hunt (Jane Mitchell), Lee Bowman (Gerald I. Ladimer), Samuel S. Hinds (Mayor Richard Daniels), Cliff Clark (Captain Lynch), Eddie Quillan (Eddie Wright), John Litel (Matty), Catherine Lewis (Bessie Wright), Nella Walker (Mrs. Daniels), Sam Ash, John Ince (card players), Leon Belasco (Chris Spyro, the cook), Roy Brent (the suspect), Eddy Chandler (detective Rosson), Ken Christy (chief of police), Paul Fix (Allison Stacy), James Flavin (detective Keenan), Edward Keane (Forsythe), Mitchell Lewis (restaurant owner), George Lloyd (Joe Bulge Salinas), Jack Sterling (Steve), Emmett T Vogan (detective Novak), Charles Wagenheim (Martin) and **Ava Gardner** (drive-in waitress, role not credited).

USA release: 12 March 1942

Mayor Richard Daniels promises to clean up the city and rid it of its racketeers. He is assisted by Gerald Ladimer who, behind a respectable front, is actually a member of a mob gang. The mayor is killed when his car is bombed. Gordon McKay, a knowledgeable chemist and Gerald's close friend, is asked to lead investigations to discover who is responsible for the sabotage. He disproves Gerald's alibi.

SUNDAY PUNCH

1942. USA 75'
Director: David Miller. *Producer:* Irving Starr (MGM). *Screenplay:* Fay and Michael Kanin, Allen Rivkin, based on a story by Kay and Michael Kanin. *Director of Photography (B/W):* Paul Vogel. *Sound:* Douglas Shearer. *Costumes:* Robert Kalloch. *Art Directors:* Cedric Gibbons, Gabriel Scognamillo. *Sets:* Edwin B. Willis. *Editing:* Albert Akst. *Distribution (USA):* MGM.

Cast: Albert Lundigan (Ken Burke), Jean Rogers (Judy Galestrum), Guy Kibbee ("Pops" Muller), Dan Dailey Jr. (Olaf Jensen), J. Carrol Naish (Matt Bassler), Connie Gilchrist (Ma Galestrum), Sam Levene (Roscoe), Leo Gorcey ("Biff"), "Rags" Ragland ("Killer" Connolly), Douglas Newland ("Baby" Fitzroy), Anthony Caruso (Nat Cucci), Tito Renaldo (José Morales), Michael Browne (Al), Dane Clark (Phil Grogan), Dick Wessel (Moxie), Dave Willock (milkman), Lester Matthews (Smith), Alfred Hall (head waiter), Floyd Shackleford (doorman), Duke York, Sammy Shack (boxers), Edward Earle (employee), Marcia Ralston (blonde), Pat West (announcer), Robin Raymond (Vivian), Lester Dorr (photographer), Al Hill, Steve Pendleton (taxi drivers), Matt McHugh (man in the park), Tom Hanlon, Cy Schindell, Frank Hagney and **Ava Gardner** (girl in the first row).

USA release: 17 April 1942

Judy lives with her aunt, who runs a boarding house for men only. The presence of the young woman rouses the passion of two aspiring boxers: the janitor Olaf Jensen, and Ken Burke, a young medical student. To lure Judy away from her two suitors, Matt Bassler offers her a job as singer on his American tour. However Olaf not only wins all of his matches, but also Judy's heart. Defeated, Ken goes back to his studies.

CALLING DR. GILLESPIE

1942. USA 84'
Director: Harold S. Bucquet. *Producer:* Jerome S. Bresler (MGM). *Screenplay:* Willis Goldbeck, Harry Ruskin, based on an original story by Kubec Glasmon, and characters conceived by Max Brand (a.k.a. Frederick Faust). *Director of Photography (B/W):* Ray June. *Technical Consultant:* Dr. Charles Mandell. *Assistant Directors:* Tom Andre, Bill Ryan. *Sound:* Douglas Shearer. *Art Directors:* Cedric Gibbons, Malcolm Brown. *Sets:* Edwin B. Willis. *Costumes:* Robert Kalloch. *Make-up:* Sydney Guilaroff. *Music:* Daniele Amfitheatrof. *Editing:* Elmo Veron. *Distribution (USA):* MGM.

Cast: Lionel Barrymore (Dr. Leonard Gillespie), Philip Dorn (Dr. John Hunter Gerniede), Donna Reed (Marcia Bradburn), Mary Nach (Emma Hope), Walter Kingsford (Dr. Walter Carew), Philip Brown (Roy Todwell), Alma Kruger (Molly Byrd), Nell Craig (Nurse Parker), Nat Pendleton (Joe Wayman), Nana Bryant (Mrs. Marshall Todwell), Jonathan Hale (Frank Marshall Todwell), Charles Dingle (Dr. Ward O. Kenwood), Ruth Tobey (Susan May Prentiss), Mary Blake (Sally), Eddie Acuff (Clifford Genet), Robin Raymond (Bubbles), Ernie Alexander (elevator boy), Hillary Brooke (Mrs. Brown), Patrick McVey (Sergeant Hartwell), Emmett T. Vogan (Lieutenant Clifton) and **Ava Gardner** (a student, role not credited).

USA release: 16 June 1942

John Hunter Gerniede, a young psychiatrist of Dutch ancestry, works under the supervision of Dr. Gillespie. One of the young intern's patients is Roy, a student suffering from mental illness. The young doctor is very pessimistic about Roy's case, though Dr Gillespie disagrees. When the patient commits a series of horrible crimes, he accuses Dr Gillespie of being responsible. The police arrest the madman in the hospital where he has asked to be admitted in order to murder Dr Gillespie.

HITLER'S MADMAN

1942. USA 85'
Director: Douglas Sirk. *Producer:* Seymour Nebenzal, Rudolph Joseph (Angelus Pictures/MGM). *Screenplay:* Peretz Hirschbein, Melvin Levy, Doris Malloy, based on a story by Emil Ludwig and Albrecht Joseph and *Hangman's Village* by Bart Lytton. Poem *The Murder of Lidice*, by Edna St Vincent

Millay. *Director of Photography (B/W):* Jack Greenhalgh, Eugen Schüfftan. *Sound:* Percy Townsend, W.M. Dalgleish. *Art Directors:* Fred Preble, Edward Willens. *Sets:* Edgar G. Ulmer. *Music:* Karl Hajos, Eric Zeisl. *Editing:* Dan Milner. *Distribution (USA):* MGM.

Cast: John Carradine (Reinhardt Heydrich), Patricia Morison (Jarmila Hanka), Alan Curtis (Karel Vavra), Ralph Morgan (Jan Hanka), Howard Freeman (Heinrich Himmler), Ludwig Stössel (Mayor Bauer), Edgar Kennedy (Nepomuk), Jimmy Conlin (Dvorak), Blanche Yurka (Mrs. Hanka), Jorja Rollins (Clara Janek), Al Shean (priest), Elisabeth Russell (Maria Bartonek), Victor Kilian (Janek), Johanna Hofer (Mrs. Bauer), Wolfgang Zilzer (S.S. Colonel), Tully Marshall (professor), Frances Rafferty (student with glasses), Natalie Draper (Julia Petschek), Betty Jaynes, Celia Travers (nurses), Lionel Royce (Captain Kleist), Dennis More (sentry), Lester Dorr (sergeant), Budd Buster (conductor), Dick Talmadge (chauffeur), Chand Brandenburg (road worker), Ernst Hausman, Sam Waagenaar (guards) and **Ava Gardner** (Katy Chotnik, role not credited).

USA release: 2 July 1943

Karel is parachuted into Lidice to organize a campaign of local resistance against the nazis occupying Czechoslovakia. Jan Hanka, the father of Jarmila, Karel's fiancée, tries to be reassuring: he tells the inhabitants of Lidice that Himmler, acting under Hitler's orders, has peaceful intentions. When a dozen philosophy students from the University of Prague are arrested and a priest is murdered during mass, however, the truth is all too clear. Karel, Jarmila and Jan plot a deadly ambush for Himmler. His car is machine gunned and plunges into a ravine. Seriously injured but still alive, he is taken to a hospital in Prague where he demands revenge. Jan Hanka is taken prisoner, Jarmila shot as she tries to escape with Karel. Himmler orders the execution of all the men in Lidice and has all women and children deported. The village is wiped off the face of the map.

REUNION IN FRANCE

1942. USA 102'
Director: Jules Dassin. *Producer:* Joseph L. Mankiewicz (MGM). *Screenplay:* Jan Lustig, Marvin Borowsky, Marc Connelly, based on a story by Ladislas Bus-Fekete. *Director of Photography (B/W):* Robert Planck. *Sound:* Douglas Shearer. *Special Effects:* Warren Newcombe. *Art Directors:* Cedric Gibbons, Daniel B. Cathcart. *Sets:* Edwin B. Willis, Henry Grace. *Costumes:* Irene. *Music:* Franz Waxman, Eric Zeisl, Mario Castelnuevo-Tedesco. *Editing:* Elmo Veron. *Distribution (USA):* MGM.

Cast: Joan Crawford (Michèle de la Becque), John Wayne (Pat Talbot), Philip Dorn (Robert Cortot), Reginald Owen (Schultz), Albert Bassermann (General Hugo Schroeder), John Carradine (Ulrich Windler), Anne Ayars (Juliette), J. Edward Bromberg (Durand), Moroni Olsen (Paul Grebeau), Henry Daniell (Emile Fleuron), Howard Da Silva (Anton Stregel), Arthur Space (Henker), Charles Arnt (Honoré), Maurice Ankrum (Martin), Edith Evanson (Geneviève), Ernest Dorian (captain), Margaret Laurence (Clothilde), Odette Myrtil (Mme. Montanot), Peter Whitney (soldier) and **Ava Gardner** (Marie, a salesgirl at Montanot, role not credited).

USA release: 1 December 1942

After a trip to Biarritz, Michèle de la Becque returns to Paris only to find the city occupied by the Germans and her Parisian townhouse requisitioned. She is bitterly disillusioned to discover that her fiancé Robert, who had no greater desire than to serve his country, is now working for the Germans. Michèle is forced to move into a tiny room and beg her dressmaker Montanot to let her work as a salesgirl in his shop. One evening Michèle agrees to help Pat, an American pilot who has escaped from a prison camp. Reluctantly, Michèle turns to Robert for help. He gets false papers for the American soldier and organizes his escape. The Germans suspect Robert, whom Michèle learns is in fact the leader of one of the most important networks of the French resistance. This discovery seals their love.

PILOT N°5

1943. USA 70'
Director: George Sidney. *Producer:* B.P. Fineman (MGM). *Screenplay:* David Hertz. *Director of Photography:* Paul C. Vogel. *Special Effects:* Arnold Gillespie, Don Jahrus. *Sound:* Douglas Shearer. *Art Directors:* Cedric Gibbons, Howard Campbell. *Sets:* Edwin B. Willis, Glen Barner. *First Assistant Director:* Sanford Roth. *Music:* Lennie Hayton. *Editing:* George White. *Distribution (USA):* MGM.

Cast: Franchot Tone (Lieutenant George Braynor Collins), Marsha Hunt (Freddie Andrews), Gene Kelly (Vito Alessandro), Van Johnson (Everett Arnold), Alan Baxter (Winston Davis), Dick Simmons (Henry W. Claven), Steven Geray (Commander Eichel), Howard Freeman (Hank Durban), Frank Puglia (Nikola Alessandro), William Tannen (American soldier), Edward Fielding (Dean Barrett), Frank Ferguson (Tully), Carl Saxe (Dutchman), Peter Lawford (Englishman), Jack Gardner (mechanic), Sara Haden (usher), James Davis, Cliff Danielson (military police), Jacqueline White (a girl at the party), Hobart Cavanaugh (boat owner), William Halligan (bar owner), Kay Medford (secretary), Billy Wayne, Eddie Acuff (cameramen), Marie Windsor, Betty Jaynes, Marilyn Maxwell (girls at the party), William Bishop, Leigh Sterling (officer cadets), John Dilson (defense trainer), Harry Semels (hairdresser) and **Ava Gardner** (an extra).

USA release: 1 April 1943

On an airbase in Java, five American pilots resist the bombings of the Japanese. One of the pilots, George Collins, is chosen to accomplish a difficult mission: with the only good plane they have left he must launch a defense. After his take off, his companions talk about him as a person. Lieutenant Davis remembers that at first he had hesitated to recruit Collins because of his bad reputation. Lieutenant Arnold recalls that Collins was in love with Freddie when they were in law school together. Vito Alessandro's story reveals the relations Collins had with a crooked politician. The men think that he decided to join the army as a sort of redemption. Just then a radio message comes over that Collins is about to bomb a Japanese tanker.

DU BARRY WAS A LADY

1943. USA 103'
Director: Roy Del Ruth. *Producer:* Arthur Freed (MGM). *Screenplay:* Irving Brecher, based on the musical comedy by Herbert Fields and Buddy G. De Sylva. *Screen Adaptation:* Nancy Hamilton. *Additional Dialogues:* Wilkie Mahoney. *Director of Photography (Technicolor):* Karl Freund. *Color Consultants:* Natalie Kalmus, Henri Jaffa. *Sound:* Douglas Shearer. *Special Effects:* Warren Newcombe. *Art Director:* Cedric Gibbons. *Sets:* Edwin B. Willis, Henri Grace. *Make-up:* Jack Dawn. *Hairstylist:* Sydney Guilaroff. *Costumes:* Irene, Howard Shoup. *Costumes (men):* Gile Stule. *Choreographer:* Charles Walters. *Music and Lyrics:* Cole Porter, Lew Brown, Ralph Freed, Burton Lane, Roger Edens, E.Y. Harburg. *Music Director:* George Stoll. *Musical Adaptation:* Roger Edens. *Arrangements:* George Bassman, Leo Arnaud, Alec Stordahl, Sy Oliver. *Music Director:* Georgie E. Stoll. *Editing:* Blanche Sewell. *Distribution (USA):* MGM.

Cast: Red Skelton (Louis Blore/Louis XV), Lucille Ball (May Daly/Mme. Du Barry), Gene Kelly (Alec Howe/Black Arrow), Virginia O'Brien (Ginny), "Rags" Ragland (Charlie/Dauphin), Zero Mostel (Rami/Cagliostro), Donald Meek (Mr. Jones/ Duc de Choiseul), Douglas Dumbrille (Willie/Duc de Rigor), George Givot (Cheezy/Comte de Rochefort), Louise Beavers (Niagara), Charles Coleman (doorman), Dick Haymes (singer), Cecil Cunningham, Harry Hayden (couple), Clara Blandick (old woman), Marie Blake (woman), Andrew Tombes (Mr. McGowan), Don Wilson (voice of speaker), Chester Clute (doctor), Jo Strafford (singer), Dick Alexander, Art Miles, Paul "Tiny" Newlan, Kay Williams, Kay Aldridge, Hazel Brooks. With Tommy Dorsey and his Orchestra. And **Ava Gardner** (a girl).

USA release: 6 May 1943

Louis Blore works as a cloakroom attendant in a nightclub. The cigarette girl Ginny is in love with Louis who only has eyes for May Daly, the star of the show. Alec, a dancer, declares his love for May Daly, but she she is looking for a man with money. It is no surprise therefore that when Louis wins 75,000 dollars at the Sweepstakes, May Daly agrees to marry him. Louis tries to weaken Alec's charm by slipping a drug in his drink, but falls prey to his own ruse when their glasses get mixed up. Instead, Louis is whisked back two hundred years in time. He suddenly finds he is King Louis XV and May Daly is Lady Du Barry. Lady Du Barry promises to offer her favors to King Louis if he revokes the sentence against a revolutionary known as "Black Arrow" (who in fact looks just like Alec). Louis' cries to stop the execution are drowned in the crowd, just when the effects of the drug wear off. Louis the cloakroom attendant regains consciousness. Afraid this vision might be a premonition, he breaks off his engagement with May Daly and instead decides he is better off with Ginny, the cigarette girl, while Alec proposes to the star.

GHOSTS ON THE LOOSE

1943. USA 65'
Director: William Beaudine. *Producer:* Sam Katzman, Jack Dietz (Banner Production). *Associate Producer:* Barney A. Sarecky. *Screenplay:* Kenneth Higgins. *Director of Photography (B/W):* Mack Stengler. *Sound:* Glen Glenn. *Art Director:* David Milton. *First Assistant Director:* Arthur Hammond. *Music Director:* Edward Kay. *Editing:* Carl Pierson. *Distribution (USA):* Monogram Pictures Corporation.

Cast: Leo Gorcey (Mugs McGinnis), Huntz Hall (Glimpy Williams), Bobby Jordan (Danny), Bela Lugosi (Emil), **Ava Gardner** (Betty Williams Gibson), Rick Vallin (Jack Gibson), Minerva Urecal (Hilda), Wheeler Oakman (Tony), Peter Seal (Bruno), Frank Moran (Monk), Stanley Clements (Scruno), Billy Benedict (Benny), Bobby Stone (Dave), Sammy Morrison (Sorina), Bill Bates (piano player), Jack Mulhall (Lieutenant Brady), Tom Herbert (employee at the Park Central Plaza), Bob Hill (wedding master of ceremonies), Blanche Payson (Mrs. "Ma" Williams) and Kay Marvis.

USA release: 8 June 1943

Jack and Betty get married. Tony, a nazi spy, tries to persuade them to sell him their future house which is connected by a secret passageway to a hideout with an underground press. When Jack refuses, Tony warns the couple not to spend their first honeymoon night there because the house is haunted. The "East Side Kids" think that the newly-weds cannot afford to fix up the house. They decide to surprise the couple by doing all the work themselves, but enter the wrong house and come face to face with Emil, the leader of a nazi spy ring. The "Kids" however are a spunky bunch. They discover the printing press and the secret passageway and hastily assume that Jack is also part of the spy ring. The former owner of the little house

reports him to the police and a warrant to search Jack's house is issued. In the meantime, the nazis are tipped off and move the printing press to Jack's house, where of course the police discover it. Nevertheless, in the end the nazis are caught in their own trap.

YOUNG IDEAS

1943. USA 77'
Director: Jules Dassin. *Producer:* Robert Sisk (MGM). *Screenplay:* Ian McLellan Hunter, Bill Noble. *Director of Photography (B/W):* Charles Lawton. *Sound:* John A Williams. *Art Directors:* Cedric Gibbons, Leonid Vassian. *Sets:* Edwin B. Willis, Mark Alper. *First Assistant Director:* George Rhein. *Music:* George Bassman. Orchestra conducted by: David Snell. *Editing:* Ralph E. Winters. *Distribution (USA):* MGM.

Cast: Susan Peters (Susan Evans), Herbert Marshall (Michael Kingsley), Mary Astor (Jo Evans), Elliot Reid (Jeff Evans), Richard Carlson (Tom Farrell), Allyn Joslyn (Adam Trent), George Dolenz (Pepe), Emory Parnell (Judge Kelly), Dorothy Morris, Frances Rafferty, Robert Emmett O'Connor, Rod Rogers, Roberta Smith, Grady Sutton and **Ava Gardner** (an extra).

USA release: 13 July 1943

Jo Evans, a writer, decides to give up her profession to marry Michael Kingsley, a chemistry professor. Her son, Jeff Evans, a novelist, and her daughter Susan, children from a previous marriage, try to keep them from getting married, until they realize how their thoughtless jokes have created true suffering.

LOST ANGEL

1943. USA 91'
Director: Roy Royland. *Producer:* Robert Sisk (MGM). *Screenplay:* Isobel Lennart, based on an idea by Angna Enters. *Director of Photography (B/W):* Robert Surtess. *Sound:* Douglas Shearer. *Art Directors:* Ceddric Gibbons, Lynden Sparhawk. *Sets:* Edwin. B. Willis, Helen Conway. *First Assistant Director:* George Rhein. *Costumes:* Irene. Music: Daniele Amfitheatrof. *Editing:* Frank E. Hull. *Distribution (USA/France):* MGM.

Cast: Margaret O'Brien (Alpha), James Craig (Mike Regan), Marsha Hunt (Katie Mallory), Philip Merivale (Professor Peter Vincent), Henry O'Neil (Professor Pringle), Donald Meek (Professor Catty), Keenan Wynn (Packy Roost), Alan Napier (Dr. Woodring), Sara Haden (Rhoda Kitterick), Kathleen Lockhart (Mrs. Catty, music professor), Walter Fenner (professor Endicott), Howard Freeman (professor Richards), Elisabeth Risdon (Mrs. Pringle), Bobby Blake (Jerry), Bobby Driscoll (boy in train), Jack Lambert (Moran, left-hander), Naomi Childers (nurse), Kay Medford, Gloria Grafton (operators), Edward McWade (old man in the park), Russel Gleason, William Bishop, Lee Phelps, Edward Hearn (reporters), Mike Mazurki (soldier), Alten Wood (heavy), All Hill (idiot), Joe Yule (tenant) and **Ava Gardner** (check-point girl, role not credited).

USA release: 27 October 1943

Abandoned by her mother, little Alpha is taken in by the Institute of Modern Psychology which uses her as a subject for its studies on mental development. The researchers do such a good job on her mind that, by the age of six, Alpha is a fount of scientific knowledge. Nevertheless, the laboratory has never given her any of the tenderness a child normally receives. Interviewed by Mike Regan, a journalist, Alpha discovers the realities of life and emotions. She runs away from the Institute and is taken in by Mike and his fiancée Katie. Katie would love to adopt Alpha if Mike were not so terrified

In 1944, MGM considers Ava's talent and offers her a supporting role in one of its series productions *Three Men in White*. In this still Lionel Barrymore, Van Johnson, and George H. Reed admire Ava.

of the little girl's excessive shows of affection. Mike flees the whole situation. He is overcome with regret, however, and finally accepts the responsibility of bringing up the child with Katie.

SWING FEVER

1943. USA 81'

Director: Tim Whelan. *Producer:* Irving Starr (MGM). *Screenplay:* Nat Perrin, Warren Wilson, based on an original story by Matt Brooks and Joseph Hoffman. *Director of Photography (B/W):* Charles Rosher. *Sound:* Frank B. MacKenzie. *Art Directors:* Cedric Gibbons, Stephen Goossom. *Sets:* Edwin B. Willis. *First Assistant Director:* Marvin Stuart. *Choreographers:* Ernst and Maria Matray. *Original Musical Soundtrack:* Nacio Herb Brown, Sammy Fain, Sunny Skylar. *Music Director:* George E. Stoll, David Snell. *Arrangements:* Earl Brent. *Orchestration:* George Dunning, Phil Moore, Wally Heglin. *Editing:* Ferris Webster. *Distribution (USA):* MGM.

Cast: Kay Kyser (Lowell Blackford), Marilyn Maxwell (Ginger Gray), William Gargan ("Waltzy" Malone), Lena Horne (as herself), Nat Pendletonon ("Killer" Kennedy), Curt Bois (Nick Serocco), Morris Ankrum (Dan Conlon), Andrew Tombes (Dr. Clyde L. Star), Maxie Rosenbloom ("Rags"), Clyde Fillmore (Mr. Nagen), Pamela Blake (Lois), Jack Roper (blacksmith), Ish Kabbible (Ish), Harry Babbit (himself), Karine Booth, Kathleen Williams, and **Ava Gardner** (girls), Mike Mazurski, Sammy Stein (wrestlers), Mantan Moreland (Woodie), William Bishop (soldier), Dan Tobey (speaker), Lou Nova (Kid Mandell), Murray Alper (bouncer), Charles Sullivan (policeman) and Merriel Abott and "The Merriel Abott Dancers" and the Orchestra of Kay Kyser with Julie Conway, Trudy Irvin and Sully Mason as themselves.

USA release: 2 December 1943

Lowell Blackford is a composer who plans to devote his life to classical music. He uses his gifts as a hypnotizer to help promote his career. Things get complicated when he is suddenly plunged into the completely unknown world of professional boxing. To make matters worse, he falls prey to his manager and his manager's fiancée, a nightclub singer. Nevertheless, everything is set right again, though he never figures out exactly how. Lowell marries the woman he loves and becomes... a famous jazzman.

THREE MEN IN WHITE

1944. USA 85'

Director: Willis Goldbeck. *Producer:* MGM *Screenplay:* Martin Berkeley, Harry Ruskin, based on characters created by Max Brand (a.k.a. Frederick Faust). *Director of Photography (B/W):* Ray June. *Sound:* John F. Dullan. *Art Directors:* Cedric Gibbons, Harry McAfee. *Sets:* Edwin B. Willis. *First Assistant Director:* Al Raboch. *Music:* Nathaniel Shilkret. *Editing:* George Hively. *Distribution (USA):* MGM.

Cast: Lionel Barrymore (Dr. Leonard Gillespie), Van Johnson (Dr. Randall Adams), Marilyn Maxwell (Ruth Edley), Keye Luke (Dr. Lee Wong How), **Ava Gardner** (Jean Brown), Alma Kruger (Molly Bird), "Rags" Ragland (Hobart Genet), Nell Craig (Nurse Parker), Walter Kingsford (Dr. Walter Carew), George H. Reed (Conover), Patricia Baker (Mary Jones), George Chandler (patient), Billy Cummings (boy in the street), Byron Foulger (a technician), Sam McDaniel (telephone operator), Addison Richards (Mr. Brown) and Celia Travers.

USA release: 26 April 1944

Dr. Gillespie puts doctors Randall Adams and Lee Wong How to a test to decide which one to choose as assistant. Dr Wong How treats a little girl who is suffering from a vitamin deficiency. Dr Adams, however, decides to treat a pretty young woman whom he has just saved from food poisoning. Dr Adams, distracted by a romantic interlude with the nurse Ruth Edley, is only able to cure his patient with the assistance of his rival, who generously offers to help. This success earns Adams the position as Gillespie's right-hand man. A similar position is also created for Dr Wong How, whose results are just as brilliant.

TWO GIRLS AND A SAILOR

1944. USA 126'

Director: Richard Thorpe. *Producer:* Joe Pasternak (MGM). *Screenplay:* Richard Connel, Gladys Lehman. *Director of Photography (B/W):* Robert Surtess A.S.C. *Sound:* Douglas Shearer. *Art Directors:* Cedric Gibbons, Paul Groesse. *Sets:* Edwin B. Willis, John Bonar. *Costumes:* Irene, Kay Dean. *Choreographer:* Sammy Lee. *Music Director:* Georgie Stoll. *Songs:* Earl K. Brent. *Vocal Arrangements:* Kay Thompson. *Editing:* George Boemler. *Distribution (USA/France):* MGM.

Cast: June Allyson (Patsy Deyo), Gloria De Haven (Jean Deyo), Van Johnson (John Dyckman Brown, III), Tom Drake (Frank Miller), Henry Stephenson (John Dyckman Brown, I), Jimmy Durante (Billy Kipp), Henry O'Neil (John Dyckman Brown, II), Ben Blue (Ben), Carlos Ramirez (Carlos), Frank Sully (Adams), Donald Meek (Mr. Nizby), Frank Jenks (Dick Deyo) and José Turbi, Gracie Allen, Lena Horne, Albert Coates, Amparo Navarro, Virginia O'Brien, Dorothy Ford, The Wilde Twins, Harry James and his Orchestra, with Helen Forrest, Xavier Cugat and his Orchestra, with Lina Romay. And **Ava Gardner** (a hostess for the soldiers).

USA release: 5 May 1944.

Patsy and Jean, who have been in show biz since they were kids, perform in a club where John, a likeable sailor, is a regular. The girls have always dreamed of opening up a club to entertain the soldiers. This dream comes true thanks to a donation from a mysterious fan. Patsy and Jean remodel a club that had been closed for twenty-five years and invite some of the greatest artists to perform: Xavier Cugat and Harry James and their orchestras, Lena Horne, the dancer Ben Blue and pianists Amparo Navarro and José Iturbi. To help out as a waiter, they hire the now retired performer Billy Kipp. Patsy and Jean are both in love with John, who doesn't know which one to choose. Patsy discovers the identity of their benefactor, who is none other than John, son and grandson of the billionaire family Dyckman Brown. Jean gives up John and consoles herself in the arms of a Texan soldier. Patsy marries John.

MAISIE GOES TO RENO

1944. USA 90'

Director: Harry Beaumont. *Producer:* George Haight (MGM). *Screenplay:* Mary C. McCall Jr., based on a story by Harry Ruby and James O'Hanlon, based on characters conceived by Wilson Collison. *Director of Photography (B/W):* Robert H. Plank. *Sound:* Douglas Shearer. *Art Directors:* Cedric Gibbons, Howard Campbeid. *Sets:* Edwin B. Willis, Helen Conway. *First Assistant Director:* Charles O'Malley. *Costumes:* Irene. *Music:* David Snell. *Songs:* Sammy Fain, Ralph Freed. *Choreographer:* Sammy Lee. *Editing:* Frank E. Hull. *Distribution (USA):* MGM.

Cast: Ann Sothern (Maisie Ravier), John Hodaik ("Flip" Hennahan), Tom Drake (Bill Fullerton), Marta Linden (Winifred Ashbourne), Paul Cavanagh (Roger Pelham), **Ava Gardner** (Gloria Fullerton), Bernard Nedell (J.E. Clave), Roland Dupree (Jerry), Chick Chandler (Tommy Cutter), Bunny Waters (Elaine), Donald Meek (Parsons), James Warren (Dr. Hanley Fleeson), Douglas Morrow (master of ceremonies), William Tannen (leader), Edward Earle (employee), Byron Foulger (Dr. Jo Cummings), Leon Tyler (waiter), Karin Booth, Dallas Worth, Lynn Arlen, Ethel Tobin, Elisabeth Dailey (girls at the reception desk), Noreen Nash (pretty girl), Dick Rich (military police), Almira Sessions (woman with bus ticket), Ray Teal (police officer), Ray Walker (bus conductor), Anthony Caruso (George, dealer), Cliff Clark (chief of police), John Hamilton (judge).

USA release: 20 July 1944

Overworked and a nervous wreck, Maisie Ravier decides to take a two-week vacation to Reno. She meets Bill Fullerton, a penniless soldier, who asks her to try to dissuade his millionaire wife from divorcing him. After a big mix-up, Maisie eventually discovers, thanks to a casino employee, that Bill's wife Gloria is the victim of a blackmailer who is after her fortune.

MUSIC FOR MILLIONS

1944. USA 107'

Director: Henry Koster. *Producer:* Joe Pasternak (Henry Koster Productions/MGM). *Screenplay:* Myles Connoly. *Director of Photography (B/W):* Robert Surtees. *Sound:* Douglas Shearer. *Art Directors:* Cedric Gibbons, Hans Peters. *Sets:* Edwin B. Willis, Helen Conway. *Costumes:* Irene, Kay Dean. *Choreographer:* Jack Donohue. *Music:* Walter Bullock, Walter Donalson, Harold Spina, Herbert Stothart, directed by José Iturbi. *Music Director:* George Stoll. *Arrangements:* Joseph Nussbaum, Ted Duncan, Calvin Jackson. *Editing:* Douglas Biggs. *Distribution (USA):* MGM.

Cast: Margaret O'Brien ("Mike"), José Iturbi (himself), June Allyson (Barbara Ainsworth), Jimmy Durante (Andrews), Marsha Hunt (Rosalind), Hugh Herbert (Uncle Ferdinand), Harry Davenport (doctor), Marie Wilson (Marie), Larry Adler (Larry), Ben Lessy (Kickebush), Ethel Griffies (Mrs. McGuff), Katharine Balfour (Elsa), Helen Gilbert (Helen), Mary Parker (Anita), Madeleine Lebeau (Jane), Eddie Jackson (singer), Jack Roth (drummer), Connie Gilchrist and **Ava Gardner** (an extra).

USA release: 1 December 1944

"Mike" is in fact a ten-year-old girl. She goes to New York one day to see her elder sister Barbara, a cellist in José Iturbi's band. The band adopts her as their mascot and tours for the troops. Barbara is married to Joe, a sergeant fighting in the Pacific, and has not had any news from him in a long time. When a telegram arrives from the Defense Department announcing Joe's death, her friends intercept it. They fear for the serious effects the shock might have on Barbara's pregnancy. Instead, they get an old drunken forger to write some false letters to reassure her. Nevertheless, to everyone's astonishment, soon a real letter arrives signed by Joe himself. The notice of his death was a terrible mistake. When he comes home, Joe discovers that Barbara has given birth to a little baby boy.

BLONDE FEVER

1944. USA 69'

Director: Richard Whorf. *Producer:* William W. Wright (MGM). *Screenplay:* Patricia Coleman, based on the play by Ferenc Molnar. *Director of Photography:* Lester White. *Art Directors:* Cedric Gibbons, Preston Ames. *Music:* Nathaniel Skilret. *Editing:* George Hively. *Distribution (USA):* MGM.

Cast: Philip Dorn (Peter Donay), Mary Astor (Delilah Donay), Felix Bressart

(Johnny), Gloria Grahame (Sally Murfin), Marshall Thompson (Freddie Bilson), Curt Bois (Brillon), Elisabeth Risdon (Mrs. Talford), Arthur Walsh (Willie) and Hume Cronyn, Jessica Tandy, **Ava Gardner** (an extra).

USA release: 5 December 1944

Peter Donay, the owner of a fashionable restaurant, has a crush on Sally. She is one of his sexy waitresses and only has an eye on his money, especially after he has won forty thousand dollars in a jackpot. Delilah, Peter's wife, is determined to win back her husband's heart by adopting the strategy "All is fair…"

James Craig, Frances Gifford, and Ava Gardner in a sequence from *She Went to the Races.*

SHE WENT TO THE RACES

1945. USA 87'
Director: Willis Goldbeck. *Producer:* Frederic Stephani (MGM), *Screenplay:* Lawrence Hazard, based on a story by Alan Friedman and De Vallon Scott. *Director of Photography (B/W):* Charles Salerno Jr. *Sound:* Douglas Shearer. *Art Directors:* Cedric Gibbons, Preston Ames. *Sets:* Edwin B. Willis. *First Assistant Director:* Al Raboch. *Music:* Nathaniel Skilkret. *Editing:* Adrienne Fazan. *Distribution (USA):* MGM.

Cast: James Craig (Steven Canfield), Frances Gifford (Dr. Ann Wotters), **Ava Gardner** (Hilda Spotts), Edmund Gwenn (Dr. Homer Pecke), Sig Ruman (Dr. Gurke), Reginald Owen (Dr. Pembroke), J.M. Kerrigan (Jeff Habbard), Charles Halton (Dr. Collyer), Chester Clute (Wallace Mason), Frank Orth (Skelly, barman), Joe Hernandez (himself), Buster Keaton (groom), Matt Morre (Duffy), John Dehner (speaker), Johnny Forrest (usher).

USA release: 5 October 1945

Hilda entrusts her horse to a group of scientists who, for twenty thousand dollars, promise to improve the horse's performance and guarantee its victory against all odds in the next race. Less lucky in love, though, Hilda is unable to lure the handsome athlete Steven away from Dr Ann Wotters.

WHISTLE STOP

1945. USA 88'
Director: Léonide Moguy. *Producer:* Seymour Nebenzal (a Nero production, in collaboration with United Artists). *Associate Producer:* Philip Yordan. *Executive Producer:* Walter Mayo. *Screenplay:* Philip Yordan, based on the novel by Maritta M. Wolff. *Director of Photography (B/W):* Russell Metty. *Special Effects:* R.O. Binger. *Sound:* Corson Jowett. *Sound Effects:* Del Harris. *Art Director:* Rudi Feld, *Assistant Art Director:* George Van Marter. *Sets:* Alfred Kegerris. *First Assistant Director:* Milton Carter. *Choreographer:* Jack Crosby. *Dialogue Supervisor:* Leon Charles. *Music:* Dimitri Tiomkin. *Music Editor:* George Emich. *Editing:* Gregg Tallas. *Distribution (USA):* Nero Films.

Cast: George Raft (Kenny), **Ava Gardner** (Mary), Victor McLaglen (Gadlo), Tom Conway (Lew Lentz), Jorja Curtright (Fran), Florence Bates (Molly Veech), Jane Nigh (Josie), Charles Judels (Sam Weech), Jimmy Ames (the barker), Charles Drake (Ernie), Carmel Myers (Estelle), Jimmy Conlin, Mack Gray.

USA release: 25 January 1946

Mary returns to Ashbury to put her house up for sale. At least that is what Molly, her ill-paying tenant, tells everyone. But Mary's real reason is that she is still very much in love with Kenny, Molly's son, considered a penniless good-for-nothing. It was because of the rivalry between Kenny and Lew, the owner of the "Flamingo", that she had in fact left the town two years before. Though Kenny still loves Mary, he is now engaged to another woman, Fran. Gadlo, the barman at the Flamingo, is hired to get rid of Lew who is smothering Mary with his attentions. The crime is planned for the "Whistle Stop", the station where Lew is catching the train to Detroit to deliver money from a country fair. Lew, who is tipped off, escapes the ambush. When Fran is killed in an accident, Kenny decides to try to win Mary back by promising to change his ways.
Lew contacts Kenny to propose a reconciliation. However, when Gadlo and Kenny arrive on the spot, they discover someone has been there before them. The body of the Flamingo bouncer is lying on the floor. Afraid of being accused of murder, Kenny and Gadlo flee the scene and, pursued by the police, escape after a chase. Kenny is wounded and Gadlo takes him to

a woman in Detroit, then goes back to Ashbury to settle his accounts with Lou. Gadlo shoots Lou after being denounced by him to the police. In the end, Mary finally goes to join Kenny in Detroit.

THE KILLERS

1946. USA 99'

Director: Robert Siodmak. *Producer:* Mark Hellinger (Universal). *Production Assistant:* Jules Buck. *Screenplay:* Anthony Veiller (with John Huston and Richard Brooks, not credited), based on the novel by Ernest Hemingway. *Director of Photography (B/W):* Elwood "Woody" Bredell. *Special Effects:* David S. Horsley. *First Assistant Director:* Melville Shyer. *Sound:* Bernard B. Brown, William Hedgcock. *Art Directors:* Jack Otterson, Martin Obzina. *Sets:* Russell A. Gausman, Edward R. Robinson. *Make-up:* Jack P. Pierce. *Hairstylist:* Carmen Dirigo. *Costumes:* Vera West. *Music:* Miklos Rozsa. *Song: The More I Know of Love:* Miklos Rozsa (Music) and Jack Brown (Lyrics). *Editing:* Arthur Hilton. *Distribution: (USA):* Universal.

Cast: Burt Lancaster (Ole Anderson, alias Peter Lunn "the Swede"), **Ava Gardner** (Kitty Collins), Edmond O'Brien (James Reardon), Albert Dekker (Jim Colfax), Sam Levene (Sam Lubinsky), Charles D. Brown (Packy Robinson), Donald MacBride (Kenyon), Phil Brown (Nick Adams), Charles McGraw (Al), John Miljan (Jack, the debauched man), William Conrad (Max), Queenie Smith (Queenie), Garry Owen (Joe), Harry Hayden (George), Bill Walker (Sam), Vincent Barnett (Charleston), Jack Lambert (Dum Dum Clarke), Jeff Corey (Blinkey Franklin), Wally Scott (Charlie), Virginia Christine (Lilly Lubinsky), Gabrielle Windsor (Ginny), Rex Dale (man), Howard Freeman (chief of police), Harry Brown (payer), Beatrice Roberts (nurse), John Berkes (Plunther), John Sheehan (doctor), Charles Middleton (Brown, farmer), Al Hill (client), Noel Cravat (Lou Tringle), Reverend Neal Dood (priest).

USA release: 21 August 1946

James Reardon, an agent for an insurance company, investigates the death of Peter Lunn, shot in cold blood in a small town in New Jersey. In Atlantic City, he questions Queenie, a former housekeeper, who has been bequeathed his inheritance. She recalls that Peter had tried to commit suicide over Kitty Collins, the mistress of criminal Jim Colfax.
Peter Lunn had been a boxer, but gave up fighting after being seriously injured in a match in Philadelphia. He let himself be accused of a jewelry robbery to cover up for Kitty. When Peter was released from prison, he participated in a hold-up set up by Jim Colfax. When they tried to cut Peter out of his share, he escaped with the money and Kitty was his accomplice. Reardon's insurance company lost 250,000 dollars in this theft. Kitty knows they are looking for her and contacts the insurance company, offering to give back 70,000 dollars. Reardon rejects this proposal and escapes an attempt on his life.
Jim Colfax is fatally wounded by one of his men who has come to claim his share. Kitty reveals that she is in fact Colfax's accomplice when she hurries to his deathbed. Two days after the hold-up, she had left Peter Lunn to turn the money over to Colfax. Lunn, having become a dangerous witness, had then been killed. Kitty begs Colfax to clear her. He refuses and dies.

THE HUCKSTERS

1947. USA 115'

Director: Jack Conway. *Producer:* Arthur Hornblow Jr. (MGM). *Screenplay:* Luther Davis, based on the novel by Frederic Wakeman. *Adaptation:* Edward Chodorov, George Wells. *Director of Photography (B/W):* Harold

The Killers with, left to right, Jeff Corey, Donald MacBride, Ava Gardner, and Sam Levene.

Rosson. *Special Effects:* Warren Newcombe, A. Arnold Gillespie. *Technical Consultant:* John Driscol. *Sound:* Douglas Shearer. *Art Directors:* Cedric Gibbons, Urie McCleary. *Sets:* Edwin B. Willis, Jack D. Moore. *Make-up:* Jack Dawn. *Hairstylist:* Sydney Guilaroff. *Costumes:* Irene. *Music:* Lennie Hayton. *Editing:* Frank Sullivan. *Distribution: (USA):* MGM.

Cast: Clark Gable (Victor Albee Norman), Deborah Kerr (Kay Dorrance), Sydney Greenstreet (Evan Llewellyn Evans), Adolphe Menjou (Mr. Kimberly), **Ava Gardner** (Jean Ogilvie), Keenan Wynn (Buddy Hare), Edward Arnold (Dave Lash), Aubrey Mather (Mr. Glass), Richard Gaines (Cooke), Frank Albertson (Max Herman), Clinton Stundberg (Michael Michaelson), Douglas Fowley (Georgie Gaver), Gloria Holden (Mrs. Kimberly), Connie Gilchrist (Betty), Kathryn Card (Regina Kennedy), Lillian Bronson (Miss Hammer), Vera Marshe (Gloria, secretary), Ralph Bunker (Allison), Virginia Dale (receptionist), Jimmy Conlin (Blake), George O'Hanlon (Freddie Callahan), Ranson Sherman (George Rockton), Tom Stevenson (Paul Evans), Anna Nagel (teletypist), John Hiestand (speaker), Jack Rice (employee), Robert Emmett O'Connor (doorman), Dianne Perine (Ellen Dorrance), Fred Sherman, John Daheim (taxi drivers), Eugene Baxtor Day (Hal Dorrance).

USA release: 27 June 1947

Mr. Kimberly, the manager of an advertising agency, asks Victor Norman to think up an idea for the launch of a new soap. Victor offers a woman, Kay Dorrance, the opportunity of using her name and image. Though the head of the agency is against the idea, the president Evans likes it.
This marks Victor's first victory, which he decides to celebrate in a nightclub where Jean, one of his ex-girlfriends, is performing. When Jean joins their table, Kay is overcome with jealousy at the woman's obvious attraction to Victor. She refuses to promote the new product. Victor has to find another idea. The agency suggests he go meet the comedian Buddy Hare.
Jean gives up all hope of getting Victor back when she discovers he is in love with Kay. Victor rejects Buddy Hare's idea and hires Jean. When he goes back to New York, Kimberly reproaches him for having used Jean, who

is a complete unknown. Nevertheless, the campaign turns out to be a tremendous success, which earns him Evans' praise and a fabulous contract. Victor, however, refuses Evans' contract and his tyrannical ways and asks Kay to marry him.

SINGAPORE

1947. USA 79'
Director: John Brahm. *Producer:* Jerry Bresler (Universal). *Screenplay:* Seton I. Miller, Robert Thoeren, based on a story by Seton I. Miller. *Director of Photography (B/W):* Maury Gertsman. *Special Effects:* David S. Horsley. *First Assistant Director:* Hal Herman. *Sound:* Charles Felstead, Jack A. Bolger Jr. *Art Directors:* Bernard Herzbrun, Gabriel Scognamillo. *Sets:* Russell A. Gausman, Olivier Emert. *Make-up:* Bud Westmore. *Hairstylist:* Carmen Dirigo. *Ava Gardner's Costumes:* Michael Woulfe. *Music:* Daniele Amfitheatrof, arranged and directed by David Tamkin. *Editing:* William Hornbeck. *Distribution: (USA/France):* Universal.

Cast: Fred MacMurray (Matt Gordon), **Ava Gardner** (Linda Graham/Ann Van Leyden), Roland Culver (Michael Van Leyden), Richard Haydn (Inspector Hewitt), Spring Byington (Mrs. Bellows), Thomas Gomez (Mr. Mauribus), Porter Hall (Mr. Bellows), George Lloyd (Sasha Barda), Maylia (Ming Ling), Holmes Herbert (Reverend Barnes), Edith Evanson (Miss Barnes), Frederick Worlock (Cadum), Lal Chand Mehra (Mr. Hussein), H.T. Tsiang (Sabar), Rudy Robles (office clerk), Philip Ahn (barman), Reginald Sheffield (travel agent), Monica Winckel, Cha-Bing (locals), Curt Conway (Pepe), Don Escobar (night worker), Norman Ainsley (immigration officer), Luke Chan (Chinese waiter), Maxine Chevelier (singer), Dick Elliott (passenger), Leyland Hodgson (British officer), David Ralston (Inspector Hewitt's assistant), Gerard Olivier Smith (Englishman) and George Sorel, Richard Abbott.

*S*ingapore with Fred MacMurray.

USA release: 12 August 1947

The police are on the alert when they see Matt Gordon back in Singapore. Inspector Hewitt suspects that Gordon has returned for some rare pearls that he left behind when he was suddenly forced to flee a Japanese attack. The bombings had wreaked havoc in the city, separating him from Linda just before their marriage.
The trafficker Mauribus is also interested in the pearls, which he offers to buy from Matt. During an evening out, Matt thinks he sees Linda, whom he thought was dead. The woman, however, claims her name is Mrs. Van Leyden and that she is married to a British plantation owner. Matt tries to evoke their past together, yet this is all completely unknown to the young woman.
The woman is intrigued that Matt is so convinced that she is this woman and tries to do a little investigating on her own. A former servant, Minh Ling, confirms that she is in fact Linda. She begs Matt not to try to see her again. Matt decides to leave Singapore with the pearls he has hidden in a room occupied by some tourists, Mr. and Mrs. Bellows.
Mauribus kidnaps Linda and keeps her hostage in his hideout, trying to force her to reveal where the pearls are hidden. Matt comes to Linda's rescue and, when he shoots Mauribus, the woman faints, overcome by the shock. Matt takes her home to her husband, Van Leyden. At the airport the Bellows are searched by inspector Hewitt who discovers the pearls that Matt has hidden in their luggage.
Linda recovers her memory. She is still in love with Matt. Van Leyden admits that he had done everything possible to stop her from curing her amnesia. Linda arrives too late at the airport, where she has rushed to join Matt. But inspector Hewitt sends out a radio message to the pilot to turn back.

ONE TOUCH OF VENUS

1948. USA 82'
Director: William A. Seiter (and Gregory La Cava, not credited). *Producer:* William A. Seiter, Lester Cowan (Universal/Artists Alliance). *Associate Producer:* John Beck. *Screenplay:* Harry Kurnitz, Frank Tashlin, based on the musical comedy by S.J. Perelman and Ogden Nash (libretto), Ogden Nash (Lyrics) and Kurt Weill (Music), based on the story *The Tinted Venus* by F. Anstey. *Director of Photography (B/W):* Frank Planer A.S.C. *Special Effects:* David S. Horsley. *Sound:* Leslie I. Carey, Joseph Lapis. *Art Directors:* Bernard Herzbrun, Emrich H. Nicholson. *Sets:* Russell A. Gausman, Al Fields. *Make-up:* Bud Westmore. *Hairstylist:* Carmen Dirigo. *Costumes:* Orry Kelly. *Choreographer:* Billy Daniels. *Music and New Lyrics:* Ann Ronell. *Dubbing of Ava Gardner's song:* Eileen Wilson. *Musical Arrangement:* Leon Arnaud. *Editing:* Otto Ludwig. *Distribution: (USA):* Universal

Cast: Robert Walker (Eddie Hatch), **Ava Gardner** (Venus, Goddess of Love/Venus Jones), Dick Haymes (Joe Grant), Eve Arden (Molly Stewart), Olga San Juan (Gloria), Tom Conway (Whitfield Savory), James Flavin (Detective Kerrigan), Sara Allgood (usher), Hugh Herbert (Mercury), Arthur O'Connell, Kenneth Patterson, Ann Nagel, Russ Conway, Jerry Marlowe, Ralph Brooks, Mary Benoit, Joan Miller, Charles Sherlock (reporters), Josephine Whittell (Brenda's mother), George J. Lewis, Eddie Parker (detectives), John Valentine (Stammers), Phil Garris (salesman), Ralph Peters (taxi driver), Pat Shade (newspaper vendor), George Meeker (Mr. Crust), Dick Gordon, Frances Mack (guests), Martha Montgomery (pretty girl), Yvette Reynard, Pat Parish (young girls), Helen Francell, Harriet Bennett (women in the park), Bob McCord (man in the park), Gino Corrado (head waiter), John Davidson (customer).

USA release: 16 November 1948

Eddie, a window dresser at Savory's Art Gallery, prepares to exhibit a statue of Venus which will be unveiled shortly. Perched on his stepladder, when he gives the goddess of love a kiss in jest, the statue suddenly comes alive. Eddie faints. He rouses in the arms of a real flesh-and-blood Venus.

Eddie is arrested after his boss, Savory, reports the statue missing and holds Eddie responsible for its disappearance. Released on bail, Eddie goes home to the apartment that he shares with his friend Joe. But just as he peers into his steamy bathroom mirror, there is Venus' face again before him. Eddie faints again. Little by little, however, he starts getting used to Venus and she grows more and more important in his life. Eddie's fiancée Gloria suspects him of having another woman and quickly turns to Joe for consolation.

Eddie is again on the run from the police. Venus comes to his rescue and, thanks to her magic powers, transforms the police's report into little paper cutouts and the officer into a dog. Eddie finally surrenders to Venus' advances during an evening in the park.

One day, however, when he goes out to buy some popcorn, he is finally arrested. In the meantime, a storm is unleashed, which signals to Venus that her time on earth is up. Venus begs the heavens to give her just a little more time. Her wish is granted. All of the clocks are set back ten minutes. Just enough time to prove that Eddie is innocent. Venus uses her power over the owner of Savory's to convince him to intervene in Eddie's favor. At midnight, Venus changes back into a statue again and the unveiling may finally be held.

The next day, a young woman wanders lost through the halls of the gallery and asks Eddie for help. She looks exactly like Venus and her name is Venus Jones. Eddie decides to walk with her for a while.

THE BRIBE

1948. USA 98'

Director: Robert S. Leonard. *Producer:* Pandro S. Berman (MGM). *Screenplay:* Marguerite Roberts, based on a story by Frederick Nebel. *Director of Photography (B/W):* Joseph Ruttenberg A.S.C. *First Assistant Director:* Bert Glazer. *Special Effects:* Warren Newcombe, A. Arnold Gillespie. *Sound:* Douglas Shearer, Fred MacAlpin. *Art Directors:* Cedric Gibbons, Malcolm Brown. *Sets:* Edwin B. Willis, Hugh Hunt. *Make-up:* Jack Dawn. *Hairstylist:* Sydney Guilaroff. *Ava Gardner's costumes:* Irene. *Music:* Miklos Rozsa. *Song: Situation Wanted* by Nacio Herb Brown and William Katz. *Arrangements:* Eugen Zador. *Editing:* Gene Ruggiero. *Distribution (U.S.A):* MGM.

Cast: Robert Taylor (Rigby), **Ava Gardner** (Elizabeth Hintten), Charles Laughton (A.J. Bealer), Vincent Price (Carwood), John Hodiak (Tug Hintten), Samuel S. Hinds (Dr. Warren), John Hoyt (Gibbs), Tito Renaldo (Emilio Gomez), Martin Garralaga (Pablo Gomez), Robert Cabal, David Cota, Pepe Hernandez, Richard Lopez (grooms), Nacho Galindo (employee), Walter A. Merrill, Frank Mayo (Americans), Marcel de la Bosse, Albert Pollet (Frenchmen), Alberto Morin (José, waiter), Felipe Turich (employee), Jerry Pina (juggler), Harry Vejar (Indian), Fernando Alvarado (flautist), Peter Cusaneli (rumba dancer), Ernesto Morelli (barman), Alfonso Pedroza (hotel owner), Julian Rivero (boat captain), Joe Dominguez, Juan Duval (waiters), Charles Gonsales (bouncer), William Hale (passerby).

USA release: 13 February 1949

FBI agent Rigby is sent on assignment to a Caribbean island to investigate the trafficking of warplane engines. On his way to Carlota, Rigby sits next to someone called Carwood. At "Pedro's" he meets a suspicious couple: Eliz-

Ava Gardner and Robert Walker in *One Touch of Venus.*

abeth Hinten, a nightclub singer who seduces him, and Tug, a pilot who has just been fired by his boss, this same Carwood.

Bealer, an ominous character, proposes a fishing trip to Rigby which ends tragically. Rigby hooks a big fish and falls overboard just as Carwood, piloting the boat, takes off at full speed. The young Emilio, who is helping Rigby with the investigation, dives in to save him and is attacked by a shark. Emilio's father, Pablo, offers to help Rigby pursue the investigation. They discover the traffickers' hideout and also that the ringleader is none other

Ava looks good even in her plain costumes. Here with John Hodiak in Robert Z. Leonard's *The Bribe*, 1948.

than Carwood. Rigby suspects Elizabeth and Tug of being involved in the trafficking.

Bealer tries to discredit Rigby in the eyes of Elizabeth, who is in love with him. Bealer reveals to her not only Rigby's mission as an FBI agent, but also that her husband is involved in the trafficking. Tug has become a cumbersome accomplice who now threatens to turn over Carwood to the police. He is found murdered, suffocated in his sleep.

Rigby gets Bealer to lure Carwood by making him believe that Elizabeth has secret information her husband revealed to her before his death. Carwood agrees to see Elizabeth, but Rigby is there to meet him instead. Carwood manages nevertheless to escape and disappears into the crowd where Carnival is in full swing. Rigby goes after him and shoots Carwood as a show of fireworks burst in the air. Now nothing can stand in the way of Rigby's and Elizabeth's happiness.

THE GREAT SINNER

1948. USA 110'
Director: Robert Siodmak. Producer: Gottfried Reinhardt (MGM). Screen-

play: Ladislas Fodor, Christopher Isherwood, based on a subject by Ladislas Fodor and René Füelöp-Miller (from *The Player* by Dostoyevsky). *Director of Photography (B/W):* George Folsey. *Special Effects:* Warren Newcombe. *Sound:* Douglas Shearer, Fred MacAlpin. *Art Directors:* Cedric Gibbons, Hans Peters. *Sets:* Edwin B. Willis, Henry Grace. *Make-up:* Jack Dawn. *Hairstylist:* Sydney Guilaroff. *Costumes (women):* Irene. *Costumes (men):* Valles. *Technical Consultant:* Paul Elbogen. *Music:* Bronislau Kaper. *Music Director:* André Prévin. *Editing:* Harold F. Kress. *Distribution: (USA):* MGM.

Cast: Gregory Peck (Feodor Dostoyevsky), **Ava Gardner** (Pauline Ostrovsky), Melvyn Douglas (Armand De Glasse), Walter Huston (General Ostrovsky), Ethel Barrymore (Granny), Frank Morgan (Aristide Pitard), Agnes Moorehead (Emma Getzel), Ludwig Stossel (hotel manager), Ludwig Donath (doctor), Erno Verebes (groom), Curt Bois (jeweler), Martin Garralaga (maharajah), Antonio Filauri (Señor Pinto), Frederick Ledebur (De Glasse's secretary), Jean Del Val (croupier), Vincent Renno (Casino inspector), William H. Hawes (nervous Englishman), André Charlot (distinguished gentleman), Sam Scar (Turk), Else Heims (woman with cigar), John Piffle (fat man), Emil Rameau (fearful man), Elspeth Dudgeon (fearful old woman), James Anderson (nervous young man), Charles Wagenheim (man with ring), Gisela Werbisek (stingy woman), Hannelore Axman (woman with the fixed stare), Lorraine Crawfod (pretty blonde), Ann Sturgis (pretty brunette), Leonid Kinskey (leader of the fanfare), Ilka Grüning (duenna), Fred Nurney (porter), David McMahon (stationmaster).

USA release: 6 July 1949

During a stormy night, Pauline goes to the dying Feodor Dostoyevsky's bedside. She gathers up some pages of a manuscript she finds scattered by the wind and begins reading *Confessions of a Sinner*. It is, in fact, the couple's own true story.

Indeed, Dostoyevsky meets the disturbing Pauline, daughter of General Ostrovsky, on a train. Fascinated by the woman, he decides to stop in the gambling city of Wiesbaden instead of continuing his journey. The world of the casinos becomes new material that inspires a novel. He tries to understand the mechanism behind the passion of gambling through a man he meets at the casino, Aristide Pitard. The gambler, on the brink of ruin, even resorts to robbery to continue gambling. Dostoyevsky thinks he has saved the man from his vice by giving him the money to leave town; instead, the writer finds Pitard that very evening betting his money in the casino. Completely ruined, Pitard commits suicide.

Pauline tries to lure Dostoyevsky into gambling, but his passion is writing and instead he transforms Pauline into a character in his novel. Pauline's father, General Ostrosky, is alarmed to see his daughter falling in love with Dostoyevsky. Indeed, he has arranged to marry her to Armand de Glasse, the casino manager, in payment of his debts. Dostoyevsky offers to pay back the general's debts himself. Luck is on his side.

In just one evening he manages to win enough money to pay back the entire sum to Armand de Glasse. The latter, however, postpones the transaction, convinced that Dostoyevsky will be tempted to gamble again with his winnings. De Glasse is right. This time the odds are against the writer and he loses everything. Dostoyevsky bets against Armand de Glasse and loses again. Forced to sign an IOU in the form of a promise to cede all profits from any future works, he takes refuge in an attic room at his hotel and falls seriously ill.

Only Pauline's very rich grandmother can now save her and her lover. But persuaded by the general, her son, to stake her entire fortune at the gambling table, she dies suddenly at the casino, having lost everything. Completely destroyed and ruined, Dostoyevky begs Pauline for forgiveness.

EAST SIDE, WEST SIDE

1949. USA 108'

Director: Mervyn LeRoy. *Producer:* Voldemar Vetluguin (MGM). *Screenplay:* Isobel Lennart, based on a novella by Marcia Davenport. *Director of Photography (B/W):* Charles Rosher A.S.C. *First Assistant Director:* Howard W. Koch. *Special Effects:* Arnold Gillespie. *Sound:* Douglas Shearer, A.N. Fenton. *Art Directors:* Cedric Gibbons, Randall Duell. *Sets:* Edwin B. Willis. *Assistant Set Designer:* Arthur Krams. *Make-up:* Jack Dawn, Robert Ewing. *Hairstylists:* Sydney Guilaroff, Betty Pedreti. *Costumes:* Hélène Rose. *Music:* Miklos Rozsa. *Arrangements:* Eugène Zador. *Editing:* Harold F. Kress. *Distribution: (USA):* MGM.

Cast: Barbara Stanwyck (Jessie Bourne), James Mason (Brandon Bourne), Van Heflin (Mark Dwyer), **Ava Gardner** (Isabel Lorrison), Cyd Charisse (Rosa Senta), Nancy Davis (Helen Lee), Gale Sondergaard (Nora Kerman), William Conrad (Lieutenant Jacobi), Raymond Greenleaf (Horace Elcott Howland), Douglas Kennedy (Alec Dawning), Beverly Michaels (Felice Backett), William Frawley (Bill, barman), Lisa Golm (Josephine), Tom Powers (Owen Lee), Paula Raymond (Joan Peterson), Jimmy Horne, Geraldine Farmer, Maria Reachi (evening guests), Lou Lubin (man in the street), Rita Lynn (woman), Wheaton Chambers, Jack Gargan (doormen), Stella Soldi (grandmother), Wesley Bly ("Del Rio" maitre d'hôtel), Peter Thompson (Jock Ardley), Stanley Waxman (John), Stanley Orr (Bournes' chauffeur), Tom P. Dillon (Dan, old policeman), Jewel Rose (girl at the check-point), Setra Spence (girl with cigarette), Wilson Wood, Ralph Montgomery, Fred Hoose, Roger Moore, Betty Taylor (reporters), Ernest Anderson (hefty guy), Harry Strang (Fred, doorman), Frank Meredith (policeman).

USA release: 7 December 1949

Brandon and Jessie Bourne are a seemingly happily married couple in New York's high society. Jessie seems to have forgiven the affair her husband had with Isabel Lorrison shortly after their marriage.

Above: With Mervin LeRoy, director of *East Side, West Side.*

However, Isabel reappears in Brandon's life one night at the "Del Rio", a club where Brandon is a regular. Her new boyfriend, Alec Dawning, surprises them talking intimately together and hits Brandon. That night Brandon tells his wife about the fight but does not mention that Isabel is back in New York. A malicious girlfriend soon fills his wife in on the rest. From that moment on Jessie feels threatened.

Jessie meets Mark Dwyer, a solid young man brought up on the poor side of town, an ex-police officer who is now a journalist. Though they are from very different backgrounds, they somehow share a great complicity. Nevertheless, Jessie believes in her marriage though she knows Brandon has started seeing Isabel again. The woman has even been to see him at his office. Jessie looks forward to her husband's promise to take a trip together to Virginia.

Isabel manages to see Jessie to let her know that she has the power to get Brandon to call off the trip. Shortly after, Isabel is found murdered in her home. Though Jessie is immediately accused of the crime, Brandon is also suspected.

Mark Dwyer helps inspector Jacobi to investigate. Near Isabel's body he finds part of a broken fingernail. It is then proven that the broken nail belongs to Dawning's new girlfriend who murdered the woman out of jealousy. Brandon tries everything to regain his wife's trust, but in vain. Jessie tells him she needs time to recover and make a new life – perhaps with Mark.

Below: With Gregory Peck in *The Great Sinner.*

MY FORBIDDEN PAST (CARRIAGE ENTRANCE)

1949. USA 81'

Director: Robert Stevenson. *Producer:* Polan Banks, Robert Sparks (RKO). *Executive Producer:* Sid Rogell. *Screenplay:* Marion Parsonnet, based on the novel by Polan Banks *Carriage Entrance*. *Adaptation:* Leopold Atlas. *Director of Photography (B/W):* Harry J. Wild. *Sound:* Phil Brigandi, Clem Portman. *Art Directors:* Albert S. d'Agostino, Alfred Herman. *Sets:* Darrell Silvera, Harley Miller. *Hairstylist:* Larry Germain. *Costumes:* Michael Woulfe. *Make-up:* Larry Germain. *Music:* Frederick Hollander. *Music Director:* Constantin Bakaleinikoff. *Editing:* George C. Shrader. *Distribution: (USA):* RKO

Cast: Robert Mitchum (Dr Mark Lucas), **Ava Gardner** (Barbara Beaurevel), Melvyn Douglas (Paul Beaurevel), Lucile Watson (Aunt Eula), Janis Carter (Corinne), Gordon Olivier (Clay Duchesne), Basil Ruysdael (Dean Cazzley), Clarence Muse (Pompey), Walter Kingsford (coroner), Jack Briggs (cousin Philippe), Will Wright (Luther Toplady), Watson Downs (receptionist), Cliff Clark (horse seller), John B. Williams (fishmonger), Louis Payne (man), Johnny Lee (toy seller), George Douglas (deputy), Kenneth MacDonald (police lieutenant), Everett Glass (old doctor), Barry Brooks (policeman), Daniel De Laurentis (boy with candle).

USA release: April 1951

Late 1800s. New Orleans. Barbara Beaurevel is very much in love with the young doctor Mark Lucas and plans to go to join him. Her cousin Paul, however, discourages the young woman from leaving her aunt Eula who took her in as a girl and brought her up after the death of her grandmother. Paul, in fact, has other plans for Barbara. That is, to marry her to Clay Duchesne, his accomplice, to get his hands on the inheritance that Barbara is unaware her old aunt has left her.

Though Mark Lucas eventually marries Corinne, he never stops loving Barbara. When she discovers this, Barbara gives a ball during which Corinne and Paul fall in love. Barbara does everything to encourage an affair between the two to separate Corinne from Mark. Paul, however, who is married, seems to only consider Corinne as a mistress. When she tells him of

her intention to divorce her husband, Paul reacts violently. Corinne falls and is killed instantly.

Barbara surprises Paul as he flees the scene, and then she discovers Corinne's body. Her cousin makes up false alibis for himself and Barbara risks being accused of murdering her rival. Nevertheless, during the trial, it is Mark who is in the dock. He watches as none of the witnesses testify in favor of his innocence. Barbara cannot bear seeing the man she loves accused unjustly. She goes to the witnesses' box and testifies against Paul to prove Mark's innocence.

PANDORA AND THE FLYING DUTCHMAN

1950. Great Britain. 123'

Director: Albert Lewin. *Producer:* Albert Lewin, Joseph Kaufman (Doskay Production associated with Romulus Films). *Production Manager:* Anthony Nelson-Keys. *Screenplay:* Albert Lewin, based on *The Legend of the Flying Dutchman*. *Director of Photography:* Jack Cardiff A.S.C. (Technicolor). *Director of Photography (2nd Unit):* Ted Scaife. *Color Consultant:* Joan Bridge. *Special Effects:* William Percy Day. *Sound:* Alan Allen. *Art Directors:* John Bryan, Tim Hopewell-Ash. *Sets:* John Hawkesworth. *First Assistant Director:* Mark Evans. *Costumes:* Beatrice Dawson. *Music:* Alan Rawsthorne. *Music Director:* Hubert Clifford. *Sound Editing:* Harry Miller. *Editing:* Ralph Kemplen. *Distribution (USA):* MGM / *(G.B.):* Independent Film Distributors Ltd. in association with British Lion.

Cast: James Mason (Hendrick Van der Zee), **Ava Gardner** (Pandora Reynolds), Nigel Patrick (Stephen Cameron), Sheila Shim (Janet Fielding), Harold Warrender (Geoffrey Fielding), Mario Cabre (Juan Montalvo), Marius Goring (Reggie Demarest), John Laurie (Angus), Pamela Kellino (Jenny Ford), Margarita d'Alvarez (Señora Montalvo), Patricia Raine (Peggy, Jenny's friend), La Pillina (Flamenco dancer), Abraham Sofaer (judge), Francisco Igual (Vicente), Guillermo Bertran (tavern owner), Lila Molnar (Geoffrey's governess), Phoebe Hodgson (dressmaker), John Carew (priest), Edward Leslie (doctor), Gabriel Carmona (banderillo), Antonio Martin (picador), Christiana Forbes (nurse), Helen Cleverley (second nurse), Gerald Welsh (nurse).

Great Britain Release: 5 March 1951. USA release: 5 April 1951

One evening in spring at the tavern "Deux Tortues", the poet Reggie Demarest commits suicide when Pandora Reynolds, an American singer with whom he is madly in love, once again refuses to marry him. Stephen, another of Pandora's admirers, even agrees to sacrifice his race car for her by driving it off a cliff. Pandora then promises to marry him the ninth day of the third month of the year.

Pandora is intrigued by a sailboat anchored in the bay of Esperanza. Her imagination is sparked by research that her friend, the archaeologist Geoffrey Fielding, is doing on a seventeenth-century text on the legend of *The Flying Dutchman*. Pandora swims out to the boat. She meets Hendrick Van der Zee, a Dutch painter, who is putting the finishing touches on a portrait of the mythical Pandora, the embodiment of woman. Pandora is shocked to see that the painting is a portrait of her, but does not fathom its profound meaning. She seizes a knife and slashes the face in the painting, an image of the person she would truly like to be, and not the one she actually is.

A very special love begins to unfold between Pandora and Van der Zee. Pandora's friend Fielding is impressed at Van der Zee's extensive knowledge as he helps translate the manuscript of *The Flying Dutchman*. The legend tells the story of a ship's captain who, returning from an expedition, murders his wife whom he suspects of adultery.

Sentenced to death, the captain escapes, thanks to a mysterious person who opens his cell door. A "voice" reveals his fate to him: despite his crime,

A̲va in a scene from *My Forbidden Past (Carriage Entrance)*.

the captain will not die but is condemned to sail the seas eternally. He may only go ashore every seven years, until a woman sacrifices herself for him and thus redeems him of his crime. Van der Zee, however, instead of reading this text, actually recites it. It is in fact the story of his own life, and he is the Flying Dutchman.

Geoffrey suddenly realizes that Pandora is in danger. The bullfighter Juan Montalvo has come back to Esperanza. He is yet another man in love with Pandora. Juan Montalvo very soon realizes that his most formidable rival is not Stephen, whom Pandora is about to marry, but the Dutchman. Montalvo is convinced that he has murdered Van der Zee when he stabs him in the back, but the next day the Dutchman reappears during a bullfight. This fearful vision paralyzes Montalvo and in that split second the bull charges and kills him.

Van der Zee is about to set sail. He does not want to make Pandora the woman to sacrifice herself for his own redemption. Thinking that Pandora is now out of danger, Fielding agrees to read the manuscript of the Flying Dutchman to her. Pandora realizes that she is the very woman who can save the Dutchman and break his curse.

A violent wind keeps the boat from setting sail and Pandora goes to Van der Zee. The boat is now free to leave the port. It is swept away by the fury of the storm and the two lovers, now united, perish at sea. Shortly afterwards, the fishermen of Esperanza discover two entwined bodies in their nets, Pandora and the Dutchman.

SHOW BOAT

1950. USA 108'

Director: George Sidney. *Producer:* Arthur Freed (MGM). *Associate Producers:* Ben Feiner Jr., Roger Edens. *Screenplay:* John Lee Mahin (and George Wells, Jack McGowan), based on the musical by Jerome Kern and Oscar Hammerstein II, adapted from the novel by Edna Ferber. *First Assistant Director:* George Rhein. *Director of Photography:* Charles Rosher A.S.C. (Technicolor). *Color Consultants:* Henri Jaffa, James Gooch. *Special Effects:* Warren Newcombe. *Sound:* Douglas Shearer. *Art Directors:* Cedric Gibbons, Jack Martin Smith. *Sets:* Edwin B. Willis, Richard A. Pefferle. *Costumes:* Walter Plunkett. *Make-up:* William Tuttle. *Hairstylist:* Sydney Guilaroff. *Original Musical Soundtrack:* Jerome Kern, Conrad Salinger. *Additional Music:* Alexander Courage. *Music Director:* Adolph Deutsch. *Orchestration:* Conrad Salinger. *Choreographer:* Robert Alton. *Editing:* John D. Dunning. *Distribution (USA):* MGM.

Cast: Kathryn Grayson (Magnolia Hawks), **Ava Gardner** (Julie La Verne), Howard Keel (Gaylord Ravenal), Joe E. Brown (Captain Andy Hawks), Marge Champion (Ellie May Shipley), Gower Champion (Frank Schultz), Robert Sterling (Stephen Baker), Agnes Moorehead (Parthy Hawks), Adele Jergens (Cameo McQueen), Leif Erickson (Pete), William Warfield (Joe), Frances Williams (Queenie), Owen McGiverney (Windy McClain), Regis Toomey (Sheriff Vallon), Sheila Clark (Kim Ravenal), Emory Parnell (Jack Green), Frank Wilcox (Mark Hallson), Chick Chandler (Herman), Ian MacDonald (drunk), Fuzzy Knight ("Trocadéro" pianist), Norman Leawitt (George).

USA release: 11 June 1951

When the Show Boat comes to dock at one of the many little Louisiana towns scattered along the Mississippi, it is met with excitement. Jovial Captain Andy Hawks presents his show while the members of his company parade through the crowds. Julie La Verne, a pretty half-caste woman, who performs with her husband, Stephen, are part of the company. There is a law in force at the time, however, that forbids half-castes from performing. Reported to the authorities by a jealous rival, Julie La Verne and Stephen are forced to leave the show.

Ava Gardner and Kathryn Grayson in a happy scene from George Sydney's *Show Boat* (1950).

The card shark Gaylord Ravenal gets himself hired to replace Stephen, and Captain Andy Hawks' daughter, Magnolia, with whom Gaylord is in love, takes Julie's place. Though Gaylord offers Magnolia a life of luxury, his passion for gambling is still all-consuming. One freezing winter in Chicago, he suffers a change of fortune. The newly-weds are forced to sneak out of their luxurious hotel to a squalid flat.

Magnolia forgives her husband, for she is hopelessly in love with him, even offering to sell her jewels to pay back his debts. Gaylord wants to try his luck again with the money. This time his losses are devastating. His gambling buddies refuse to give him any credit. Gaylord is forced to sell all of his wife's possessions. Overcome with shame he leaves Magnolia.

The years pass. Magnolia auditions for a job at the cabaret where Julie la Verne is performing. Julie is now an alcoholic after her separation from

Ava Gardner stars again with Clark Gable, in the uninspired *Lone Star*.

Stephen. She pleads the club owner to hire Magnolia and leaves the show in which she is the star. That New Year's Eve, Captain Andy Hawks goes to see his daughter perform. She decides to go back to join the Show Boat. Gaylord learns from Julie that he has a little daughter named Kim and decides to return to Magnolia. Julie's drunken gaze follows the Show Boat as it leaves the port carrying aboard it the now happily reunited family.

LONE STAR

1951. USA 90'
Director: Vincent Sherman. *Producer:* Z. Wayne Griffin (MGM). *Screenplay:* Borden Chase, based on his own novella. *Adaptation:* Howard Estabrook. *Director of Photography (B/W):* Harold Rosson A.S.C.. *Special Effects:* A. Arnold Gillespie, Warren Newcombe. *Sound:* Douglas Shearer. *Art Directors:* Cedric Gibbons, Hans Peters. *Sets:* Edwin B. Willis, Alfred E. Spencer. *First Assistant Director:* Sid Sidman. *Costumes:* Gile Steel. *Make-up:* William Tuttle. *Hairstylist:* Sydney Guilaroff. *Music:* David Buttolph. *Editing:* Ferris Webster, Peter Ballbusch. *Distribution (USA):* MGM.

Cast: Clark Gable (Devereaux Burke), **Ava Gardner** (Martha Ronda), Broderick Crawford (Tom Craden), Lionel Barrymore (Andrew Jackson), Beulah Bondi (Minniver Bryan), Ed Begley (Claude Demmet), James Burke (Luther Kilgore), William Farnum (Tom Crockett), Lowell Gilmore (Captain Elliot), Moroni Olsen (Sam Houston), Russell Simpson (Senator Maynard Cole), William Conrad (Mizette), Lucius Cook (Seth Moulton), Ralph Reed (Bud Yoakum), Ric Roman (Gureau), Victor Sutherland (President Anson Jones), Jonathan Cott (Ben McCullogh), Charles Cane (Mr. Mayhew), Nacho Galindo (Vincente), Trevor Bardette (Sid Yoakum), Harry Woods (Dellman), Dudley Sadler (Ashbel Smith), Emmett Lynn (Josh), James Burke (Luther Kilgore), George Hamilton (Noah), Roy Gordon, Stanley Andrews, William E. Green (men), Earl Hodgins (Windy Barton), Warren Mac Gregor (ranch owner), Rex Lease, Davidson Clark (Senators), Chief Yowlachie (Indian chief), Tony Roux (Chico).

USA Release: 18 December 1951

1845. The state of Texas is not yet part of the United States of America because there is strong internal opposition, led by Tom Craden, clamoring for independence. Former U.S. President Andrew Jackson, however, supports the unification of all the States. He needs the support of his old friend, General Sam Houston, who has withdrawn from political life. Devereaux Burke, a rich breeder, is sent on a mission to find Sam Houston, now living among the Comanches, to rally him to the support of the cause.

Those for and against the independence of Texas hold increasingly heated meetings in the little town of Austin. Burke meets Martha Ronda, editor-in-chief of the town's newspaper. This is a press organ used solely to support Tom Craden's cause, now that Martha is the leader's mistress. During a dinner with senators, an enraged Tom Craden takes them hostage to force their signature of an act of independence. They are only released after Burke's intervention. Though he and Martha are attracted to each other, Burke admits that he does not agree with her position in the conflict. Burke continues his mission and crosses the desert to Sam Houston's retreat. Houston writes a letter declaring that he is in favor of the annexation of Texas to the United States. Though Tom Craden and his men surprise Burke and seize the document, Burke manages to recover it and, exhausted, finally reaches Austin. Burke also convinces Martha of the validity of his cause, supported by General Houston's declaration.

The next day, Burke presents the document to the Senate and organizes the siege of the city occupied by Tom Craden's troops. Defeated, Tom Craden surrenders to the cause of his enemies. A new star is now added to the American flag.

THE SNOWS OF KILIMANJARO

1952. USA 114'
Director: Henry King. *Producer:* Darryl F. Zanuck (20th Century Fox). *Screenplay:* Casey Robinson, based on the novel by Ernest Hemingway. *Director of Photography (Technicolor):* Leon Shamroy A.S.C. *Technicolor Color Consultant:* Leonard Doss. *Special Effects:* Ray Kellogg. *Director of Photography (2nd Unit):* Charles Clarke, Robert Snody. *Sound:* Bernard Freericks, Roger Heman Sr. *Art Directors:* John de Cuir, Lyle Wheeler. *Sets:* Thomas Little, Paul S. Fox. *Costumes:* Charles Le Maire. *Choreographer:* Antonio Triana. *Make-up:* Ben Nye. *Technical Consultant:* Major Ramsay Hill. *French Unit:* Michel Boisrond (Production Manager), Jacques Gibault (Studio Manager), Jean Benezech (Assistant Cameraman). *Music:* Bernard Herrmann, Alfred Newman. *Song: You Do Something To Me*: Cole Porter. *Editing:* Barbara McLean A.C.E. *Distribution (USA):* 20th Century Fox.

Cast: Gregory Peck (Harry Street), Susan Hayward (Helen), **Ava Gardner** (Cynthia Street), Hildegarde Neff (Countess Liz), Leo G. Carroll (Uncle Bill Swift), Torin Thatcher (Johnson), Ava Norring (Beatrice), Helen Stanley (Connie), Marcel Dalio (Emile), Vicente Gomez (guitarist), Richard Allan (Spanish dancer), Leonard Casey (Dr. Simmons), Paul Thompson (magician), Emmett Smith (Molo), Victor Wood (Charles), Bert Freed (American soldier), Agnès Laury (Margot), Janine Grandel (Annette), John Dodworth (Compton), Charles Bates (Harry at 17), Lisa Ferraday (saleswoman), Maya van Horn (princess), Ivan Lebedeff (marquis), Benny Carter (saxophonist), Monique Chantal (Georgette), Salvador Baguez, George Navarro (stretcher bearers), George Davis (waiter), Nicole Regnault.

Release USA: 17 December 1952

At the foot of the great Kilimanjaro, vultures circle over an encampment where writer and adventurer Harry Street lies wounded. His wife Helen is by his side. They both know that he is dying. Through his delirium, the specter of

A scene from *The Snows of Kilimanjaro* with Greory Peck.

approaching death and an overcoming sense of failure plunges him into vivid recollections.

The writer, seventeen and suffering his first heartbreaks, receives a present from his uncle and mentor Bill. Uncle Bill gives him a Springfield rifle saying, "Go hunt tigers now instead of women".

In Paris, in 1920, Harry falls in love with Cynthia, a woman he meets in a nightclub. An American like himself, she occasionally models for the Montmartre painters and says her only ambition is to one day find happiness.

The couple move into a little apartment on the Place de la Contrescarpe. Harry publishes his first book. With his insatiable quest for adventure, he persuades Cynthia to leave for Africa with him. Cynthia is growing tired of their tumultuous life. When she discovers she is pregnant, she decides not to tell her husband and gets an abortion, afraid of being an obstacle to his career as a writer.

In Spain, Harry lands an assignment to cover a story in war-torn Damascus. When Cynthia reproaches him for his ambitions, Harry decides against it and turns down the offer. In the meantime, however, his wife betrays her husband in despair and then leaves him.

Years later, Harry is living a dissolute life with a woman, the countess Liz, on the French Riviera. He has now gained fame as a writer of popular novels, yet is plagued by the dissatisfaction of having opted for easy success. Painfully aware of the emptiness of his life, Harry suffers a breakdown and begins to question his entire past. Cynthia's memory haunts him to the point of obsession. One evening, on the Place Vendôme, he even rushes up to a woman, convinced that she is Cynthia. Yet it is another woman, Helen. Harry finally discovers where Cynthia is living. She is in Madrid. When Harry discovers that the countess Liz has intercepted a compromising letter written to him and has destroyed the return address, he leaves her. Harry goes to Spain, at the height of the Civil War, and enlists in the Republican Army. As combat rages, he sees an ambulance overturn. Rushing to the rescue of the driver lying under the vehicle, he realizes it is Cynthia. Harry tells her how much he has always loved her, but she dies en route to the hospital.

Back in Paris, Harry goes to his dying uncle Bill's bedside. In his will, his uncle Bill bequeaths Harry a riddle: How can he explain the presence of a leopard's body on the western peak of the highest mountain of Africa, Kilimanjaro? Harry decides to marry Helen, perhaps because of her strong resemblance to Cynthia. He takes her to the foot of the Kilimanjaro on a trip. It is during this journey that he discovers the key to the riddle of the leopard. For, just as the leopard, Harry has ventured too far and lost his way. Lying wounded, Harry suddenly realizes how important Helen is in his life. His wife cuts open his wound to avoid gangrene. Harry loses consciousness. As Helen dozes, at dawn, the sound of a plane is heard approaching. The rescuers have arrived and Harry is saved.

RIDE, VAQUERO!

1952. USA 90'

Director: John Farrow. *Producer:* Stephen Ames (MGM). *Screenplay:* Frank Fenton. *Director of Photography* (Anso Color-Technicolor): Robert Surtees. *Color Consultant:* Alvord Eiseman. *Special Effects:* A. Arnold Gillespie. *Sound:* Douglas Shearer. *Art Directors:* Cedric Gibbons, Arthur Lonergan. *Sets:* Edwin B. Willis, F. McLean. *First Assistant Director:* Jerry Thorpe. *Costumes:* Walter Plunkett. *Make-up:* William Tuttle. *Hairstylist:* Sydney Guilaroff. *Music:* Bronislau Kaper. *Editing:* Harold F. Kress. *Distribution (USA):* MGM.

Cast: Robert Taylor (Rio), **Ava Gardner** (Cordelia Cameron), Howard Keel (Tom Cameron), Anthony Quinn (José Esqueda), Kurt Kasznar (Father Antonio), Ted de Corsia (Sheriff Parker), Charlita (singer), Jack Elam (Barton), Walker Baldwin (Adam Smith), Joe Dominguez (Vincente), Frank McGrath (Pete), Charles Stevens (waiter), Rex Lease, Tom Greenway (Sheriff Deputies), Percy Helton (trader), Paul Fierro (Valero), Movota Castenada (Hussy), Almira Sessions (woman), Monte Blue (barman), Kay English (woman in the park), Stanley Andrews (General Sheridan), Joey Ray (croupier), Italia De Nubila (dancer), Norman Leavitt (dentist), Philip Van Zandt (dealer) and Jim Hayward.

USA release: 15 July 1953

Though the Civil War is over, Texas is still living in a state of chaos. José Esqueda is the leader of a gang of outlaws terrorizing the new settlers, who are trying to develop government land. Tom Cameron is one of these settlers. When his wife Cordelia joins him on the ranch he has just built, the outlaws burn it to the ground.

Brownville's sheriff resigns and Tom calls a public meeting to denounce the outlaws' crimes and get the people to defend themselves. Father Antonio intervenes to avoid a fight between Tom and José. Shortly after, Tom's ranch is threatened again. Tom, however, makes José's men retreat and even defeats the outlaw's right-hand-man, Rio. The man, who is attracted to Cordelia, agrees to work for Tom rather than be turned over to the sheriff. Tom and Rio go to Mexico to buy horses. While crossing a river, Rio saves Tom from drowning.

Tom's ranch is now prosperous. He travels to Dodge City for supplies and leaves Cordelia with Rio. Ever since Rio saved her husband's life, Cordelia totally trusts him. Cordelia persuades Rio to take her to see José to get him to stop his hateful attacks. She threatens the bandit with a gun, but cannot bring herself to shoot. Breaking down, Cordelia falls into Rio's embrace. Rio's love for the young woman is so strong that he decides to leave the ranch.

He is arrested and the sheriff threatens to run him out of town if he does not reveal José's hideaway. José, who has never forgiven Rio's betrayal, decides to act. He gets a band of outlaws together to attack Brownville. The bank is sacked and in a shoot-out Tom is wounded and the sheriff killed. José and Rio have a showdown in the saloon. Both men are killed. As Father Antonio prays for the two dead men, Cordelia and Tom return to a life of peace.

MOGAMBO

1953. USA 114'

Director: John Ford. *Producer:* Sam Zimbalist (MGM). *Production Manager:* Roy Parkinson. *Screenplay:* John Lee Mahin, based on the play by: William Collison, *Red Dust*. *Directors of Photography (Technicolor):* Robert Surtees, Frederick A. Young. *Color Consultant:* Joan Bridge. *Cameramen:* Cecil R. Cooney, Graham Kelly. *Director of Photography* (gorilla sequences): Jack Whitehead, Freddie Cooper, Jackson Drury, Doug Wolf. *Sound:* A.W. Watkins, Amy Fisher. *Special Effects:* Tom Howard, Bert Monk. *Art Director:* Alfred Junge. *2nd Unit Directors:* Richard Rosson, Yakima Canutt, James C. Havens. *Assistant Directors:* Wingate Smith, Cecil Ford. *Script Girl:* Angela Martelli. *Make-up:* Colin Garde. *Hairstylist:* Maude Onslow. *Costumes:* Helen Rose. *Editing:* Frank Clarke. *Distribution (USA/France):* MGM.

Cast: Clark Gable (Victor Marswell), **Ava Gardner** (Eloise Y. "Honey Bear" Kelly), Grace Kelly (Linda Nordley), Donald Sinden (Donald Nordley), Philip Stainton (John Brown-Pryce), Eric Pohlman (Leon Boltchak), Laurence Naismith (captain), Denis O'Dea (Father Joseph), Asa Etuia (young native girl), Kikunyu Chemsabom Arap Maategit (Moontala), and the tribes: Samburu (Kenya), Wagenia (Belgian Congo), Bahaya (Tanganyika), M'Bandi (French Equatorial Africa).

Release: USA: October 1953

Vick lives the adventurous and carefree life of an incorrigible bachelor in Africa, where he captures tigers for zoos and circuses. He is irritated to hear that an old acquaintance, Eloise Kelly, will be arriving. The woman is a young widow whose husband was killed in a plane crash very soon after their marriage. Though Vick soon arranges for her to leave, the boat is shipwrecked and Eloise shows up again at a welcoming party that Vick gives in honor of the anthropologist Donald Nordley and his wife Linda.
Vick, under Linda's charms, is finally persuaded to lead an expedition into a region where gorillas live. Eloise is to accompany them up to Kina and then be taken to the airport. Kina, however, turns out to be completely abandoned. As they arrive, the group is suddenly blocked by a tribe of Samburu. Father Joseph urges Vick to turn back, since the rebel Samburu tribe is unstoppable. Vick, Eloise and the Nordleys, in fact, barely escape the attack. Vick eventually manages to set up camp in the region of the gorillas. The group, accompanied by guides, ventures into the jungle. While Nordley films a family of gorillas, Vick tries to capture one, but because of Nordley's clumsiness it escapes.
Linda is no longer able to conceal her feelings for Vick nor her uncontrollable jealousy of Eloise. One evening, while Eloise and Vick share a quiet moment together, Linda grabs a rifle and wounds Vick. Eloise covers up for Linda and makes Donald Nordley believe it was an accident.
The Nordleys and Eloise prepare their departure. Vick decides to stay in the region to try to capture a gorilla again. As Eloise is about to leave, however, Vick asks her to marry him. She refuses, but as the pirogue pushes further and further from the bank, she is overcome by regret. Suddenly, she dives into the water and returns to Vick.

THE BAND WAGON

1953. USA 112'

Director: Vicente Minnelli. *Producer:* Arthur Freed (MGM). *Associate Producer:* Roger Edens. *Screenplay:* Betty Comden, Adolph Green. *Director of Photography* (Technicolor): Harry Jackson (and George Folsey). *Color Consultants:* Henri Jaffa, Robert Brower. *Special Effects:* Warren Newcombe. *First Assistant Director:* Jerry Thorpe. *Art Directors:* Cedric Gibbons, Preston Ames. *Sets:* Edwin B. Willis, Keogh Gleason. *Costumes:*

Above: A scene from *Mogambo.* *Opposite page:* With Robert Taylor in *Ride, Vaquero!*

Mary Ann Nyberg. *Choreographer:* Michael Kidd. *Music:* Arthur Schwartz. *Lyrics:* Howard Dietz. *Music Director:* Adolphe Deutsch. *Orchestration:* Conrad Salinger. *Editing:* Albert Akst. *Distribution (USA):* MGM.

Cast: Fred Astaire (Tony Hunter), Cyd Charisse (Gabrielle Gérard), Jack Buchanan (Jeffrey Cordova), Oscar Levant (Lester Marton), Nanette Fabray (Lily Marton), James Mitchell (Paul Byrd), Robert Gist (Hal Bentyon), Thurston Hell (Colonel Tripp), Le Roy Daniels (shoe shiner), Myrna Hansen, Dee and Eden Hartford, Julie Newman (ballet girls in "Girl Hunt Ballet"), Sue Casey (woman at slot machine), Steve Forrest (man on the quay), Matt Mattox (classical dancer), Herbert Vigran, Emory Parnell (two travelers), Douglas Fowley (auctioneer), Roy Engel, Frank Scannel, Stu Wilson (reporters), John Lupton (Jack, prompter), Bobby Watson (Tony's valet) and **Ava Gardner** as herself.

USA release: 3 July 1953

Tony Hunter is a has-been singer and dancer. His friends in New York, Lester and Lily Marton, producers of musical comedies, want to create a comeback for him by having Tony star in a new show directed by Jeffrey Cordova.
Tony is delighted at the prospect, but perplexed when Cordova starts changing the Martons' musical into a new version of Faust's tragedy. Nor does he agree with the choice of his partner: the classical dancer Gabrielle Gérard. Not only is she much too tall for him, but their styles are completely incompatible. Rehearsals are tense and end up in a big argument.
Tony and Gabrielle eventually make up, though, and even fall in love. Tony's fears, nevertheless, are confirmed on opening night when the show conceived by Cordova is a huge flop. Tony then takes things into his own hands. He takes the show back to the composers' original idea. As they tour, they work out the show which turns out to be a smash hit on Broadway. The show's whole company, led by Gabrielle herself, organizes a surprise party in gratitude to Tony.

KNIGHTS OF THE ROUND TABLE

1953. Great Britain. 115'
Director: Richard Thorpe. *Producer:* Pandro S. Berman (MGM). *Screenplay:* Talbot Jennings, Jan Lustig, Noel Langley, based on *Le Morte d'Arthur*, by Sir Thomas Malory. *Directors of Photography:* Frederick A. Young, Stephen Dade. (Cinemascope/Technicolor). *Sound:* A.W. Watkins. *Special Effects:* Tom Howard. *Director 2nd Unit:* Yakima Canutt. *Art Directors:* Alfred Junge, Hans Peters. *Costumes:* Roger K. Furse. *Make-up:* Charles E. Parker. *Music:* Miklos Rozsa. *Arrangements:* Eugene Zador. *Editing:* Frank Clarke. *Distribution (USA/France):* MGM.

Cast: Robert Taylor (Sir Lancelot), **Ava Gardner** (Queen Guinevere), Mel Ferrer (King Arthur), Anne Crawford (Morgane, the fairy), Stanley Baker (Modred), Felix Aylmer (Merlin), Maureen Swanson (Elaine), Gabriel Woolf (Perceval, the Gaul), Anthony Forwood (Gareth), Robert Urquhart (Gauvin), Niall MacGinnis (the Green Knight), Ann Hanslip (Anne), Jill Clifford (Brangaine), Stephen Vercoe (Agravaine), Howard Marion Crawford (Simon), John Brooking (Bedivere), Peter Gawthorne (the bishop), Alan Tilvern (steward), John Sherman (Lambert), Dagmar Wynter (Vivien), Mary Germaine (Brigid), Martin Wyldeck (John), Barry MacKay, Derk Tansley (squires of the Green Knight), Roy Russsell (Leogrance), Gwendoline Evans (Enid), Michel de Lutry (dancer).

USA Release: 7 January 1954

Ever since the death of King Uther, power struggles between the great Lords have been tearing fifth-century England asunder. Merlin gathers together the pretenders to the throne to put them to a test to choose the new king. Each must try to extract the sword of Excalibur, which has been plunged into an anvil. Modred fails, Arthur Pendragon is successful.
Lancelot rallies to the side of the new King Arthur and wages battle against Modred who contests the new king's sovereignty. Modred is defeated. Lancelot refuses to be sworn into an Order of Knights to which Modred belongs. He leaves Camelot and King Arthur's castle. As he escorts the beautiful Guinevere to the Green Knight, Lancelot falls hopelessly in love with her. Upon his return to Camelot, Lancelot attends the coronation of King Arthur of England who marries Guinevere and takes the oath of the Order of the Knights of the Round Table. The Order sets as its mission to bring peace to the kingdom.
Modred and the fairy Morgane try to discredit Lancelot when they discover that he is secretly in love with the queen. Lancelot marries Elaine, the sister of Perceval the Gaul, to quell these rumors. He then departs for battle against the Pictes who have revolted in the North. Modred and Morgane poison Merlin who is against Lancelot's return to Camelot until the Pictes have been defeated. Modred makes a pact with the King of the Pictes making Lancelot's return possible, thus luring him into a trap.
Elaine has died in childbirth, leaving a son to Lancelot. Lancelot's loyalty to the king triumphs. His love for the queen remains chaste and pure. His apparent indifference finally drives the queen to a thoughtless, desperate act. One night she goes to his chambers. The king is immediately warned of what is considered, in the eyes of the entire court, to be proof of their adulterous liaison.
King Arthur gathers together the Knights to decide the fate of the lovers. Even as the Knights are about to pronounce their verdict, Lancelot cries out his innocence once again. Modred demands Lancelot be put to death, but in his magnanimity the king condemns Lancelot to exile, and the queen to enter a convent.
The king's prestige is seriously undermined by the scandal. The kingdom is again rife with civil war. Arthur is fatally wounded in battle. Lancelot receives the king's last dying wish. Indeed, King Arthur, realizing Modred's betrayal, pardons Lancelot and commands him to eliminate Modred. He asks him to carry news to the queen that she is absolved. Lancelot defeats Modred during a bloody battle and is comforted by Perceval who discovers the Grail.

THE BAREFOOT CONTESSA

1954. Italy/USA 128'
Director: Joseph L. Mankiewicz. *Producer:* Joseph L. Mankiewicz (Figaro Incorporated), in association with Angelo Rizzoli, Robert Haggiac. *Production Manager:* Forrest E. Johnston. *Production Assistants:* Franco Magli, Michael Wasynski. *Director of Photography* (Technicolor): Jack Cardiff. *Sound:* Charles Knott. *Art Director:* Arrigo Equini. *First Assistant Director:* Piero Mussetta. *Costumes:* Fontana Sisters (Rome). *Music:* Mario Nascimbene. *Editing:* William A. Hornbeck A.C.E. *Distribution (USA):* United Artists.

Cast: Humphrey Bogart (Harry Dawes), **Ava Gardner** (Maria Vargas), Edmond O'Brien (Oscar Muldoon), Marius Goring (Alberto Bravano), Valentina Cortesa (Eleanora Torlato-Favrini), Rossano Brazzi (Vincenzo Torlato-Favrini), Elizabeth Sellars (Jerry), Warren Stevens (Kirk Edwards), Mari Aldon (Myrna), Franco Interlenghi (Pedro), Alberto Rabagliati (nightclub owner), Enzo Staiola (waiter), Maria Zanoli (Maria's mother), Renato Chiantoni (Maria's father), Bill Fraser (J. Montague Brown), John Parrish (Mr. Black), Jim Gerald (Mr. Blue), Diana Decker (drunken blonde), Riccardo Rioli (gypsy dancer), Tonio Selwart (pretender to the throne), Margaret Anderson (wife of pretender), Gertrude Flynn (Lulu McGee), John Horne (Hector Eubanks), Bessie Love (Mr. Eubanks), Robert Christopher (Eddie Black), Anna Maria Paduan (lady-in-waiting), Carlo Dale (chauffeur), Nino Capozzi (wedding guest), Enzo Staiola (bus driver), Sonia Baladin (roulette player), Ivo Garrani (Kirk Edwards's pilot), Manno de Guido, Olga San Juan, Robert James Brown.

USA release: 30 September 1954

The millionaire American producer Kirk Edwards, film director Harry Dawes, and press agent Oscar Muldon, are scouting for an actress to play the lead role in their next film. The men's wanderings lead them to a little club in Madrid where the Spanish dancer Maria Vargas performs. Maria has known almost nothing but civil war, misery and suffering. She is looking for a way to get as far away as possible from her family, her mother especially, whose bitterness has meant only a life of unhappiness for her father.
Maria is sent for screen tests and they are impressive. She eventually stars in three of Harry Dawes' films over the years. Harry is not only her director, but also becomes a loyal friend and confidant. Her first film, *Black Dawn*, is a box-office hit and Maria becomes the very popular film star known as Maria d'Amata. Then a tragic event in Maria's family occurs. Press agent Oscar Muldoon immediately fears the bad publicity could compromise the star's career.
Maria's father is accused of murdering his wife and is brought to trial. During the proceedings, Maria's brother Pedro describes the petty and rather pathetic quarrel which sparked the argument between the parents. On the witness stand, Maria gives a moving account of the suffering her father has endured over the years. The jury decides her father acted in self-defense and acquits him. Despite the Studio's fears, the trial turns out to be the film's best publicity. Maria's phenomenal success and dream life has not brought her happiness, however. Somehow her fairy tale come true has a bitter taste. The glamorous parties bore her. More often than not, while waiting for her unlikely prince charming to appear, Maria slips away, usually barefoot, to meet casual lovers, gypsies, who remind her of her poor origins.
She is full of contradictions, though, and at one of the countless dazzling evenings she is forced to attend, Maria leaves one night on the arm of billionaire Alberto Bravano. She breaks off her relationship with her producer, the despicable Kirk Edwards. Bravano takes Maria to the French Riviera in a whirl of sumptuous living. Though she is not his mistress, Bravano is happy

166

Maria escapes the movie world and rediscovers her true self during this unexpected encounter with a group of gypsies. Ava Gardner completely identified with her character in *The Barefoot Contessa*.

just to let people think she is. Nevertheless, one evening in a casino, when Maria offers part of her winnings to a gypsy friend, Bravano accuses her of stealing and molests the actress. Having witnessed the whole shocking scene, Count Torlato-Favrini defends Maria and takes her away with him.

The heirless Count, who lives in a magnificent castle, is the last descendant of a noble Italian family. He asks Maria to marry him and become Contessa Torlato-Favrini. Overjoyed, Maria announces the incredible news to Harry, who is in Italy shooting a film. Though Harry agrees to be her witness, he is gnawed by a feeling of ominous foreboding.

Three months later, a tragedy occurs. The marriage has never been consummated. The Count, because of an injury suffered during the war, is impotent. Maria confides in Harry. In her innocent desire to give the Count an heir, she has become pregnant by one of the men in his service. Harry rushes to the castle but it is too late: the Count shoots twice, killing Maria and her lover, then lets himself be arrested by the police.

AROUND THE WORLD IN EIGHTY DAYS

1955. USA 175'

Director: Michael Anderson. *Producer:* Michael Todd. *Screenplay:* S.J. Perelman, James Poe, John Farrow based on the work by Jules Verne. *Director of Photography:* Ellis W.Carter (Technicolor). *Sound:* Ted Bellinger. *Special Effects:* Lee Zawitz. *Art Director:* Ken Adams, James W. Sullivan. *Sets:* Ross Dowd. *Costumes:* Miles White. *Make-up:* Gustaf Norin. *Hairstylist:* Edith Keon. *Editing:* Gene Ruggiero. *Distribution:* MGM.

Cast: David Niven (Phileas Fogg), Cantinflas (Passepartout), Finlay Currie (whist partner), Robery Morley (Mr. Ralph), Trevord Howard (Denis Fallentin), Charles Boyer (Monsieur Gasse), John Gielgud (Mr. Foster), Harcourt Williams (Hinshaw), Martine Carol (tourist), Fernandel (carriage driver), Luis Miguel Dominguin (as himself), Shirley MacLaine (Princess Aouda), Peter Lorre (Japanese organizer), Red Skelton (drunk), Marlene

With Stewart Granger in George Cukor's *Bhowani Junction* (1955).

Dietrich (hostess), Buster Keaton (train conductor), Frank Sinatra (pianist).

Accepting a bet by members of his club, Phileas Fogg departs for a trip around the world in 80 days. **Ava Gardner** (not credited) is among the crowd of spectators who have come to applaud toreador Luis Miguel Dominguin in the sequence set in Spain.

BHOWANI JUNCTION

1955. USA 110'

Director: George Cukor. *Producer:* Pandro S. Berman (MGM). *Screenplay:* Sonya Levien, Ivan Moffat, based on the novel by John Masters. *Director of Photography* (Cinemascope-Eastman Color): Frederick A. Young. *Color Consultant:* George Hoyningen-Huene. *Special Effects:* Tom Howard. *Sound:* A.W. Watkins. *Art Directors:* Gene Allen, John Howell. *Make-up:* Charles E. Parker. *Costumes:* Elisabeth Haffenden. *Hairstylist:* Pearl Tipaldi. *Music:* Miklos Rozsa. *Musical Arrangements:* Eugene Zador. *Editing:* Frank Clarke, George Boemler. *Distribution (USA):* MGM

Cast: **Ava Gardner** (Victoria Jones), Stewart Granger (Colonel Rodney Savage),

Bill Travers (Patrick Taylor), Abraham Sofaer (Surabhai), Francis Matthews (Ranjit Kasel), Marne Maitland (Govindaswami), Peter Illing (Ghanshyam, "Davay"), Edward Chapman (Thomas Jones), Freda Jackson (Mrs. Sadami), Lionel Jeffries (Lieutenant Graham McDaniel), Vida St-Romaine (Mrs. Jones), Anthony Bushell (Lanson), Alan Tilvern (Ted Dumphy), Ronald Swire and Harold Kasket.

USA release 23 April 1956

India 1947. Under Gandhi's instigation, members of Congress want to take power and hasten the departure of the British. Extremists, however, led by "Davay", transform their passive resistance into bloody riots. Colonel Savage is sent to work with the civil authorities with a mission to protect the railways. He requisitions an Anglo-Indian woman, Victoria Jones, though she is reluctant. She has in fact just returned to Bhowani after serving for four years in the British army.

When untouchables paralyze the railways by laying across the tracks, Colonel Savage orders buckets of urine to be poured over the protesters. Victoria is disgusted by these humiliating methods. When her fiancé, Patrick Taylor, an Anglo-Indian like herself, finds the incident amusing, she angrily breaks off their engagement. In the meantime, she begins to feel closer to the Indian side of her background through a growing friendship with Ranjit Kasel.

One evening, when Lieutenant McDaniel is sent to arrest Victoria, he tries to molest her. Her resistance turns into a violent fight. Victoria seizes an iron bar to defend herself and hits the officer, who is killed by the blow. Victoria seeks refuge with Mrs. Sadani, Ranjit's mother, who is also hiding the terrorist Davay. Mrs. Sadani urges Victoria to marry Ranjit, and she accepts. The day of their wedding, however, she is overcome by doubt and flees the temple.

An inquest is underway concerning the death of Lieutenant McDaniel. Colonel Savage tries to help Victoria who, because of her pro-Indian leanings, risks unfair treatment. The military court decides that she has acted in self-defense and Victoria is freed. Nevertheless, she is suspected of having participated in a terrorist attack that caused the derailing of a train.

Davay kidnaps Victoria and tries to force her to be an accomplice in another terrorist attack to blow up the train in which Gandhi is travelling. Colonel Savage and Patrick Taylor are alerted and rush to the scene. They seize Davay in a tunnel where he is getting ready to plant the bomb. Davay shoots and kills Patrick Taylor. Colonel Savage manages to save Gandhi and shoots Davay. Victoria realizes she is in love with Colonel Savage. When he returns to England, she leaves India to join him.

THE LITTLE HUT

1956. Great Britain. 90' (G.B) / 78' (USA)
Director: Mark Robson. *Producers:* F. Hugh Herbert, Mark Robson (MGM). *Screenplay:* F. Hugh Herbert, based on the play by André Roussin (1947) and the English adaptation by Nancy Mitford. *Director of Photography:* Frederick A. Young (Eastman-Color). *Cameraman:* Robert Walker. *Photographic Special Effects:* Tom Howard. *Sound:* A.W. Watkins, P. Cavazutti. *Art Director:* Elliot Scott. *Screenplay:* Angela Allen. *First Assistant Director:* David Middlemas. *Costumes:* Christian Dior. *Hairstylist:* Riccardo Spinaci. *Make-up:* Cesare Gambarelli, Mario Van Riel. *Music:* Robert Farnon. *Song: The Little Hut* (*Lyrics:* Eric Mashwitz, Marcel Stellman. *Music:* Peggy Cochrane). *Editing:* Ernest Walter. *Distribution (USA):* MGM.

Cast: **Ava Gardner** (Lady Susan Ashlow), Stewart Granger (Sir Philip Ashlow), David Niven (Henry Brittingham-Brett), Walter Chiari (Mario), Finlay Currie (Reverand Brittingham-Brett), Jean Cadell (Mrs. Brittingham-Brettt), Jack Lambert (Captain MacWade), Henry Oscar (Mr Trollope), Viola Lyel (Miss Edwards), Jaron Yaltan (Indian gentleman).

USA release: 31 December 1956

In this lighthearted comedy Lady Susan feels unhappy and neglected by her busy husband, Sir Philip Ashlow. To reassure his wife, Sir Philip finds the time to organize a Caribbean dream cruise. Among the guests there is Henry who, in addition to being a family friend, has also been a secret admirer of Susan for years.

The yacht, swept away in a violent storm, is shipwrecked. Susan, Sir Philip and Henry end up on a desert island. Sir Philip faces the situation with his usual pragmatic good sense: he builds two huts, a small one for Henry and a big one for he and his wife. He improvises a watch tower at the top of a palm tree. Day after day, Henry repeats the entry "nothing to report" in his diary.

Finally, Henry suggests to Sir Philip that in all fairness they should share Susan. Sir Philip of course refuses, and Henry reveals that he has in fact been his wife's admirer for many years. Susan confirms the fact. A vexed Sir Philip, after having heard Henry, the sole witness, and Susan's accusations that her husband had not even noticed her new negligee after his return from the United States, declares their divorce.

Sir Philip realizes what a thoughtless husband he has been. He asks forgiveness and tries to make amends to Susan. Much to Henry's disappointment, his wife is touched by Sir Philip's words of love.

One day a native suddenly appears. Though he speaks an incomprehensible tongue, he manages to make it understood what he wants. That is, Susan. The native captures Sir Philip and Henry in a fishing net and drags Susan to the little hut, after having adorned her with a garland of flowers. The native gives himself away, however, when he slips into a few words of English. Susan recognizes him as Mario, the yacht's cook. She makes him her accomplice to keep her "ex-husband" and admirer jealous. Suddenly, they all hear the burst of a canon that announces the arrival of a British ship. The shipwrecked survivors are saved.

Back in London, Henry goes to see Sir Philip and Lady Ashley. Sir Philip's wife is now busy knitting a layette. The couple inform him that the divorce declared on the island had no legal value.

THE SUN ALSO RISES

1957. USA 129'
Director: Henry King. *Producer:* Darryl F. Zanuck (20th Century Fox). *Screenplay:* Peter Viertel, based on the novel by Ernest Hemingway. *Director of Photography* (Cinemascope-De Luxe Colors): Leo Tover. *Color Consultant:* Leonard Doss. *Sound:* Bernard Freericks, Frank Moran. *First Assistant Director:* Stanley Hough. *Art Directors:* Lyle R. Wheeler, Mark-Lee Kirk. *Sets:* Walter M. Scott, Paul S. Fox, Jack Stubbs. *Costumes:* Charles Le Maire. *Ava Gardner's costumes* designed by: Fontana Sisters (Rome). *Make-up:* Jack Obrienger. *Hairstylist:* Gladys Rasmussen. *Music:* Hugo Friedhofer, Vicente Gomez. *Musical Arrangements:* Edward B. Powell. *Music Director:* Lionel Newman. *Editing:* William Mace. *Distribution (USA):* 20th Century Fox.

Cast: Tyrone Power (Jake Barnes), **Ava Gardner** (Lady Brett Ashley), Mel Ferrer (Robert Cohn), Errol Flynn (Mike Campbell), Eddie Albert (Bill Gor-

Ava Gardner plays a domineering woman in a man's world (*The Sun Also Rises*).

The intuitive and experienced actress Ava Gardner and Anthony Franciosa, a student of the Actors Studio: two completely opposing ways of approaching a role. (*The Naked Maja*).

ton), Gregory Ratoff (Count Mippipopoulos), Juliette Greco (Georgette), Marcel Dalio (Zizi), Henry Daniell (army doctor), Bob Cunningham (Harris), Danik Patisson (girl), Robert J. Evans (Pedro Romero), Eduardo Noriega (Mr. Braddock), Jacqueline Evans (Mrs. Braddock), Carlos Murquiz (Montoya), Rebecca Iturbide (Frances Cohn), Carlos David Ortigos (Romero's brother), Lilia Guizar (Jake's secretary), Lee Morgan (American at the bullfight), and the Niños Cantoros de Morelia.

USA release: 23 August 1957

The American journalist Jake Barnes, correspondent for the *New York Herald,* goes to live in Paris right after World War I. Lady Brett Ashley has just returned from a trip to Europe. Jake Barnes and Lady Brett had met in a military hospital during the war. The widow of an English Lord, she had volunteered for the army as a nurse. Though Jake Barnes and Lady Ashley had been close, a physical relationship was never possible because of Jake's injury during the war.

Lady Ashley had never accepted this bitter fate and though she is about to marry Mike Campbell, an English aristocrat and penniless adventurer, she is still in love with Jake. When Jake goes to Pampelona to follow the bullfighting season, he runs into Lady Ashley with Mike at a café terrrace. Robert Cohn, a friend of Jake's, has also ended up in Pampelona. His heavy advances to Lady Ashley are even embarrassing. The stifling heat and alcohol aggravate the jealousy as Romero, a brilliant young bullfighter, adds another name to the list of Lady Ashley's admirers.

Lady Ashley is attracted to the charming Romero. Jake encourages their love affair. Mike resigns himself to it, while Robert, who cannot bear the thought of the budding love between Lady Ashley and the bullfighter, humiliates young Romero. However, the matador regains his dignity in the arena by offering spectators, and particularly Lady Ashley, a magnificent show in the art of bullfighting.

Robert leaves Pamplona and goes back to his wife in the United States. Romero shatters all high hopes his admirers had in him and his career by giving up bullfighting to live his passionate love for Lady Ashley.

When Jake makes a stopover in Biarritz on his way home, however, he receives a desperate telegram from Lady Ashley and a call for help. Her affair with Romero was a terrible mistake and all is lost. Jake rushes to join her in Madrid. As Lady Ashley is comforted in his arms, she cannot help nurturing hopes of their impossible love.

THE NAKED MAJA

1958. Italy/USA 111'
Director: Henry Koster. *Producer:* Goffredo Lombardo (Titanus/United Artists/Société Générale de Cinématographie). *Executive Producer:* Silvio Clementelli. *Screenplay:* Norman Corwin, Georgio Properi, based on a story by Oscar Saul and Talbot Jennings. *Director of Photography* (Technirama-Technicolor): Giuseppe Rotunno A.I.C. *Sound:* Mario Messina. *Art Directors:* Piero Filippone, Georgio Giovannini. *Sets:* Gino Brosio, Emilio d'Andria. *Assistant Directors:* Paolo Cavara, Mimola Girosi. *Costumes:* Dario Cecchi, Maria Baroni. *Make-up:* Euclide Santoli, Franco Freda, Alma Santoli, Alfio Meniconi. *Ava Gardner's Hairstylist:* Sydney Guilaroff. *Choreographer:* Alberto Lorca. *Music:* Angelo Franscesco Lavagnino. *Editing:* Mario Serandrei. *Distribution (USA):* MGM.

Cast: **Ava Gardner** (Duchess of Alba), Anthony Franciosa (Francisco Goya), Amedeo Nazzari (Manuel Godoy), Gino Cervi (Charles IV), Lea Padovani (Queen Marie-Louise), Massimo Serato (Sanchez), Carlo Rizzo (Junanito), Renzo Cesana (Bayeu), Ivana Kislinger (Pepa), Audrey MacDonald (Anita), Patrick Crean (Enrique), Tonio Selvart (Aranda), Peter Meersman (Dr. Peral), Enzo Fiermonte (Navarra), Yamido Fullwood (Maria de la Luz), Carlo Giustini (José), John Karlsen (Inquisitor), Renata Mauro, Pina Bottin (Majas), Amru Sani (singer), Carmen Mora (dancer), Clayton Hall (Goya's assistant), Stella Vitelleschi (Maria Josepha), Paul Muller (French Ambassador), Gustavo de Nardo (priest), André Esterhasi (Count De Fuentes), Leonardo Botta (Prince Ferdinando), Roberta Primavera (Princess of Portugal), Pamela Sharp (Maria Isabella), Alberto Plebani (Don Antonio), Nadia Balabin (Carlota Joaquins), Giuseppe Giardina (Luigi de Parme), Erminio Spalla (innkeeper), Amina Pirana Maggi (Asuncion the governess).

USA release: 16 April 1959

As the Inquisition continues to wield its ironclad power under the reign of Charles IV, King of Spain, the painter Goya meets Maria Cayetana, the Duchess of Alba, in the streets of Madrid. Despite her noble origins, Maria is a colorful supporter of the people. She enjoys the company of men in taverns where she plots against Queen Marie-Louise, aided by her lover, the military chief Godoy. Both Maria Cayetana and Godoy are supporters of Napoleon.

Maria seriously endangers her life, however, when she participates in a popular protest movement to overthrow the existing rulers. Queen Marie-Louise banishes Maria into exile. Goya goes to see her where she is living in Jolinar. She was his model for *The Naked Maja*, one of his masterpieces.

Maria fears that her political activities might compromise Goya's position as the Court's official painter. Out of love, she therefore decides to deny her strong feelings for him and openly accepts the advances of a young officer. Tremendously disillusioned, Goya falls ill. He begins to paint only the ugliness of the world. His works are soon condemned by the Inquisition and he is persecuted.

Maria returns to Madrid and intervenes in Goya's favor before the king to obtain the painter's acquittal. It is Godoy, however, secretly in love with Maria, who grants her request, hoping thus to obtain Maria's favors. Despite his gesture of clemency, Maria rejects Godoy, who is threatened with destitution by the queen. With the help of the servants, he poisons Maria.

Napoleon's troops invade the city. The royal family flees into exile. Spain is in agony as Goya rushes to Maria's deathbed.

ON THE BEACH

1959. USA 134'

Director: Stanley Kramer. *Producer:* Stanley Kramer (Lomitas Productions, Inc/ United Artists. *Screenplay:* John Paxton and James Lee Barrett, based on the novel by Nevil Shute. *Director of Photography* (Cinemascope. B/W): Giuseppe Rotunno. *Special Effects:* Lee Zavitz. *Cameraman:* Ross Wood. *Sound:* Hans Wetzel. *Art Director:* Fernando Carrere. *Sets:* Rudolph Sternad. *Costumes:* Joe King. *Ava Gardner's costumes designed by:* Fontana Sisters - Rome. *Make-up:* John O'Gorman, Frank Prehoda. *Hairstylist:* Jane Shugrue. *Music:* Ernest Gold. *Editing:* Frederic Knudtson. *Distribution (USA):* United Artists.

Cast: Gregory Peck (Captain Dwight Towers), **Ava Gardner** (Moira Davidson), Fred Astaire (Julian Osborne), Anthony Perkins (Lieutenant Peter Holmes), Donna Anderson (Mary Holmes), John Tate (Admiral Bridie), Lola Brooks (Lieutenant Hosgood), Guy Doleman (Farrel), John Meillon (helmsman Swain), Harp McGuire (Sundstrom), Lou Vernon (Davidson), Ken Wayne (Benson), Richard Meikle (Davis), Joe McCormick (Ackerman), Grant Taylor (Morgan), Peter Williams (Professor Jorgenson), Jim Barrett (Chrysler), John Casson (Captain of the Salvation Army), Basil Buller-Murphy (Froude), Paddy Moran (man at the port), Kevin Brennan (Dr Foster), Keith Eden (Dr. Fletcher), John Royle (superior officer), Frank Gatcliff (radio officer), C. Harding Brown (Dykers), Harvey Adams (Sykes), Stuart Finch (Jones), Audine Leith (Betty), Jerry Ian Seals (Fogarty), Carey Paul Beck (young boy).

USA release: 18 December 1959

1964. An atomic war has devastated part of the earth. An American submarine carrying Commander Dwight Towers and his crew surfaces along the coast of Australia. They are the survivors of the catastrophe.

Commander Dwight Towers goes ashore and is met by Lieutenant Peter Holmes and his wife Mary. Among the members of the welcoming party he meets scientist Julian Osborne who speaks at length about the perilous situation. There is also Moira Davidson who, as she reaches forty, is overcome by the realization of her failed life and loneliness.

Peter Holmes remarks to Moira that Commander Towers has lost his wife and children during the war. However, it is Dwight Towers who suddenly makes Moira feel like living again. The Commander is haunted by the past and Moira, now very much in love, is discouraged by having to compete with memories of the dead. She starts drinking again and turns to Julian Osborne for comfort, though she has repeatedly refused his proposals of marriage.

Commander Towers, Lieutenant Holmes and Julian Osborne leave for the coast of California on a reconnaissance mission. They must try to ascertain the Australians' true chances of survival. At Cap Barrow, the level of radioactivity is extremely high. In San Francisco there is not one survivor. Helmsman Swain disembarks, having decided to die in his hometown. The submarine heads for San Diego to identify a mysterious signal that turns out to be a simple Coca-Cola bottle hanging from the cord of a blind swinging in the wind.

The submarine returns to Melbourne. Lieutenant Holmes is reunited with his wife Mary, who very soon begins to show the first signs of radiation. Dwight and Moira fall in love, but their moments of fulfillment and happiness are short-lived. Soon the Government orders that euthanasia pills be distributed to the population. Peter and Mary Holmes take the pills, whereas Julian Osborne commits suicide by carbon monoxide.

Ava Gardner, in the role of the prostitute Soledad, and Dirk Bogarde as a defrocked priest, are the moving couple in *The Angel Wore Red*.

Commander Towers hopes to spend the last hours of his life by Moira's side, but the submarine's crew decides otherwise, and prefers to return to American waters. The submarine leaves Melbourne as Moira gazes out to sea in despair.

THE ANGEL WORE RED

1959. Italy/USA 99'

Director: Nunnally Johnson. *Producer:* Goffredo Lombardi (Titanus-Spectator). *Production Manager:* Silvio Clementelli. *Screenplay:* Nunnally Johnson, based on *The Fair Bride*, by Bruce Marshall. *Director of Photography* (B/W): Giuseppe Rotunno A.I.C. *Cameraman:* Nino Cristiani. *Sound:* Mario Messima. *Art Director:* Piero Filippone. *Sets:* Gino Brosio, Nedo Azzino. *Assistant Directors:* Mario Russo, Carlo Lastricati. *Costumes:* Maurizio Chiara. *Make-up:* Euclide Santoli. *Ava Gardner's Hairstylist:* Sydney Guilaroff. *Music:* Bronislau Kaper. *Music Director:* Robert Armbruster. *Editing:* Louis Loeffler. *Distribution (USA):* MGM.

Cast: **Ava Gardner** (Soledad), Dirk Bogarde (Arturo Carrera), Joseph Cotten (Hawthorne), Vittorio de Sica (General Clave), Aldo Fabrizi (Canon Rota), Arnoldo Foa (rebel major), Finlay Currie (bishop), Rosanna Rory (Mercedes), Enrico Maria Salerno (Captain Botargas), Robert Bright (Father Idelfonso), Franco Castellani (José), Bob Cunningham (Mac), Gustavo de Nardo (Major Garcia), Nino Castelnuevo (Captain Trinidad), Aldo Pini (chaplain) and Leonardo Porzio, Renato Terra Caizzi.

USA release: September 1960

1936. At the dawn of the Civil War, Father Arturo Carrera renounces his vows of priesthood, disillusioned by the Church which he feels no longer responds to the needs of the faithful. The Republican troops invade the churches, arrest, torture, and kill the priests, whom they accuse of treason. Before his death, the

With Paul Lucas (Dr. Steinfeldt). The Baroness Ivanoff becomes involved in the conflict between China and the Western powers in *55 Days at Peking*. She volunteers as a nurse, just as Lady Ashley in *The Sun Also Rises*.

bishop entrusts the precious relic of St. John to Father Cannon Rota. The relic was to be delivered to the Falangists, partisans of General Franco.

The Republicans are searching for Arturo Carrera whom they suspect of having the relic. More than a symbol, the relic is in fact a veritable weapon of war that has the power to rally the masses. Carrera takes refuge in a nightclub where a prostitute, Soledad, works. He had once met the woman on the bombed and gutted streets of the city. Soledad is attracted to Carrera but, though she offers him protection, he is eventually arrested.

An American journalist, Hawthrone, warns General Botargas about the Republicans' violent methods against the priests. He suggests rehabilitating Arturo Carrera and making him a model of a new secularism. Carrera has now become a socialist and activist for the Republican army. Soledad wants to change her life and they become lovers.

Carrera refuses to help Father Rota, who is in hiding, fearing that this would endanger his position. Indeed, Arturo Carrera has been closely watched ever since his release. He is soon overcome with remorse, however, and asks Soledad to take the priest some food. Soledad is arrested in the ruined cathedral where Father Rota is hiding. General Clave, who is against the atrocious methods being used by the Republicans, keeps her from being tortured by General Botargas.

Father Rota is sentenced to death. Shortly before his execution he tells Carrera that the relic of St. John is hidden in the altar of the cathedral. He asks him to make sure the relic gets to the Falangists. Upon orders from General Clave, Soledad and Carrera are sent to join a group of prisoners who are escorted to the gates of the city to fight the Falangists. Carrera agrees to confess the many prisoners. Soledad, seeing him, fears that in the act of giving confession his vocation as a priest might be reawakened. She is afraid this may be an obstacle to their love.

Carrera recovers the holy relic and asks Soledad to take it to the Republicans. However, Soledad is shot and killed by the Falangists. The journalist Hawthorne manages to recover the relic. He takes it back to Carrera who sets it in a shrine along a country road.

55 DAYS AT PEKING

1962. USA 150'

Director: Nicholas Ray (and Guy Green). *Producer:* Samuel Bronston. *Associate Producer:* Alan Brown. *Screenplay:* Philip Yordan, Bernard Gordon. *Additional Dialogues:* Robert Hamer. *Director of Photography* (Technicolor-Super Technirama 70mm): Jack Hildyard. *Sound:* Milton Burrow. *Special Effects:* Alex Weldon. *Casting:* Maud Spector. *Screenplay:* Lucie Lichtig. *Sets:* Veniero Colasanti, John Moore. *Make-up:* Mario Van Riel. *Hairstylist:* Grazia de Rossi. *Ava Gardner's Hairstylist:* Alexandre. *Costumes:* Veniero Colasanti. *Music:* Dimitri Tiomkin. *Editing:* Robert Lawrence. *Mixing:* David Hildyard. *Credits:* Dong Kingman. *Distribution (USA):* Allied Artists.

Cast: Charlton Heston (Major Matt Lewis), **Ava Gardner** (Baroness Natasha Ivanoff), David Niven (Sir Arthur Robertson), Flora Robson (Empress Tzu Hsi), John Ireland (Sergeant Harry), Harry Andrews (Bearn's father), Leo Genn (General Jung-Lu), Robert Helpmann (Prince Tuan), Ichizo Itami (Colonel Shiba), Kurt Kasznar (Baron Sergei Ivanoff), Philippe Leroy (Julliard), Paul Lukas (Dr. Steinfeld), Lynne Sue Moon (Teresa), Elizabeth Sellars (Lady Sarah Robertson), Massimo Serato (Garibaldi), Jacques Sernas (Major Bobrinski), Jerome Thor (Lieutenant Andy Marshall), Geoffrey Bayldon (Smythe), Joseph Furst (Captain Hanselman), Walter Gotell (Captain Hoffman), Alfred Lynch (Gerald), Alfredo Mayo (Spanish Ambassador), Martin Miller (Hugo Bergmann), Conchita Montes (Mme Gaumaire), Robert Esterhazy (Austrian Ambassador), Carlos Casaravilla (Japanese Ambassador), José Niando (Italian Ambassador), Eric Pohlmann (Baron Von Meck), Aram Stephan (Gaumaire), Robert Urquhart (Captain Hanley), Félix Defauge (German Ambassador), Fernando Sancho (Belgian Ambassador), Michael Chow (Chiang), Mitchell Kowal (American sailor), Nicholas Ray (Maxwell), Mervyn Jones (priest).

USA Release (New York): 29 February 1963

Peking 1900. The city is occupied by eleven foreign powers. The Empress Tzu Hsi, the last descendant of the Manchu dynasty, rules in the Forbidden City, seconded by her advisors Prince Tuan and General Jung-Lu. The two men have clashing views on foreign policy. Jung-Lu, head of the Imperial Army, is a moderate. Prince Tuan is a sympathizer of the Boxers, a secret society guilty of terrorist attacks on foreign delegations.

Major Lewis, leading a battalion of marines, has returned to Peking to protect the American delegation. As the men enter the city, a Boxer is killed. The British diplomat, Sir Robertson, reproaches the Major for the murder, as it risks poisoning relations with the Chinese.

At a grand ball given in honor of Major Lewis, Jung-Lu appears accompanied by the Baroness Ivanoff, "infamous" for her pro-Chinese affinities. The Baroness wears a magnificent necklace which arouses the envy of the dignitaries' wives. When Prince Tuan interrupts the ball to demonstrate the superiority of the Boxers, Major Lewis bitterly mocks him and the Boxers, and humiliates the prince.

In an absurd and vengeful act, Prince Tuan has the Boxers assassinate the German ambassador. Sir Robertson goes before the Empress Tzu Hsi and protests against the brutal attack. To demonstrate her goodwill, the Empress has the murderers executed immediately. She pretends to be unaware that the person behind the murder was the prince himself, despite Sir Robertson's claims.

As tension mounts, the Empress issues a formal ultimatum for all foreign states to leave Peking. In any case, foreign diplomats and military chiefs are increasingly reluctant to remain at their posts under the Boxers' violent attacks. When Sir Robertson declares that reinforcement troops led by General Sydney are on their way, however, they rally to support the diplomat. War is officially declared. Baroness Ivanoff, under the protection of her powerful friend Jung-Lu, tries to flee Peking but fails. When she is offered refuge by a doctor, the Baroness helps him treat the countless wounded. Major Lewis mounts a siege against Peking. With Sir Robertson's help, he sabotages a Chinese ammunitions depot and blows it up. The Empress then orders Jung-Lu to join the Boxers too. The Western forces lose all hope when they learn that General Sydney's troops have been delayed by heavy combat with the Chinese army.

Baroness Ivanoff tries to barter her fabulous necklace for opium needed to relieve the suffering of the wounded, but she is shot at the gates of the city. The Chinese launch an attack with a formidable war machine that emerges out of the night and spits fiery missiles. At dawn all seems lost for the Western forces whose siege has lasted 55 days. The army led by General Sydney suddenly appears, however, and total disaster is avoided when he successfully enters Peking. This moment marks the fall of the Chinese imperial dynasty.

SEVEN DAYS IN MAY

1963. USA 120'
Director: John Frankenheimer. *Producer:* Edward Lewis (Seven Arts/Joel Productions Inc.). *Production Manager:* Hal Polaire. *Screenplay:* Rod Serling, based on the novel by Fletcher Knebel and Charles W. Bailey II. *Director of Photography (B/W):* Ellsworth Fredericks A.S.C. *Cameraman:* John Mehl. *Sound:* Joe Edmondson. *Art Director:* Cary Odell, assisted by Phil Jeffries. *Sets:* Edward G. Boyle. *Assistant Directors:* Hal Polaire, Dale Hutchinson, Robert J. Anderson. *Screenplay:* John Franco. *Make-up:* David Grayson, Art Jones. *Ava Gardner's Hairstylist:* Sydney Guilaroff. *Costumes:* Wes Jefferies. *Music:* Jerry Goldsmith. *Editing:* Ferris Webster. *Distribution (USA):* Paramount.

Cast: Burt Lancaster (General James M. Scott), Kirk Douglas (Colonel Martin Jerome Casey, called "Jiggs"), Fredric March (President Jordan Lyman), **Ava Gardner** (Eleanor Holbrook), Edmond O'Brien (Senator Raymond Clark), Martin Balsam (Paul Girard), George Macready (Christopher Todd), Whit Bisell (Senator Prentice), Hugh Marlowe (Harold McPherson), Bat Burns (Arthur Corwin), Richard Anderson (Colonel Murdock), Jack Mullaney (Lieutenant Hough), Andrew Duggan (Colonel "Mutt" Henderson), John Larkin (Colonel Broderick), Malcolm Atterbury (White House doctor), Helen Kleeb (Esther Townsend), John Houseman (Admiral Barnswell), Collette Jackson (barmaid), Ferris Webster (General Barney Rutkowski), Charles Watts (host of the party), Fredd Wayne (Whitney), William Challee (army staff officer), Rodolfo Hoyos (Spanish officer), Charles Meredith, Stuart Homes (members of the Commssion).

USA release: 12 February 1964

The signing of a disarmament treaty between the United States and the USSR causes clashes between peace demonstrators in support of President Lyman and opposers to the treaty led by General Scott, Chief of Staff of the Armed Forces.
Colonel Casey discovers the existence of a clandestine military base where three thousand men are training for an attack against the Communists. He suspects a military plot hatched by General Scott, whose political ambitions are a secret to no one. President Lyman decides to conduct his own investigation. He meets with his most trusted aides and appoints Raymond Clark, Georgia Senator, to head a reconnaissance mission. The men are sent to the region of El Paso where the secret base is believed to be located. As Clark and his men penetrate the forbidden zone, however, they are taken prisoner.

Colonel Casey discovers compromising letters in the possession of Eleanor Holbrook, General Scott's former mistress. The loyal Secretary, Paul Girard, obtains irrefutable evidence of a plot against President Lyman, thanks to the confession of Admiral Barnswell. Unfortunately, Girard is killed in a plane crash shortly after. The letter containing Admiral Barnswell's confession is discovered among the debris of the aircraft in a cigarette case where Paul Girard had carefully hidden it.
The document is photocopied and distributed to the generals involved in the affair. Letters of resignation are also distributed to them which they are asked to sign by President Lyman. During a press conference, the President's popularity is again at its peak as General Scott is relieved of his duties.

THE NIGHT OF THE IGUANA

1963. USA 118'
Director: John Huston. *Producer:* Ray Stark (a John Huston/Ray Stark production for Seven Arts - MGM). *Executive Producer:* Abe Steinberg. *Associate Producer:* Alexander Whitelaw. *Production Manager:* Clarence Eurist. *Screenplay:* Anthony Veiller, John Huston, based on the play by Tennessee Williams. *Director of Photography (B/W):* Gabriel Figueroa. *Sound:* Basil Fenton-Smith. *Production Coordinator:* Emilio Fernandez. *Assistant Directors:* Tom Shaw, Terry Morse, Jaime Contreras. *John Huston's Assistant:* Gladys Hill. *Script Girl:* Angela Allen. *Art Director:* Stephen Grimes. *Make-up:* Jack Obrienger. *Wardrobe*

In 1963, in *The Night of the Iguana*, based on Tennessee Williams' play, John Huston films a realistic Ava. Here with Richard Burton.

The slave Hagar gives Abraham a descendant instead of his wife Sarah, who is barren. (*The Bible... In the beginning*).

174

Mistress: Dorothy Jeakins. *Hairstylist:* Sydney Guilaroff, accomplished by Agnes Flanagan. *Music:* Benjamin Frankel. *Sound Editing:* Leslie Hodgson. *Editing:* Ralph Kemplen. *Distribution (USA):* MGM.

Cast: Richard Burton (Reverend T. Lawrence Shannon), **Ava Gardner** (Maxine Faulk), Deborah Kerr (Hanna Jelkes), Sue Lyon (Charlotte Goodall), Grayson Hall (Judith Fellows), James "Skip" Ward (Hans Prosner), Cyril Delevanti (Nonno), Emilio Fernandez (barman), Mary Bolan (Miss Peebles), Gladys Hill (Miss Dexter), Billie Matticks (Miss Throxton), Eloise Hardt, Thelda Victor, Betty Proctor, Dorothy Vance, Liz Rubey, Barbara Joyce, Bernice Starr (tourists), Fidelmar Duran (Pepe), Roberto Leyva (Pedro), C.G. Kim (Chang).

New York Release: 15 June 1964

Reverend Shannon, accused of sexual relations, is forced to leave the church when hostility from his congregation becomes unbearable.

As a tour guide, he crosses Mexico on a coach with a group of retired school-teachers. The leader of their group, Miss Fellows, is also chaperoning a precocious teenager named Charlotte. Tormented by the memory of his past, Shannon resists Charlotte's advances though the girl constantly harasses him. When the group is forced to make a halt by the sea because of a flat tire, the girl swims enticingly near to him. That night Charlotte enters his hotel room while Shannon is busy writing a formal letter explaining his reasons for leaving the ministry.

Miss Fellows unjustly accuses Shannon of seducing Charlotte. In revenge, he forces the bus off its course and decides to have them driven to a nearby clifftop where one of his friends, Maxine, runs a hotel. Shannon makes sure the bus cannot leave by tampering with the motor, and the group of elderly ladies is obliged to spend the night in the hotel. Just then, Miss Jelkes and her grandfather, Nonno, turn up too. The two describe themselves as drifters. They live off of her portrait sketches and his poems. Maxine offers the strange couple shelter for the night.

Shannon locks himself in his room to keep Charlotte from coming to him, and also to escape the fierce rivalry now developing between Maxine and Miss Fellows. When Charlotte sees the ex-priest mortifying his feet by walking over broken glass, the shocked teenager befriends Maxine's two sons, Pepe and Pedro. She finds the missing spare part for bus driver Hank, who gets his bus back on the road.

In a desperate act, Shannon tries to commit suicide by hurling himself into the sea from the cliff. Pedro and Pepe save him from drowning and tie him up exactly like the iguana that they caught just a little while before. Thus begins a vigil that lasts through the night. While Maxine, seething with jealousy, goes to take a midnight swim with her two sons, Miss Jelkes begins to recount her chaste romantic adventures to Shannon. Her story completely shatters his preconceived ideas of love. Thanks to this encounter, by dawn, Shannon has regained inner peace.

Maxine proposes to Miss Jelkes and Shannon to take over the hotel. Miss Jelkes decides she would prefer to continue her journey. Shannon, however, accepts the offer under the condition that Maxine stays too.

THE BIBLE... IN THE BEGINNING

1964. Italy/USA 175'
Director: John Huston. *Producer:* Dino de Laurentiis, Luigi Lurashi (20th

Century Fox/Seven arts). *Production Manager:* Bruno Todini. *Screenplay:* Christopher Fry, assisted by Jonathan Griffin, Ivo Perilli, Victorio Bonicelli. *Director of Photography:* Giuseppe Rotunno (70mm / De Luxe Colors). *Cameraman:* Giuseppe Maccari. *Special Effects:* Augie Lohman. *First Assistant Directors:* Vana Caruso, Ottavio Oppo. *John Huston's assistant:* Gladys Hill. *Script Girl:* Yvonne Axworthy. *Sound:* Basil Fenton-Smith. *Art Directors:* Mario Chiari, Stephen Grimes, assisted by Pasquale Romano. *Sets:* Enzo Eusepi, Bruno Avesani. *Costumes:* Maria de Matteis, Tigano, Lo Varo. *Ava Gardner's costumes designed by:* Fontana Sisters. *Make-up:* Alberto de Rossi, Giuliano Laurenti. *Hairstylist:* Elda Magnanti. *Music:* Toshiro Mayuzumi. *Sound Editing:* Leslie Hodgson. *Editing:* Ralph Kemplen. *Mixing:* Mario Celentano. *Distribution (USA):* 20th Century Fox.

Cast: Michael Parks (Adam), Ulla Bergryd (Eve), Richard Harris (Cain), John Huston (Noah, the voice of God/Narrator), Stephen Boyd (Nemrod), George C. Scott (Abraham), **Ava Gardner** (Sarah), Peter O'Toole (three angels), Zoe Sallis (Hagar), Gabriele Ferzetti (Lot), Eleanora Rossi Drago (Lot's wife), Franco Nero (Abel), Alberto Lucantoni (Isaac), Eric Leutzinger (Japheth), Pupella Maggio (Noah's wife), Robert Rietty (Liezer), Peter Heinze (Cam), Grazia Maria Spina (Adriana Ambesi (Lot's daughters), Gabriella Pallota (Cam's wife), Angelo Boschariol (Sem), Claudie Lange (the Queen), Anna Maria Orso (Sem's wife), Luciano Conversi (Ishmael), Rossana di Rocco (Japheth's wife), Flavio Nennati (the snake), Amru Sani (woman with goat), Marie-Christine Pratt (girl with goat), Aviva Israeli, Palla Ambrosi, the members of the Living Theatre, the crow professor, the elephants Candy and Bonnie, the giraffes Ada and Roma, the hippos Nikita and Pippo, the zebu Ludwig.

USA release: 26 October 1966

After having created the heavens, the earth, the plants and the animals, God created Adam, a being after his own image, to rule the world. Adam tended the Garden of Eden. To give him a helper similar to himself, God created the first woman: Eve. Eve surrendered to temptation and ate of the forbidden fruit from the Tree of Knowledge of Good and Evil and God banished Adam and Eve from Paradise.

Two sons, Cain and Abel, were born from their union. The two brothers grew up together; Cain became a farmer and Abel a shepherd. God accepted Abel's offerings and rejected Cain's. In a jealous rage, Cain murdered his brother. Before Abel's blood-soaked body, Cain cried out in despair and suffering. God put an eternal curse upon him and condemned him to wander the earth forever.

Mankind had become cruel. God decided to destroy all humanity by a Great Flood that would cover the entire earth. Noah and his family escaped the deluge when God told them to build an ark and to take with them one male and female of each species. After it had rained for forty days and forty nights, upon God's command the rains ceased and the waters began to recede. Noah's ark ran aground on Mount Ararat. The survivors of the Flood discovered, much to their horror, a world of desolation where all other traces of life had been destroyed.

The descendants of old Noah built a tower which was so high it could reach the sky. God decided to punish them for their pride. He created a multitude of different tongues. Having become strangers to one other, they were then scattered to the four corners of the globe.

The slave Hagar gave birth to her first child, Ishmael, for Sarai, Abraham's wife, who was barren. But Sarai could not bear the presence of Hagar and chased her from the house, banishing her to live in the desert. Abraham undertook a long pilgrimage with his family, facing the desert with its enemies.

God decided to destroy the cities of Sodom and Gomorrah, whose inhabitants were sinful and corrupt, by causing fire and brimstone to rain down upon them. Only one family escaped the catastrophe, that was the family of Abraham's nephew, Lot. God commanded them to flee to the neighboring mountain without looking back. Lot's wife, however, did not respect this command and she was immediately turned into a pillar of salt.

Fourteen years after the birth of Ishmael, Abraham's house was joyfully expecting the arrival of another child. It was Sarai, now called Sarah, his previously barren wife, who, despite her age, gave birth to their son Isaac, "he who has laughed".

But when Isaac was a young boy, God commanded Abraham to sacrifice him. Abraham, in blind faith, led Isaac to a mountaintop in the land of Moriah and built an altar upon which he bound the boy up. Just when Abraham was about to deal the fatal blow, an angel of God stopped Abraham's hand.

MAYERLING

1967. Great Britain/France. 140'
Director: Terence Young. *Producer:* Robert Dorfmann (Les Films Corona/Winchester Film Production). *Delegate Producer:* Eugène Tucherer. *Associate Producer:* Maurice Jacquin. *Director 2nd Unit:* Bernard Farrel. *Screenplay:* Terence Young, based on the novel by Claude Anet, *Mayerling*, and historical documents, including the novella by Michael Arnold, *The Archduke*. *Additional Dialogues:* Denis Cannan, Joseph Kessel. *Director of Photography* (Panavision 35mm, Eastmancolor): Henri Alekan. *Cameramen:* Henri Tiquet, Raymond Picon-Borel. *Sound:* Jacques Carrère, Jean Neny, Joe de Bretagne. *Script Girl:* Betty Elvira. *Sets:* Georges Wakhewitch. *Costumes:* Marcel Escoffier. *Make-up:* Odette Berroyer, Marie-Madeleine Paris. *Hairstylists:* Simone Knapp, Alain Scemama. *Music:* Francis Lai. *Editing:* Monique Bonnot. *Distribution (USA):* MGM.

Cast: Omar Sharif (crown prince Rudolph), Catherine Deneuve (Maria Vetsera), James Mason (Emperor François-Joseph), **Ava Gardner** (Empress Elisabeth), James Robertson Justice (Edward, Prince of Wales), Geneviève Page (Countess Larisch), Ivan Desny (Count Josef Hoyos), Andréa Parisy (Princess Stéphanie), Fabienne Dali (Mizzi Kaspar), Maurice Taynac (Moritz Szeps), Moustache (Bratfisch), Bernard Lajarrige (Loschek), Véronique Vendell (Lise Karolyi), Charles Millot (Count Taafe), Roger Pigaut (Count Karolyi), Mony Dalmès (Baroness Helen Vetsera), Lyne Chardonnet (Hannah Vetsera), Alain Saury (Baltazzi), Irene Von Meyendorff (Countess Stockau), Jean-Claude Bercq (Duke Michel de Braganza), Jacques Berthier (Prince John Salvator), Howard Vernon (Prince Montenuevo), Jean-Michel Rouzière (chief of police), Roger Lumont (Inspector Losch), Jacqueline Lavielle (Marinka), Jacques Dorfmann (student rebel), Anthony Stuart (head gardener), Pierre Verneti (imperial tailor), Richard Latke (McTavish), Fred Vellaca (Lawson), Beatrice Costantini, Carole Noe, Fiona Gelin, Ludia Lorenz, Beatrice Romand, Ylia Chagall, Jacques Toulouse and the Grand Ballet Classique de France.

USA release: 31 December 1968

From the windows of his palace, Emperor François-Joseph observes his troops putting down a student riot. As a believer in severe measures, the Emperor does not intend to let himself be intimidated by a people he disdains and that he considers a threat to the Austro-Hungarian Empire. Indeed, his son, the crown prince Rudolph, is being kept out of political life precisely because of his associations with liberals and his sympathies with certain enlightened thinkers.

Rudolph has grown completely apathetic and suicidal. He is not in good health and his marriage to Princess Stephanie – they are about to celebrate their fifth wedding anniversary – is not a happy one. The only person he can turn to, his mother the Empress Elisabeth, spends little time in Vienna. Rudolph manages to contact Caroli, the leader of the Hungarian rebellion. The crown prince offers his support of Hungary's autonomy under the condition that it remain part of the Empire.

When Rudolph sets eyes on Maria Vetsera, it is love at first sight. Maria's father, however, in a calculated move to obtain a post as ambassador, betroths her to a high-ranking Spanish dignitary. The Emperor François-Joseph, in an attempt to get his son away from Maria, appoints him Inspector General, a post that demands extensive traveling. Rudolph agrees to leave Maria under the condition he be allowed to spend one month in her company. The lovers go to Mayerling, a little village outside of Vienna, where the Budapest revolt is about to break out.

During a ball, Rudolph again tries to change his father's mind by presenting Maria to him. But it is useless. The Budapest uprising is a complete failure. Caroli commits suicide. Rudolph and Maria return to Mayerling and vow eternal love to each other. On the morning of 30 January 1889, Rudolph kills himself after shooting Maria.

THE DEVIL'S WIDOW/THE BALLAD OF TAM LIN

1969. Great Britain 106'
Director: Roddy McDowall. *Producers:* Alan Ladd Jr., Stanley Mann (in association with Wincast Film Productions: Jerry Gershwin/Elliott Kastner). *Executive Producers:* Henry T. Weinstein, Anthony B. Unger. *Associate Producer:* Denis Holt. *Production Manager:* Colin Brewer. *Screenplay:* William Spier, based on the poem *The Ballad of Tam Lin* by Robert Burns. *Director of Photography* (Technicolor): Billy Williams. *Cameraman:* David Harcourt. *Sound:* Bill Daniels, Gordon K. McCullum. *Art Director:* John Graysmark. *Sets:* Don Ashton. *First Assistant Director:* Kip Gowans. *Screenplay:* Penny Daniels. *Costumes:* Beatrice Dawson. *Ava Gardner's costumes designed by:* Balmain. *Music:* Stanley Meyers. *Songs composed and performed by:* The Pentangle. *Editing:* John Victor Smith. *Distribution* (Great Britain): National Telefilm Associates. *Distribution* (USA): American International Pictures.

Cast: **Ava Gardner** (Michaela Cazaret), Ian McShane (Tom Lynn), Richard Wattis (Elroy), Cyril Cusack (Julian Ainsley), Stéphanie Beacham (Janet Ainsley), David Whitman (Olivier), Fabia Drake (Miss Gibson), Sinead Cusack (Rose), Joanna Lumley (Georgia), Jenny Hanley (Caroline), Madeleine Smith (Sue), Bruce Robinson (Alan), Pamela Farbrother (Vanna), Rosemary Blake (Kate), Michael Bills (Michael), Peter Hinwood (Guy), Hayward Morse (Andy), Julian Barnes (Terry), Olivier Norman (Peter), Virginia Tingwell (Lottie) and Jan Dinnen, Andrew Grant, Don Hawkins, Delia Lindsay, Linda Marlowe, Michael Mundell, Yvonne Quenet, Erika Raffael, Jocelyne Sbath, Christopher Williams, Jimmy Winston.

USA release: November 1972. Great Britain Release: May 1977

Michaela Cazaret, a wealthy middle-aged widow, lives surrounded by a court of young men and women at her beck and call. Among them is her young lover Tom Lynn. One morning they all flock to her castle in Scotland. Tom soon becomes bored with Michaela, however, and falls in love with a pastor's daughter, Janet Ainsley. Michaela's private secretary, Elroy, warns Tom of the danger of leaving Michaela, for Tom's two predecessors both mysteriously died in car accidents. Still very much under Michaela's influence, Tom decides against marrying Janet, unaware that she is pregnant. Janet borrows some money and leaves to have an abortion in Edinburgh.

Tom manages to convince Michaela to grant him a week of complete freedom. He goes to join Janet, hoping to finally be alone with her. He is soon discovered by Michaela's henchmen, though, and is forced to return to the castle.

During a party, Michaela and her guests play a "game of murder". Michaela is the detective and Tom the victim. That night the game is continued on the castle grounds. Tom is hunted down by Olivier and the horde of jubilant players. After being drugged, Tom starts hallucinating. First he is convinced he is being consumed by flames, then drowning in a river and, finally, that he has become a bear and then a snake.

Janet arrives just in time to bring him back to his senses and saves him from committing suicide. Michaela has failed in her attempt to kill Tom. She consoles herself with Olivier, no doubt her next victim.

THE LIFE AND TIMES OF JUDGE ROY BEAN

1972. USA 124'
Director: John Huston. *Producer:* John Foreman (First Artists/Coleytown Productions). *Delegate Producer:* Frank Caffey. *Screenplay:* John Milius. *Director of Photography* (Technicolor/ Panavision): Richard Moore. *Special Effects:* Butler-Glouner. *Sound:* Larry Jost. *Art Director:* Tambi Larsen. *Sets:* Robert Benton. *First Assistant Director:* Mickey McCardle. *John Huston's Assistant:* Gladys Hill. *Screenplay:* John Franco. *Make-up:* William Tuttle, Monty Westmore. *Hairstylists:* Jane Shugrue, James Markham. *Costumes:* Edith Head, Yvonne Wood. *Music:* Maurice Jarre. *Sound Editing:* Keith Stafford. *Editing:* Hugh S. Fowler. *Mixing:* Richard Portman *Distribution* (USA): National General Pictures Corporation.

Cast: Paul Newman (Judge Roy Bean), Jacqueline Bisset (Rose Bean), **Ava Gardner** (Lily Langtry), Tab Hunter (Sam Dodd), John Huston (Adams), Stacy Keach (Dirty Bad Boy), Roddy McDowall (Frank Gass), Anthony Perkins (Reverend La Salle), Victoria Principal (Maria-Elena), Anthony Zerbe (swindler), Ned Beatty (Hector Crites), Jim Burk (Bart Jackson), Matt Clark (Nick, "The Worm"), Steve Kanaly (Lucky Jim), Bill McKinney (Fermel Parlee), Francesca Jarvis (Mrs. Jackson), Karen Carr (Mrs. Grub), Dolores Clark (Mrs. Jim), Lee Meza (Mrs. Parlee), Neil Summers (Rufus Krile), Jack Colvin (pimp), Howard Morton (photographer), Billy Pearson (miner and stationmaster), Stan Barrett (killer), Don Starr (main inspector of the opera), Alfred G. Bosnos (opera box office), John Hudkins (doorman), David Sharpe (doctor), Barbara J. Longo (fat woman), Frank Soto (Mexican chef), Roy Jenson, Gary Combs, Fred Brookfield, Ben Dobbins, Dick Farnsworth, Leroy Johnson, Fred Krone, Terry Leonard, Dean Smith (outlaws), Margo Epper, Jeannie Epper, Stephanie Epper (prostitutes), Bruno (guard).

USA release: December 1972

At Vinegaroon, a lawless territory located near the Texan border, Roy Bean is beaten up and run out of town by a gang of outlaws. He returns to get revenge, appointing himself judge and promises to bring law and order to the territory. Roy Bean rounds up a gang of bandits and makes them his henchmen. He marries some passing prostitutes to make up the original population of the town. He himself marries a Mexican woman, Maria-Elena.

Roy Bean renders summary justice with the help of a Colt 44, a Bible and the law. He earns the nickname "the executioner" for his frequent use of the rope. Dirty Bad Boy, one of his fierce opponents, falls victim to his methods and dies, shot by a bullet in his back. The judge makes money from the many hangings, and swindles his friends to become rich and powerful.

The years pass and when railway tracks come to town, he renames the town "Langtry", after Lily Langtry, an actress he idolizes. Roy Bean even goes to San Antonio to see Langtry perform once, but discovers the show is all sold out. In his desperation, he is even fooled by a crook, who has him believe he can watch the show from the wings.

When Roy Bean returns, he is met with hostility. The people now all stand behind Frank Cass, a corrupt attorney, who has won over all the now self-righteous ex-prostitutes. Judge Roy Bean's wife Maria-Elena dies giving birth to a baby girl, Rosa. The judge is obliged to leave town.

1919. Langtry has become a thriving industrial city thanks to oil discovered nearby. The crowded streets are lined with impressive buildings. Many of the inhabitants of the original Langtry are now wealthy. Judge Roy Bean reappears amidst this hustle and bustle. Though very old now, he rises up against promoters who threaten his daughter Rosa with expropriation. He dies as he sets the city ablaze.

A few years later, Lily Langtry visits the city that bears her name.

EARTHQUAKE

1974. USA 129'

Director: Mark Robson. *Producer:* Mark Robson (Universal/Filmmakers Group). *Executive Producer:* Jennings Lang. *Production Manager:* Wallace Worsley. *Screenplay:* George Fox, Mario Puzo. *Director of Photography:* Philip Lathrop (Technicolor/Panavision). *Photographic Special Effects:* Albert Whitlock. *Special Shots:* Clifford Stine. *First Assistant Director:* Fred R. Simpson. *Sound:* Melvin M. Metcalfe, Ronald Pierce ("Sensurround" process created by M.C.A. for Universal). *Art Director:* E. Preston Ames. *Sets:* Alexander Gotizlen. *Sets Assistant:* Frank McKelvy. *Stunts:* John Daheim. *Models:* Glen Robinson. *Visual Effects:* Ross Hoffman. *Special Effects:* Frank Brendel. *Costumes:* Burton Miller. *Music:* John Williams. *Editing:* Dorothy Spencer. *Distribution (USA):* Universal.

Cast: Charlton Heston (Stewart Graff), **Ava Gardner** (Remy Royce-Graff), George Kennedy (Slade), Lorne Greene (Sam Royce), Geneviève Bujold (Denise Marshall), Richard Roundtree (Miles), Marjoe Gortner (Jody), Barry Sullivan (Stockle), Lloyd Nolan (Dr. Vance), Victoria Principal (Rosa), Walter Matthau (drunk), Monica Lewis (Barbara), Gabriel Dell (Sal Amici), Pedro Armendariz (Chavez), Lloyd Gough (Cameron), John Randolph (Mayor), Kip Niven (Walter Russell), Scott Hylands (assistant caretaker), Tiger Williams (Carry), Donald Moffat (Dr. Harvey Johnson), Jess Vent (Buck), Alan Vent (Ralph), Lionnel Johnston (Hank), John Elerick (Carl Leeds), John S. Ragin (head inspector), George Murdock (Colonel), Donald Mantooth (Sid), Michael Richardson (Sety), Alex A. Brown (first billiard player), Bob Cunningham (Dr. Frank Ames), John Dennis (Brawny Foreman), Gene Dynarski (dam caretaker), Bob Gravage (Mr. Griggs), H.B. Haggerty (2nd billiard player), Tim Herbert (Las Vegas man), Dave Morick (technician), Inez Pedroza (Laura).

USA release: November 1974

A slight tremor is felt in the Los Angeles area.
Stewart Graff and his wife Remy are having an argument. Remy accuses her husband of having an affair with Denise Marshall, the widow of one of his deceased employees. Policeman Lew Slade is being suspended after hitting another officer who reproached him for using his authority outside his jurisdiction. Miles Quade, "the world's greatest motorcyclist", is working out a new stunt with his mate, Sal Amici. In a grocery store, Jody flirts with Sal's sister, Rosa.
A worker is then found drowned in the elevator of the dam where he works. At the Institute of Seismology, though assistant Walter Russell predicts a very severe second earthquake, his chief is skeptical and decides not to reveal anything to the city's authorities. One of the Institute's eminent researchers, however, perishes while taking readings. The police, the national guards and reserves are immediately mobilized and young Jody is among them.
Stewart Graff's wife Remy confides in her father Sam, head of the company where her husband works. Her father appoints his son-in-law to an important position in the company. He is obliged to cancel a long business trip on which he had in fact intended to take his mistress Denise.
The city is suddenly hit by a terrifying earthquake. As the earth splits, electricity poles sway, crashing to the ground, and the façades of buildings suddenly crack. Widespread panic overtakes the city, workers rush to take overloaded elevators and plunge to their deaths. The streets are buried under tons of debris as entire buildings collapse. In a matter of seconds the city is completely devastated.
Stewart and his wife Remy survive the disaster. Remy's father Sam, who is trapped on the upper floor of his office building, helps his employees reach the ground floor. But the effort is too much for the elderly man and he suffers a heart attack. Stewart rushes to his side, but Sam dies shortly after his arrival at the hospital.

Ava Gardner in *Permission to Kill* (1975).

A mother goes looking for her son and finds him lying unconscious, but still breathing. Miles Quade and his buddy Sal help her to save the boy. Jody, enjoying the sudden power of his uniform, takes advantage of it. Heading a rescue team, he spots a group of youngsters who had once made fun of him and shoots at them. When he tries to molest Rosa, officer Slade shoots him.
Stewart and officer Slade manage to free people blocked in an underground tunnel, including Remy. The dam gives way, however, and its waters hit Los Angeles like a tidal wave. Stewart has almost reached the end of the tunnel and safety. Denise is waiting for him there. He suddenly realizes his wife Remy is trapped behind him in the tunnel. He decides to go back to save her, but it is all in vain for she is swept away by the swirling current.

PERMISSION TO KILL

1975. Austria/Great Britain/USA 157'

Director: Cyril Frankel. *Producer:* Paul Mills (Warner Bros/Sascha-Films). *Executive Producers:* Robert Jungbluth, Heinz Lazek. *Production Manager:* Denis Johnson. *2nd Unit Director:* Gerhard Janda. *Screenplay:* Robin Estridge, based on his own novel. *Director of Photography* (Technicolor): Frederick Young. *Director of Photography (2nd Unit):* Sepp Roff. *Sound:* James Mack, Kurt Schwarz. *Art Directors:* Theo Harish, Herwig Libowitzky. *Sets:* Elliot Scott. *First Assistant Director:* Elisabeth Fisher. *Make-up:* George Partleton. *Costumes:* Peppi Wanke, Emmi Minnich. *Ava Gardner's costumes designed by:* Franka. *Stunts:* Alf Joint. *Music:* Richard Rodney Bennett. *Music Director:* Robert Opratko. *Sound Editing:* Winston Ryder. *Editing:* Ernest Walter.

Cast: Dirk Bogarde (Alan Curtis), **Ava Gardner** (Katina Petersen), Bekim Fehmiu (Alexander Diakim), Timothy Dalton (Charles Lord), Nicole Calfan (Melissa Lascade), Frederic Forrest (Scott Allison), Klauss Wildbolz (Muller), Anthony Dutton (Jennings), Peggy Sinclair (Lily), Dennis Blanch (Brewer), John Levene (Adams), Alf Joint (MacNeil), Vladimir Popovic (Kostas), Rastilav Plamenac (Pavlos), Oliver Schott (François Diderot), Erna Riedl-Tichy (Mme Diderot),

Paul Maxwell (American), John Serret (Frenchman), Anthony Forwood (Englishman), François Baudet (Dr. Giraud), Bob Sessions (Pete), Peter Garell (Carlo), Friedrich Monning (Cliff), Fritz von Friedl, Erwin Fischer (security agents), Erwin von Gross (hotel manager).

USA release: November 1975

Alexander Diakim, a political leader exiled in Austria, is planning to return to his country to join the fight against the fascists and block the communists from seizing power. However, the "Western Liaisons Service", a spy ring led by Alan Curtis, is working to undermine his plans. Curtis gets people close to Diakim together to form a group, either voluntarily or by force. They all owe the politician either a favor or money. Among them there is the journalist Scott Allison, the Foreign Office civil servant Charles Lord, his ex-wife Katina Peterson, François Diderot, who is actually Diakim's son though his father is unaware of this, and Melissa, a veteran revolutionary.

Pressured by blackmail or other manipulation, the group, incited by Scott Allison, revolts against Curtis. Charles Lord makes Curtis believe that Diakim has been bribed to give up his cause and has accepted Lord's payoff of 500,000 dollars. Charles Lord in fact has secretly given the money to Melissa to buy Diakim's freedom after her revolutionary group makes him their target. Alan Curtis discovers the hoax and fatally wounds Charles Lord. He then recovers the money and forces Melissa to prepare Diakim's murder on his orders.

Diakim gives a press conference at the airport just before leaving Austria. Katina Peterson and Scott Allison try to warn him of Curtis' plot to have him murdered. But it is too late. Diakim dies in an explosion. Melissa is shot. Curtis arranges to make it appear that Melissa's revolutionary movement is responsible for the attack

THE BLUE BIRD

1975. USA/USSR 99'

Director: George Cukor. *Producer:* Paul Malanvsky (20th Century Fox/Sovin Film/Len Film). *Executive Producer:* Aleksandr Archansky, in association with Robert H. Greenberg and Harry N. Blum. *Co-Producers:* Paul Radin, Lee Savin. *Screenplay:* Hugh Whitmore, Alfred Hayes, based on the play by Maurice Maeterlinck, *L'Oiseau Bleu*. *Directors of Photography* (De Luxe Colors): Frederick Young, Jonas Gritsius. *Cameraman:* Freddie Cooper. *Special Effects and Visual Effects:* Wayne Fitzgerald, Gregori Senotov, Aleksandr Zavyalov, Roy Field, Lev Cholmov, Boris Michailov, Leonid Kajukov. *Sound:* Gordon Everett, Gregory Elbert, John Bramall. *Art Director:* Walery Urkevich. *Costumes:* Edith Head, Marina Azizyan. *Make-up:* Vasily Gorjunov, John O'Gorman, Tom Smith, Sofia Smirnova. *Elizabeth Taylor's Hairstylists:* Giancarlo Noueli, Arthur Bruckel. *Ava Gardner's Hairstylist:* Sydney Guilaroff. *Choreographers:* Igor Belsky, Leonid Jakobson. *Music:* Irwin Kostal. *Sound Editing:* William Hertman, Edward Rossi. *Editing:* Tatyana Shapiro, Stanford G. Allen. *Editing Supervisor:* Ernest Walker. *Mixing:* Theodore Soderbeg. *Distribution (USA):* 20th Century Fox.

Cast: Elizabeth Taylor (mother, Witch, Light, Maternal Love), Jane Fonda (Night), **Ava Gardner** (Lust), Cicely Tyson (Tylette, the cat), Tood Lookinland (Tyltyl), Patsy Kensit (Mytyl), George Cole (Tyle, the dog), Richard Pearson (Bread), Margareta Tereckhova (Milk), Georgi Vitzin (Sugar), Yevgeny Scherbakov (Fire),

Ava Gardner as Nicole Dressler in *The Cassandra Crossing*.

Valentina Ganibalova (Water), Will Geer (Grandfather), Mona Wasbourne (Grandmother), Oleg Popov (Clown), Harry Andrews (Oak Tree), Leonid Nevedomsky (father), Steve Warner, Monique Kaufman, Russel Lewis, Grant Bardsley, Ann Mannion ("children to be born"), Robert Morley (Father Time), Nadezda Pavlova (the Blue Bird), Pheona McLellan (the little patient), and the dancers of the Ballet of the Kirov Company of Leningrad and the Choreographic Ensemble of the Miniatures of Leningrad.

USA release: May 1976

Tyltyl and Mytyl, two impish children whose parents are lumberjacks, are sent to bed without dinner as punishment for crossing a dangerous suspension bridge. In a dream, they watch enviously as a wonderful party lights up the forest at night. Fireworks burst in the sky as rich, spoiled children greedily eat delicious cakes. Their mother appears, dressed like a witch, and sends them on a quest for the Blue Bird, which will bring earthly bliss. The good fairy Light gives them a hat adorned with a magic diamond that they may use against any dangers along their way.
In the land of memory, Tyltyl and Mytyl meet their grandparents who have a bird whose plumage immediately turns blue. Yet, as soon as the children seize it, the bird turns black again. Tyltyl and Mytyl also meet the good fairy Light who makes Fire, Water, Bread, and Sugar come to life. She also gives the dog Tylo and cat Tylette the gift of speech. All of them join the two children in their search for the Blue Bird.
Night gives them the key to the underworld where ghosts are imprisoned and where there is a fabulous garden filled with blue birds. Unfortunately, the birds die as soon as they are exposed to daylight. Lust, a ravishing woman, sweeps Tyltyl away on a white horse. Her castle is a microcosmic universe of laziness, lust and ignorance. Thanks to the magic diamond, Tyltyl manages to escape this world of debauchery.
The little company enters the Evil Forest, just barely escaping death, and discovers the kingdom of "children to be born". Here again a blue bird in the sky turns out to be only an illusion that soon vanishes before their very eyes.
Tyltyl and Mytyl now realize how impossible their mission is. Back home again, they discover the true happiness of being with their mother and father.

THE CASSANDRA CROSSING

1976. Germany/Italy/Great Britain 120'
Director: George Pan Cosmatos. *Producers:* Sir Lew Grade, Carlo Ponti (Associated General Films). *Production Manager:* Maria Blasetti. *Executive Producer:* Giancarlo Pettini. *Screenplay:* Tom Mankiewicz, Robert Katz, George Pan Cosmatos, based on a story by Robert Katz and George Pan Cosmatos. *Director of Photography* (Technicolor/Panavision): Ennio Guarnieri. *Cameraman:* Cesare Allione. *Special Effects:* Aldo Gasparri, Roberto Pignotti. *Sound:* Carlo Palmieri, Piero Fondi. *Dialogues Supervisor:* José Villaverde. *Assistant Directors:* Joe Pollini, Tony Brandt, Antonio Gabrielli. *Screenplay:* Marion Mertes. *Art Director:* Aurelio Crugnola. *Sets:* Mario Liverani. *Costumes:* Andriana Berselli. *Ava Gardner's costumes designed by:* Franka (London). *Ava Gardner's accessories:* Christian Dior (Paris), Gucci (Rome). *Make-up:* Giuseppe Blanchelli, Mario Van Riel, Marisa Tilli. *Hairstylists:* Gisa Favella, Ada Palombi. *Music:* Jerry Goldsmith. *Sound Editing:* Leslie Hodgson, Vernon Messenger. *Editing:* Françoise Bonnot, Roberto Silvi. *Mixing:* Fausto Ancillai. *Distribution (USA):* AVCO Embassy Pictures.

Cast: Sophia Loren (Jennifer Rispoli-Chamberlain), Richard Harris (Dr Jonathan Chamberlain), **Ava Gardner** (Nicole Dressler), Burt Lancaster (Colonel Stephen MacKenzie), Martin Sheen (Robby Navarro), Ingrid Thulin (Dr Elena Stardner), Lee Strasberg (Herman Kaplan), John Phillip Law (Commander Starck), Ann Turkel (Susan), O.J. Simpson (Father Haley), Lionel Stander (Max, train conductor), Ray Lovelck (Tom), Alida Valli (Mrs. Chadwick), Tom Hunter (Captain

With Cristina Raines in *The Sentinel.*

Scott), Lou Castel (fugitive terrorist), Caro de Mejo (patient), Fausta Avelli (Katherine) and Stefano Patrizi, Angela Goodwin.

USA release: February 1977

The Swedish Movement for Peace protests against the manipulation of certain viruses. In Geneva, three terrorists manage to get into the headquarters of the World Health Organization and sabotage a research laboratory. Caught by the guards, one of them is shot, the second wounded, and the third escapes, infected with a lung virus.
Colonel MacKenzie, in charge of the search operations, suspects the fugitive is on the Continental Express to Stockholm. MacKenzie asks for the train's passenger list. Among the passengers are Dr. Chamberlain and his wife Jennifer, and a Mrs. Hugo Dressler, the wife of an arms manufacturer. Mrs. Dressler is on a trip with Robby, a young lover. Colonel MacKenzie is in contact by radio with Dr. Chamberlain who has spotted a man hiding in the baggage car. The fugitive and Mrs. Dressler's dog both show symptoms of the illness, and both need to be evacuated. This fails when the train enters a tunnel just when the fugitive is about to be hoisted away by a helicopter.
The train is diverted towards a vast wasteland in Poland. Any passengers who have come into contact with the fugitive are left in quarantine in a former concentration camp. During a stop in Nuremberg, the doors and windows are sealed and the convoy is supplied with enriched oxygen. The express resumes its journey, with Captain Scott and his men now aboard, under Colonel MacKenzie's orders. The train must cross a dilapidated bridge, the Cassandra Crossing, which has not been used since the war.
Dr. Chamberlain discovers that the enriched oxygen is in fact the antidote for the illness. It is now no longer necessary to isolate the train, nor run the risk of crossing the perilous bridge. However, Robby tampers with the transmitter which ensured communication between MacKenzie and Chamberlain. Robby is accused of being a heroine dealer. A police inspector, disguised as a priest, has put him under arrest.

Captain Scott insists upon carrying out Captain MacKenzie's final orders to the letter and nothing can stop him from accomplishing his mission. However, Dr. Chamberlain leads a rebellion, taking command of the train. He splits the convoy in two by causing the gas cylinders in the restaurant car to blow up. The first part of the train continues its course and, as it crosses the bridge, the entire structure collapses under the weight of the cars. The back of the train, however, stops just before plunging over precipice. All of the passengers are saved.

THE SENTINEL

1976. USA. 92'

Director: Michael Winner. *Producers:* Michael Winner, Jeffrey Konvitz (Universal, in association with Jeffrey Konvitz Productions). *Production Manager:* Bob Grand. *Screenplay:* Michael Winner, Jeffrey Konvitz, based on the novel by Jeffrey Konvitz. *Director of Photography* (Technicolor/Panavision): Dick Kratina. *Special Effects:* Albert Whitlock. *Sound:* Les Lazarowitz, Hugh Strain. *Art Director:* Philip Rosenberg. *Sets Assistant:* Ed Stewart. *Assistant Directors:* Charles Okum, Ralph Singleton, Larry Albucher. *Costumes:* Peggy Farrell. *Make-up:* Dick Smith, Bob Laden. *Hairstylist:* Bill Farley. *Music:* Gil Mellé. *Editing:* Bernard Gribble, Terence Rawlings. *Sound:* Ted Mason. *Distribution (USA):* Universal.

Cast: Chris Sarandon (Michael Lerman), Cristina Raines (Alison Parker), Martin Balsam (professor), John Carradine (Father Halliran), José Ferrer (ecclesiastical dignitary), **Ava Gardner** (Miss Logan), Arthur Kennedy (Monsignor Franchino), Burgess Meredith (Charles Chazen), Sylvia Miles (Gerde), Deborah Raffin (Jennifer), Eli Wallach (detective Gatz), Christopher Walken (Rizzo), Jerry Orbach (director), Beverly d'Angelo (Setra), Hank Garrett (Brenner), Robert Gerringer (Hart), Nana Tucker (woman), Tom Berenger (man), William Hickey (Perry), Gary Allen (Malcolm Stinnett), Tresa Hughes (Rebecca Stinnett), Kate Harrington (Mrs. Clark), Jane Hoffman (Lillian Clotkin), Elaine Shore (Emma Clotkin), Sam Gray (Dr. Aureton), Reid Shelton (priest), Fred Stuthman (Alison's father), Lucie Lancaster (Alison's mother), Anthony Holland (evening guest), Jeff Goldblum (Jack), Zane Lasky (Raymond), Mady Heflin (professor), Diane Stillwell (Brenner's secretary), Ron McLarty (real estate agent).

USA release: February 1977

The model Alison Parker lives with Michael Lerman, an attorney whose first wife was a suicide victim. Inspector Gatz suspects Lerman of having had something to do with the woman's death. When Alison's father dies, she is overcome by painful childhood memories. In fact, the young woman had once tried to kill herself when she had found her father with two prostitutes. Alison now feels a desperate need to be alone. She rents an apartment in a large Victorian-style house despite the vision of a man's ominous silhouette standing in the window: Father Halliran. She meets her next door neighbors, Chazen, a curious little man who lives with his cat and canary, and Gerde and Sandra, two lesbians.
As soon as she moves into the place, Alison is gripped by a feeling of anguish. At night she is kept awake by footsteps coming from the empty apartment on the floor above. Miss Logan, the real estate agent, insists that there is no one living in the huge house other than Father Halliran. Nevertheless nevertheless the noises continue. One night Alison gets up and goes to explore the house. She discovers the terrifying sight of her father's body, half-naked and in a state of decomposition. Despite her fear, she violently attacks the corpse. In a state of shock, Alison is hospitalized. To investigate the mystery, Michael Lerman hires his friend, detective Brenner. A short while later, however, Brenner is killed in an accident. These events convince Inspector Gatz to reopen the case involving Michael.

In the meantime, Michael breaks into the archives of the diocese to consult Father Halliran's file. He finds that the man is actually a former schoolteacher by the name of O'Rourke, and that this O'Rourke had in fact disappeared more than thirty years before, after attempting to commit suicide. Father Halliran belongs to a long line of Sentinels whose mission is to protect the world against evil. Alison has been designated the next "sentinel" and is given the name of Sister Theresa.
Inspector Gatz finds proof that Michael had Brenner murder his wife. As Michael investigates the haunted house, however, he is killed. His spirit becomes one of the damned that haunt the spot. Alison is being watched by a girlfriend but manages to escape and goes back to the big house where Michael, now one of the living-dead, reveals his fate to her. Leading a horde of the damned, her neighbor Chazen commands Alison to slash her wrists to reign as queen in hell. Father Halliran suddenly appears holding a crucifix and pleads her not to listen. The forces of good triumph over the forces of evil as Alison becomes the new Sentinel.

CITY ON FIRE

1978. USA/Canada. 105'

Director: Alvin Rakoff. *Producer:* Claude Héroux (Astral Bellevue-Pathé). *Executive Producers:* Sandy Howard, Harold Greenberg. *Associate Producers:* Howard Lipson, Larry Nesis. *Screenplay:* Jack Hill, David P. Lewis, Céline La Frenière. *Director of Photography* (Eastmancolor): René Verzier. *Visual Special Effects:* William Cruse. *Special Effects:* Cliff Wenger Sr., Carol Lynn. *Sound:* Key Heeley-Ray. *Art Directors:* William McCrow, Claude Marchand. *Sets:* Csaba Andras Kertész, Myles Clarke. *Script Girl:* Susanna David. *Stunts:* Grant Page. *Make-up:* Michèle Dion. *Special Make-up:* John Alese. *Costumes:* Yvon Duhaine, Mario Davignon. *Hairstylist:* Pierre David. *Casting:* Ann Hunter Bell. *Music:* William and Matthew McCauley. *Editing:* Jean-Pol Passet, Jacques Clairoux. *Distribution (USA):* AVCO Embassy Pictures.

Cast: Barry Newman (Dr. Frank Whitman), Susan Clark (Dina Brockhurst-Lautrec), Shelley Winters (Andrea Harper), Leslie Nielsen (William Dudley, mayor), **Ava Gardner** (Maggie Grayson), Henry Fonda (Albert Risley, fire brigade chief), Mavor Moore (John O'Brien), Jonathan Welsh (Herman Stover), Richard Donat (Captain Harrison Risley), Ken James (Andrew), Donald Pilon (Dr. Matwick), Terry Haig (Terry James), Cec Linder (Counselor Paley), Hilary Lebow (Mrs. Adams), Jeff Mappin (Beezer), Earl Pennington (Mr Clark), James Franciscus (Jimbo), Sonny Forbes (Tom), Bronwen Mantel (Sarah Watts), Janice Chaikelson (Debbie Watts), Steven Chaikelson (Gerald Watts), Murray Cruchley (Tony Miller), Jérôme Tiberghein (fireman Waller).

USA release: September 1979

Herman Stover sabotages a refinery after his promotion to supervisor is rejected. In a matter of minutes the fire sets the oil-filled pipes aflame and a series of blasts shake the city.
To face the magnitude of the catastrophe, Harrison Risley, Captain of the fire brigade, dispatches all units and calls for reinforcements. The victims are rushed to a newly opened hospital owned by the billionaire Diana Brockhurst-Lautrec, a former mistress of its director Frank Whitman. The city's mayor, William Dudley, who has always supported having the refinery in the city, now fears the catastrophe will also destroy his political career.
The Captain of the fire brigade, the mayor and the hospital's director struggle to coordinate their efforts, owing to the blackout in all communications. The wind keeps the helicopters from landing. The flames begin to surround the hospital and it must be evacuated. The firemen create a tunnel of water so that the patients may be taken to safety. Everyone is eventually saved except for the arsonist Herman Stover and the head nurse, who is crushed by scaffolding that collapses as efforts are underway to save them.

At dawn, the army rescue teams arrive. The mayor, for having successfully dealt with the crisis, regains the support of the people as he speaks before television cameras, interviewed by journalist Maggie Grayson.

THE KIDNAPPING OF THE PRESIDENT

1979. Canada/USA 113'
Director: George Mendeluk. *Producer:* George Mendeluk, John Ryan, (Sefel Pictures International for Presidential Productions). *Executive Producer:* Joseph Sefel. *2nd Unit Directors:* Larry Paul, Barry Pearson. *Screenplay:* Richard Murphy, based on the book by Charles Templeton. *Screenplay Consultant:* Barry Pearson. *Director of Photography* (De Luxe Colors): Michael Malloy. *Color Consultant:* Robert Borics. *Cameraman:* Bob New. *Special Effects:* Peter Hutchinson, Richard Albain. *Sound:* Douglas Ganton. *Art Director:* Douglas Higgins. *Sets:* Henry Ciolcynski. *First Assistant Director:* Andreas Blackwell. *Screenplay:* Pauline Harlow. *Costumes:* Angie Vastagh. *Make-up:* Lee Kruse, Helen Crocker. *Hairstylists:* Victoria Truscott, Jocelyn McDonald. *Music:* Paul J. Zaza. *Electronic Music:* Nash the Slash. *Sound Editing:* John Kelly, Kevin Townshend. *Editing:* Michael McLaverty. *Distribution (USA):* Crown International.

Cast: William Shatner (Jerry O'Connor), Hal Holbrook (President Adam Scott), Van Johnson (Vice-President Ethan Richards), **Ava Gardner** (Beth Richards), Miguel Fernandes (Roberto Assanti), Cindy Girling (Linda Steiner), Michael J. Reynolds (MacKenzie), Elisabeth Shepherd (Joan Scott), Gary Reineke (Dietrich), Maury Chaykin (Harvey Cannon), Murray Westgate (Archie Strandler), Michael Kane (Herb Morris), Jackie Burroughs (woman agent), Aubert Pallascio (Prime Minister), Virginia Podesser (Prime Minister's wife), Elias Zarou (middle-aged man), Larry Duran (hotel employee), Patrick Brymer (Jesus Freak), Gershom Resnik (Marvin), John Stocker (Herman), Chapelle Jaffe (Valerie Martinelli), John Romain (TV presenter), Ken Anderson (Willis), Sully Boyar (FBI chief), David Cadiente (Mendoza), Bob Collins (Jack, police officer), Michael Fairman (Harrison), Buddy Ferrens (garage employee), Mike Fortman (James Walker), Frederick Franklyn (Herbert Thurcow), Michael Kirby (Calvin), Paul Larson (McCrory).

USA release: 13 August 1981

Roberto Assanti is a dissident in the Marxist revolutionary group, The Green Hand. Under the pretext of certain ideals, however, the man is actually a criminal working in his own interests. He plots to kidnap the President of the United States during an official visit to Toronto. Jerry O'Connor, Security Chief, is warned of the threat thanks to information received by the embassy of Argentina.
Assanti puts his plan into action. He gets two members of an American revolutionary organization, Harry Cannon and Linda Steiner, to be his accomplices. They also supply him with an armored van filled with explosives. The group are caught in a gas station. During the shoot-out, Assanti's accomplice Harry and two police officers are killed.
In Toronto, Assanti manages to approach the President by pretending he is a journalist. The terrorist, belted heavily with dynamite, takes the President hostage in the van. If his demands are not met, Linda has been ordered to blow it up. Assanti wants several million dollars in diamonds and a plane. The Vice-President of the United States, Richards, who aspires to the presidency himself, gets the money for the ransom in order to gain popularity among voters.
The police chief of Toronto does not agree with the way Security Chief O'Connor is handling the crisis. He decides to take things into his own hands and arrests Linda who is spotted in a crowd. Linda nevertheless manages to activate the countdown mechanism: the van will explode at midnight. O'Connor hands over the diamonds to Assanti and the terrorist has

the plane take off. Linda shoots Assanti after the shocking discovery that her sister, also an activist, was in fact murdered by Assanti in Argentina. Linda does not know how to stop the timer. After failing to break into the van through the floor, O'Connor finally makes a passage by ripping out the motor and saves the President just seconds before the explosion.

PRIEST OF LOVE

1980. Great Britain. 93'
Director: Christopher Miles. *Producers:* Christopher Miles, Andrew Donally (Milesian Film Production for Ronceval). *Executive Producers:* Stanley J. Seeger, Penelope Midgley. *First Assistant Director:* Graham Fowler. *Screenplay:* Alan Plater, based on the biography *The Priest of Love* by Harry T. Moore and the letters and writings of D.H. Lawrence. *Director of Photography (Color):* Ted Moore. *Cameraman:* Mike Roberts. *Sound:* Robin Gregory. *Assistant Director:* Graham Fowler. *Script-girl:* Pamela Mann. *Art Directors:* Ted Tester, David Brockhurst. *Sets:* Peter Young. *Costumes:* Anthony Powell. *Make-up:* George Frost and Olga Riviseco (Mexico), Adonella de Rosi (Italy). *Hairstylist:* Christopher Taylor. *Music:* Joseph James. *Music Director:* Alexander Faris. *Sound Editing:* Rusty Coppleman. *Editing:* Paul Davis, Ann Chegwidden. *Distribution (G.B.):* Enterprise.

Cast: Ian McKellen (D.H.Lawrence), Janet Suzman (Frieda Lawrence), **Ava Gardner** (Mabel Dodge Luhan), Penelope Keith (Dorothy Brett), Jorge Rivero (Tony Luhan), Maurizio Merli (Angelo Ravagli), John Gielgud (Herbert G. Muskett), James Faulkner (Aldous Huxley), Mike Gwilym (John Middleton Murry), Massimo Ranieri (Piero Pini), Marjorie Yates (Ada Lawrence), Wendy Alnutt (Maria Huxley), Jane Booker (Barbara Weekley), Elizabeth Spender (Elsa Weekley), Elio Pandolfi (Pino Orioli), Shane Rimmer (Head of Immigration), Sarah Brackett (Achsah Brewster), Adrienne Burgess (Katherine Mansfield), Patrick Holt (Arthur

Ava as she appears in *Priest of Love* in 1980.

Lawrence), Derek Martin (sergeant), Burnel Tucker (Earl Brewster), Mary Gifford (leader of the Puritan League), John Hudson (employee), Daniel Chatto (officer of the Aquitania), Roger Sloman (reporter on the Aquitania), Paco Mauri (immigration officer), Adrian Montano (Tinsmith), Herminio Carrasco (Milta guide), Mike Morris (Dr Uhlfelder), Gareth Forwood (photographer on the Aquitania), Natasha Buchanan (Jessis Chambers), Anne Dyson (Lydia Lawrence), Julian Fellowes (Barbara's fiancé), Graham Faulkner (farmer), Niall Padden (English soldier), Andrew McCulloch (British sergeant), Andrew Lodge (British officer), Sarah Miles (film star), Sean Mathias (film star's secretary), Franscesco Carnelliti, Cyrus Elias (Italian reporters), Madeleine Todd (Harwood Brewster), Wolf Kahler (German officer), Graziana Cappellini (Giulla Pini), Andrea Occhipinti (young printer), John Flint, Brian McDermott (police officers), Duccio Dogone, Roberto Bonnani (French gendarmes), Roy Herrick, David Glover (reporters), Mella Mitchell (Aga Khan). The Frank Marcus Indian Dancers.

USA release: October 1981. Great Britain Release: 1981

1915. On the recommendation of The National Puritain League, D.H. Lawrence's most recent work, *The Rainbow*, condemned as an outrage to public decency, is burnt in a public square in London.
1924. D.H. Lawrence accepts the invitation of a wealthy American woman living in Mexico, Mabel Dodge Luhan. Lawrence's wife Frieda accompanies him as well as the couple's friend, Dorothy Brandt. Mrs. Brandt pays for the trip thanks to her wealthy husband. During Lawrence's stay at the vast ranch in Taos, the writer savors the peace in which he can devote himself to writing. Nevertheless, this life is also like being a bird in a gilt cage and he soon feels restless.
In New Mexico he finishes *The Plumed Serpent* and discovers that he has tuberculosis. Realizing he is going to die soon, Lawrence goes back to England to visit all the places of his childhood: he remembers his mother, who encouraged him to write, and the day he met Frieda. He recalls the problems his uninhibited ways caused with neighbors when he was evicted from his cottage in Cornwall after swimming nude in the river.

With Anna Karina and Anthony Quinn in *Regina Roma*.

To escape the harsh English winter, Frieda takes her ailing husband to Italy. The couple stays in a Florentine villa owned by Angelo Ravagli. There, D.H. Lawrence writes two of his most important works: *Women in Love* and *Lady Chatterley's Lover*, first released in Italy by a publisher friend. Indeed, the writer is still under bitter attack from righteous Anglo-Saxon society. Refusing to see a doctor, D.H. Lawrence leaves Italy for France and dies in Vence, in March 1930. At his bedside are Frieda, and close friends, Aldous Huxley and his wife.
Frieda marries Angelo Ravagli. Together they take the novelist's ashes to New Mexico but, in a moment of forgetfulness, they forget them on the platform of the train station.
Note: In a new version, Christopher Miles cut the sequence of Lawrence's return to England and also the epilogue involving the ashes, thus shortening the film's running time to 1 hour 33 minutes.

TELEFILMS AND SERIES

REGINA ROMA

1982. USA. 86' (U.S.A) 101' (France)
Director: Jean-Yves Prate. *Producer:* David Amiri, Serge Roux (Bognor Ltd./Curiator Spiritus Company Ltd./Galia International Inc). *Production Coordinator:* Gianni Sarago for Genesis Productions (Rome). *Screenplay:* Pierre Rey. *Production Manager:* Maurizio Pastrovich. *Delegate Producer:* Anis Nohra. *Director of Photography:* Serge Haignere. *Cameraman:* Adolfo Bartoli. *First Assistant Director:* Carlo Quinterio. *Casting:* Barbara Johnson. *Sound:* Roberto Petrozzi. *Special Effects:* Enrico Vagniluca. *Make-up:* Giancarlo Del Brocco, Mario Michisanti. *Screenplay:* Vivalda Vigorelli. *Hairstylist:* Rita Innocenzi. *Ava Gardner's Hairstylist:* Sydney Guilaroff. *Costumes:* Maria Spigarelli. *Music and Orchestration:* Lorin Maazel. *Music composed and arranged by* Carlo Savina. *Sound Editing:* Sandro Peticca. *Editing:* Roberto Silvi. *Mixing:* Jean Neny.

Cast: **Ava Gardner** (mother), Anthony Quinn (father), Ray Sharkey (Carry), Anna Karina (Regina).

An aging couple waits for their only son Carry to celebrate Twelfth Night. Carry is a bachelor, nearing forty, brought up by his domineering mother whose affection has been suffocating. When Carry finally arrives, he is with his girlfriend Regina, an awkward, ungracious, and inarticulate girl.
During the meal, the conversation is entirely devoted to Carry and his future career moves. His mother totally ignores Regina. When, in the Twelfth Night custom of designating his queen, Carry chooses Regina instead of his mother, he also announces that the two intend to get married. When his mother hears this announcement she is shattered.
A little later, Regina listens dumbfounded as a dark family secret is revealed: the mother's loss of an illegitimate child through abortion pills. Regina cannot bear to listen any further. Held back by his mother's grasp, Carry watches helplessly as Regina rushes away. Carry's father, however, intervenes and gets his son to break free. Carry runs to join his fiancée. Epilogue (French version): Carry returns to the shelter of his mother's arms.

A.D.

1984. USA. 6 x 95'
Director: Stuart Cooper. *Producer:* Vincenzo Labella (Procter and Gamble Productions Inc/International Film Production). *Executive Producers:* Jack Wishard, George Jensen. *Delegate Producer:* John A. Martinelli. *Screenplay:* Anthony Burgess and Vincenzo Labella. *Director of Photography:* Ennio Guarnieri (A.I.C.). *Cameraman:* Giorgio Urbinelli. *Sound:* Ivan Sharrock. *Spe-*

cial Effects: Albert J. Whitlock. *Screenplay:* Marion Mertes. *Sets:* Bruno Cesari. *Make-up:* Guiliamo Laurenti. *Costumes:* Enrico Sabbatini. *Hairstylists:* Elda Magnanti, Renata Magnanti. *Music:* Lalo Schifrin. *Editing:* John A. Martinelli A.C.E.

Cast (in alphabetical order): Anthony Andrews (Nero), Colleen Dewhurst (Antonia), **Ava Gardner** (Agrippina), David Hedison (Festus), John Houseman (Gamaliel), Richard Kiley (Claudius), James Mason (Tiberius), John McEnery (Caligula), Ian McShane (Sejanus), Jennifer O'Neil (Messalina), Millie Perkins (Mary), Denis Quilley (Peter), Fernando Rey (Seneca), Richard Roundtree (Serpenius), Susan Sarandon (Livilla), Ben Vereen (Ethiopian), Tony Vogel (Aquila), Jack Warden (Nerva), Anthony Zerbe (Pilate), Neil Dickson (Valerius), Cecil Humphreys (Caleb), Amanda Pays (Sarah), Philip Sayer (Paul), Diane Venora (Corinna), Ralph Arliss (Samuel), Mike Gwilym (Pallas), David Harries (Thomas), Peter Howell (Atticus), Harold Kasket (Caiphe), Norma Martinelli (Apicata), Vincenzo Ricotta (man from Essene), Rebecca Saire (Ruth), Michael Wilding (Jesus), Bruce Winant (Seth).

1 – Two days after his crucifixion, Christ has risen. The apostles gather around Peter who tells them of the miracle. Thomas does not believe him. Then Jesus appears to them. Tiberius, the aging emperor, has withdrawn to the Isle of Capri as rampant corruption reigns in Rome. The prefect Sejanus plots against him. His niece, Agrippina, is involved in an intrigue to place her third son, Caligula, at the head of the Roman Empire. The Romans persecute the Hebrews. Pontius Pilate orders the arrest of Caleb and has his two sisters Ruth and Sarah kidnapped. Ruth is exiled, Sarah is offered as a slave to Sejanus. Jesus gives more signs of his presence, but Paul doubts that he is the Son of God. Peter calls the faithful to be baptized.

2 – Ruth rebels. She is stabbed by a Roman on the boat of exile. Sejanus is named Consul by Tiberius. Valerius acts under the command of Sejanus. He is responsible for keeping watch over Antonia, who wants to warn Tiberius against Sejanus. Back in Rome, Tiberius has arrested Sejanus, and dies, suffocated by Caligula. Peter has performed many miracles. The priests of Israel doubt that Jesus is truly the Son of God. Paul leaves to wage war against the apostles and has Etienne stoned to death. Etienne becomes Christ's first martyr.

3 – Paul persecutes the Nazarenes and carries out arrests in the name of the priests of Israel. As he is struck by a great light, he is blinded and hears the voice of the Lord. Paul converts to Christianity on the road to Damascus. Baptized, he can suddenly see again and begins to preach. Upon his return from exile, Caleb becomes a gladiator and nurtures his ambition to destroy the Romans' power. He meets Corinna, a female gladiator, and is reunited with his Sarah whom he reproaches for being in love with the Roman Valerius. Caligula is interested in the Christian concept of monotheism since he feels he himself is this God. Little by little he is overcome by madness. He wants his armies to invade Britain only so that the soldiers might bring him back seashells.

4 – Valerius wins back Sarah and marries her. They have a daughter whom they name Ruth. Valerius participates in a plot to assassinate Caligula. Claudius is made Emperor. The persecutions of the Christians grow worse. Peter performs miracles and is arrested by King Herod. God appears to him and sets him free, opening the doors of his prison.

5 – Valerius serves under the command of the Empress Messalina who tries to overthrow Emperor Claudius, her husband. Agrippina, niece and mistress of Claudius, also plots to make her son Nero Emperor of Rome instead of Britannicus, the son of Claudius and Messalina. Claudius dies, poisoned by Agrippina. Nero becomes Emperor and befriends Tijelinus, an Epicurian tavern owner whom he makes his right-hand man instead of the philosopher Seneca. When Agrippina reproaches her son for his behavior, unworthy of an Emperor, he has her murdered.

With Anthony Andrews in the telefilm *Anno Domini*.

6 – Valerius converts to Christianity. He is baptized by Paul whom he has escorted to Rome to be judged. The cruel aesthete Nero dreams of rebuilding Rome according to his own vision. The members of the Senate declare their opposition and Nero sets the city afire. He enjoys watching the spectacle of the city in flames and accuses the Christians of the crime. Tijelinus suggests to the Emperor that he should use Christians for their games. Valerius revolts

against the Roman emperor and saves the Christian children from the arena. Peter is crucified and Paul is arrested and executed with an axe. Nevertheless, Christ's teaching begins to spread. It is the dawn of the Christian era.

KNOTS LANDING

1977/1993. USA 344 x 55'

Producer: Lawrence Kasha (Roundelay-M.F. Production, in association with Lorimar Telepictures). *Associate Producer:* Mary-Catherine Harold. *Executive Producers:* Michael Filerman, David Jacobs. *Created by* David Jacobs. *Screenplay:* Allison Hock, Lynn Marie Latham, Diane Messina Stanley, James Stanley, Rogers Turrentine. *Story Continuity Editing:* James Stanley, Chuck Bulot, M.J. Cody. *Director of Photography:* Hugh K. Gagnier (A.S.C.) Panavision/Metrocolor. *Sound:* Doug Grindstaff. *Casting:* Cami Hursey. *Art Director:* Ray Markham. *Sets:* Sal Blydenburgh. *Costumes:* Travilla. *Make-up:* Leigh Mitchell, William O'Reynolds. *Hairstylists:* Barbara Kaye, Minster, Georgina Williams. *Theme Song by* Jerrold Immel.

Cast: Ted Shackelford (Gary Ewing), Joan Van Ark (Valene Erwing Gibson Waleska), Don Murray (Sid Fairgate), Michele Lee (Karen Fairgate Mac Kenzie), John Pleshette (Richard Avery), Constance McCashin (Laura Avery Sumner), James Houghton (Kenny Ward), Kim Lankford (Ginger Ward), Claudia Lonow (Dina Fairgate), Steve Shaw (Eric Fairgate), Donna Mills (Abby Cunningham Ewing Sumner), Alec Baldwin (Joshua Rush), William Devane (Gregory Sumner), Kevin Dobson (Marion Patrick MacKenzie), Julie Harris (Lilimal Clements), Lisa Hartman (Ciji Dunne/Cathy Geary Rush), Douglas Sheehan (Ben Gibson).

And **Ava Gardner** in the role of Ruth Sumner Galverston, the widow of a Congressman, for six episodes of the series 1984-85.

1 - The Deluge
2 - A Piece of the Pie
3 - Four No Trump
4 - A Price to Pay
5 - One Day in a Row
6 - Vulnerable

The romantic adventures of four families in a little town in California. Gary Ewing and his wife Valene, from Dallas, move to the West Coast. They become friends with their neighbors Kenny and Ginger Ward, Richard and Laura Avery, a newly-wed couple, and Sid and Karen Fairgate. Abby Fairgate, Sid's sister, seduces Gary. Gary divorces Valene to marry Sid. Things become complicated when Valene discovers she is pregnant by Gary…

THE LONG HOT SUMMER

1985. USA 2 x 95'

Director: Stuart Cooper. *Producer:* Dori Weiss. *Executive Producers:* Leonard Hill, John Thomas Lenox. *Associate Producers:* Daniel Cahn, Bobbi Kronowitz. *Screenplay:* Rita Mae Brown, based on the novel by Faulkner, *The Hamlet,* and on the screenplay by Irving Ravetch, Harriet Frank Jr. *2nd Unit Director:* David Gaines. *Assistant Directors:* Martin Walters, Scott White. *Directors of Photography:* Reed Smoot, Steve Yaconelli. *Special Effects:* Greg Curtis. *Sound:* Mark Ulano, Patrushka Mierzwa. *Sets:* Jan Scott. *Costumes:* Shay Cunliff. *Make-up:* Jo Ann Wabisca. *Hairstylist:* Tammy Kusian. *Music:* Charles Bernstein. *Editing:* Dann Cahn.

Cast: Don Johnson (Ben Quick), Jason Robards (Will Varner), Judith Ivey (Noel Varner), Cybill Shepherd (Eula Varner), **Ava Gardner** (Minnie Littlejohn), William Russ (Jody Varner), Wings Hauser (Wilson Mahood), Alexandra Johnson (Agnes Stewart), Charlotte Stanton (Mrs. Stewart), Albert Hall (Armistead Howlett), William Forsythe (Isaac), James Gammon (Billy Quick), Rance Howard (Wilk), Bill Thurman (Houstin), Robert Wentz (Ratliff), Irma Hall (Cécilia Howlett), Joe Berryman (Deputy Hampton), Patricia Rendleman (Lisa), Stephen Davies (Alan Stewart), Norman Bennett (auctioneer), Jerry Haynes (Lew).

1 – Ben Quick comes to a little town in Mississippi and gets a job as a tenant farmer through Jody Varner, whose father, Will Varner, is the most powerful man in the region. When Will Varner is released from hospital, he is not at all happy to find Ben Quick on his land. He has heard rumors that Quick is suspected of being an arsonist. Nevertheless, Will, despite himself, soon takes a liking to this free-wheeling young man, wishing that his own son Jody had the qualities he sees in Ben. Will even prefers to appoint Ben manager of his store instead of Jody, and expresses hopes that the young man will eventually marry his daughter Noel. Jody's wife Eula is as worried as her husband over Ben's growing power in the family, though Ben also fascinates her. Ben rescues her when she is molested by Wilson, her secret lover. That very evening a fire breaks out in a barn and Wilson is found dead.

2 – The entire town rises up against Ben and accuses him of starting the fire. Fortunately, he is saved when Will Varner vouches for his innocence. Ben knows who is responsible for the fire: it is his own father who has been seen recently in the area. As a show of goodwill Ben organizes a village celebration for the rebuilding of the barn. Ben's feelings for Will Varner's eldest daughter Noel are becoming more and more obvious. Noel and Ben grow closer after Alan, a writer whom the girl had in fact preferred, admits that he is a homosexual. Though suspicions concerning Ben are now a thing of the past, Jody still feels animosity towards his rival, whom he holds responsible for being kept out of the family business. When the mentally retarded Isaac testifies that he had surprised Ben hiding Wilson's body, renewed hatred is sparked against Ben, which leads to his arrest. He escapes when there is an accident as he is driven to prison and hides out on his land. A fight breaks out between Ben and Jody. Overcome by rage Jody sets fire to the house. Alerted by the flames, the people in the village run to the house and are ready to lynch Ben. The Varners arrive just in time. They prove that the person responsible for Wilson's death was none other than Isaac.

HAREM

1986.USA 2 x 90'

Director: Billy Hale. *Producer:* Highgate Pictures Inc. *Executive Producer:* Martin Manulis. *Production Manager:* William Deneen. *Screenplay:* Karol Ann Hoeffner. *Historical Consultant:* Prince Michael of Greece. *First Assistant Director:* Paddy Carpenter. *Director of Photography:* Don Morgan. *Cameramen:* Gordon Hayman, Trevor Coop. *Sound:* Dave Allen, Don Worthman. *Sets:* Clinton Cavers. *Sets Assistant:* Disley Jones. *Make-up:* Anna Dryhurst, Mary Hillman. *Hairstylist:* Wendy Rawson, accomplished by Anne McFeyden, Patricia Kirkman. *Costumes:* Yvonne Blake. *Sound Editing:* Paul Smith, Phil Bothamley, Bob Risk, Chris Lancaster. *Music Editing:* Brian Lintern. *Editing:* Peter Boita, Jason Krasucki, John F.Link. *Mixing:* Dean Humphries.

Cast: Nancy Travis (Jessica Grey), Art Malik (Tarik), Omar Sharif (Sultan), **Ava Gardner** (Kadin), Sarah Miles (Lady Ashley), Cherie Lunghi (Usta), Julian Set (Forest Pinkerton), Yaphet Kotto (chief of the eunuchs), Georgine Anderson (Aunt Lily), Shirley Cain (embassy hostess), George Camiller (Vizier Bly), Jojo Cole (Emily), James Coyle (Sultan's spy), Sarah Crowden (Charlotte), Caroline Dorian (Victoria), David Grant (Commander in Chief), Michael Gwilym (Salim), Barrie Houghton (astrologer), Stephen Jenn (Moslem spy), Ian Jentle (doctor), Robert Lang (Ambassador Grant), George Savides (Misha), Josette Simon (Geisla), Jeremy Sinden (Randolph), Liz Smith (Mrs. Pendleton), John L. Stevens (Radik), Philip Stone (Arthur Grey), James Taylor (Mr. Pendleton), Tony Spiridakis (Murat).

In *Harem* with Sarah Miles.

1- London 1906. Jessica Grey is about to marry the English diplomat Forest Pinkerton, who has been posted to Damascus. On their trip their lives are endangered when the rebel Tarik leads an attack against the ruling Sultan. The couple is only saved thanks to the intervention of Lady Ashley, a respected figure in Constantinople. On an excursion to the ruins of ancient Palmyra, Jessica is kidnapped by Tarik and taken to the rebels' camp. Despite herself, the young woman is strongly attracted to her kidnapper and his fiery seductiveness. Tarik offers her to the Sultan in exchange for some of his own men who are being held prisoner. Jessica rebels against the laws of the harem and tries to escape during an outing to the bazaar. As a warning, Kadin, the official sultana, holds up a disobedient "wife" as an example, having the woman executed before Jessica's very eyes. The Sultan, fascinated by Jessica's beauty, makes her his favorite. This privilege arouses Kadin's jealousy and he plots her murder. Lady Ashley brings Forest the proof that his fiancée is being held prisoner in the harem. Tarik agrees to save Jessica under the condition that Forest support the Turkish revolution. Tarik sneaks into the palace disguised as a eunuch. Jessica, however, recognizes him just as she is about to enter the Sultan's chambers, beautifully dressed and perfumed.

2 - In the Sultan's private chambers, Jessica thinks up a ruse to delay their night of love: she agrees to become his bride under the condition that she marry as a virgin. The eunuch assigned to Jessica is none other than Tarik. The revolutionary rebel tells her he will help her escape and saves her life by killing the two murderers sent by Kadin. This adventure suddenly has a liberating effect on both of them as they reveal their passionate feelings for each other and confess their love. Jessica becomes increasingly important in the Sultan's life. Indeed, under the woman's influence, he is opening up to Western culture and its progressive ideas. Despite Tarik's pressuring, Jessica refuses to spy on the Sultan or betray his trust. Nevertheless, during a trip to Brusa, Jessica discovers the Sultan's plans to put down the revolutionaries and begs Tarik to leave the palace. The sultana Kadin discovers the couple's liaison. Jessica and Tarik are brought before the Sultan and condemned to death. Tarik is to be hanged and Jessica drowned. However, the eunuch appointed to drown Jessica makes sure the bag is not completely closed. A British ship rescues Jessica at sea. She joins the rebels and helps free Tarik before he is hanged. Tarik is again in command of his troops which now unite with the palace army and together bring down the regime. The Sultan is removed from power and democracy is brought to the country. Jessica has become a woman of action who has fought for her ideals. She is no longer content to stay with her betrothed Forest and decides against returning to England. Tarik then arrives to carry her away on his black stallion.

MAGGIE

1986. USA 60'

Director: Warris Hussein. *Producer:* William Hill (Warner Bros TV & Karoger Prods). *Screenplay:* Katherine Craddock, Rod Browning. *Director of Photography:* Tony Imi. *Music:* Charles Fox.

Cast: Stephanie Powers (Maggie Webb) and **Ava Gardner**, Herb Edelman, Jeremy Lloyd, Ian Ogilvy, Paul Geoffrey, Barry Corbin, Deborah Foreman, Alley Mills, Don Fellows, Betsy Blair, Marshall Colt and Lucy Aston.

USA Broadcast: CBS TV (19 July 86).

Recently widowed, Maggie not only inherits a vast estate, but also a mountain of debts from her deceased journalist husband. To face the situation, she goes to work for her sister-in-law who runs an international public relations agency.
Her first assignment is to accompany a group of wealthy Texans to London. Yet these Texans are all criminals, each one plotting to murder the other. Maggie becomes a detective and must foil a plot that threatens the life of one of the murderers, who is himself guilty of two other murders.

Suggested reading

David Hanna, *Ava: Portrait of a Star* (Anthony Gibbs and Phillips Ltd, London, 1961).
An invaluable testimony by David Hanna who was not only Ava Gardner's agent, but also longtime friend and confidant. The book covers the period from 1954 to 1959, though Hanna did not collaborate on all of Ava's films during those years. This portrait, as the title suggests, is also doubled by a daily journal that describes the making of *The Barefoot Contessa* (including the film's preparation, shooting and ambitious worldwide promotion). The book also describes the turning point in 1958-59 when, on David Hanna's advice, Ava signed her first independent contract with Stanley Kramer for *On the Beach*.
The author, however, never completely loses sight of Ava, his friend. He recalls times spent together in Rome, London and Paris, sometimes meeting just by chance. He relates their countless conversations and the actress' doubts and fears. Hanna evokes Ava's happiness in working on such films as *Bhowani Junction* and *The Sun Also Rises* and her disappointments, such as *The Little Hut* and *The Naked Maja*. The author recounts it all with warmth, admiration, obvious honesty and great concern for objectivity. An essential book, perhaps the best approach to Ava there is.

Charles Higham, *Ava, a Life Story* (Delacorte Press, New York, 1974).
Charles Higham holds the privilege of being Ava Gardner's first biographer. Though never reprinted, *Ava, a Life Story* reconstructs the actress' life with respect for chronological detail. It also draws upon many unpublished testimonies and thus still today remains one of the best books on Ava Gardner. Charles Higham gives equal space to Ava's life and films. Indeed, the author became her best advocate in the many controversies which the actress sparked. The author includes moving and admiring (apart from Charlton Heston's) quotes from Mickey Rooney, Howard Duff, Philip Yordan, Robert Siodmak, Walter Chiari, Fred Astaire, Anthony Franciosa, John Huston, and Nunnally Johnson. *Ava, a Life Story* has served as a working document for many subsequent publications on the actress. The book's point of view and those of the many directors, actors, and screenwriters it includes are often cited. It was unfortunate that Ava Gardner did not wish to participate in the project.

André Bernard, *Ava Gardner* (PAC, Collection Têtes d'Affiche, Paris, 1976).
Under the direction of André Bernard, this was the first French publication to compile and reference texts that had previously appeared in *Éditions du Cerf* (Jacques Siclier), *Nef* (Edgar Morin), *Les Cahiers du Cinéma* (Claude Gauteur) and in *L'Express* (Jean Cau).
These admirable portraits and sharp analyses of the woman and actress as expressed through her most important roles, confirm the fascination which Ava exerted upon these authors. It is also a demonstration of the essential contribution of French criticism to the understanding of cinema and its myths. The collection concludes with a contribution by François Guérif, who retraces the milestones of Ava Gardner's career and draws upon the works by David Hanna and Charles Higham. There is also a filmography prepared by Olivier Eyquem. The volume is illustrated with 107 photos. Out of print.

Judith M. Kass, *Ava Gardner, an Illustrated History of the Movies* (Harvest/HBJ Édition, New York, 1977).
This book, unfortunately out of print, is part of an American paperback series. Ava Gardner's films take a predominant place here, with details of her private life serving only as points of reference. The author offers her personal criticism and expresses pertinent observations on Ava's performances and films. She also provides concise summaries. The book is divided into four parts which correspond to the four decades of the actress' career. 100 photos illustrate this rather mediocre text. There is a basic filmography, bibliography and index.

James Robert Parish, *The Hollywood Beauties* (Arlington House Publishers, 1978).
Ava Gardner very naturally takes her place in this album, a homage to seven of Hollywood's most beautiful women: Dolores del Rio, Kay Francis, Jean Harlow, Grace Kelly, Elizabeth Taylor and Lana Turner. One chapter is devoted to each actress, illustrated with a few (sometimes rare) photos and completed by a detailed filmography. J.R. Parish does not add anything to material already contained in the books previously mentioned in this Suggested Reading. Charles Higham is heavily cited. Parish covers Ava Gardner's career film by film, and presents critical excerpts from *Time Magazine*, *The New York Times* and *Newsweek*. Certain films from Ava's earlier period are curiously missing from his filmography, though they are cited in the text. One example is *Reunion in France*.

Matthew Rampling, *Les Plus Belles Histoires d'Amour de Hollywood: Ava Gardner* (Balland, Paris, 1981).
This is certainly an eye-catching title for a series that devotes one of its volumes to Ava Gardner. Indeed, the actress' private life offers phenomenal material. Ava's eight husbands and partners are included: Mickey Rooney, Artie Shaw, Howard Hughes, Howard Duff, Frank Sinatra, Mario Cabre, Luis Miguel Dominguin and Walter Chiari. The book is written in the form of a screenplay, with scenes complete with dialogue, just like a B-movie: "He (Sinatra) took his Colt out of his suitcase – he had a gun licence – and dialed the number for 'Bop City'. He asked for Ava. *"Hello, darling,"* she said almost immediately, *"I hope you"* – *"I'm going to kill myself,"* he said. Like a detective story, a romance, and a gossip magazine all rolled into one.

John Daniell, *Ava Gardner* (W.H. Allen, London, 1982).
By far the most impersonal of all the books on Ava Gardner, John Daniell does not contribute anything new. The book includes a study of her films, for which the author seems content to systematically cite *Picture Goer* and an analysis of the Ava Gardner myth. It would appear that the book was published in 1982 simply to fill a demand in the market, since most of the books on Ava Gardner were out of print. Yet this "Ava Gardner" suffers by comparison. It contains a filmography, selected bibliography and index, and 102 photos.

Roland Flamini, *Ava* (Coward McCann & Geoghegan, New York, 1983).
Everything contributes to make this a biographical novel more than a biography strictly speaking. There is the book's presentation (bound), the print quality, the chapter headings, the complete absence of technical information (filmography, index, etc.) and, of course, the style. Flamini seems to have had access to new sources, since his version of certain facts differs strikingly from that of his predecessors.
For example, he is the only author who dates Ava's first trip to New York in 1940 (all the others have it occur in 1941). This would suggest that Ava had a year to finish her studies before accepting MGM's offer. We would be tempted to believe this less hasty version of the facts if the author did not also date Ava's visit to the plastic surgeon McIndoe as occurring in 1957. Indeed, all evidence seems to show that she had no facial injuries yet at that time. However, a number of legal details (signatures, reworking of contracts, negotiations with MGM) and the use of Wayne Miller's cover photo of an Ava Gardner more woman than star, contribute to the book's originality.

Gilles Dagneau, *Ava Gardner* (PAC, Collection Grand Écran Paris, 1984).
Michel Pérez (*Le Matin de Paris*, 2 May 1985) wrote: "Gilles Dagneau chose the enviable task of putting up a new pedestal for the "barefoot contessa". His *Ava Gardner* gives equal attention to costumes, hairstyles, make-up, lighting effects as to the funny or melodramatic trials and tribulations invented to justify the diva's appearances. The author also offers the opportunity to recall what he so nicely refers to as "the most pleasurable of our 'bad memories'". These are the sparkling flops that studded the careers of all stars of Hollywood's golden age. Indeed, they often inspire us with deeper tenderness than the stars' most prestigious performances. Thanks to Dagneau's study, which is one of the most honest and best documented to have been published in France on any Hollywood star, the masters of MGM, from George Sidney to Richard Thorpe, return to the forefront. 262 pages. 248 separately printed photos. Out of print.

Ava Gardner with Alan Burgess and Kenneth Turan, *Ava, My Story* (Bantam Books, New York, 1990 / Presses de la Renaissance, Paris, 1991).
When all hope seemed lost, it happened, out of necessity perhaps. While Ava was home bedridden and unable to work in 1987-88, she finally agreed to write her memoirs (no doubt also for the money). The book was highly anticipated. It would finally set the records straight and disprove the many anecdotes blown out of proportion and distorted over the years. It might even contain some scathing accusations against Hollywood.
In short, we would finally have the truth. And yes, we do learn that Ava never slept with Howard Hughes, though he had always been considered one of her lovers. However, for the most part Ava is content to simply draw on what has already been written about her without giving any other version of the facts. Almost as if she had simply read up on her own self. This impression might be explained by the circumstances that forced two journalists to complete the work after Ava's death. And this is perhaps what gives the book its ambivalence, for it is neither an autobiography nor a biography.
The films Ava evokes are for the most part those which have gone down in film history in any case. Yet it is surprising to note, for example, that in the chapter on *Pandora and the Flying Dutchman* there are more details about what the actress had against Mario Cabre than on the making of the film itself. Which just goes to show us how great Ava truly was in Lewin's film.

And, if need be, that the fondest memories of film buffs are not necessarily those of the leading actors or actresses concerned.
The book also includes rare testimonies by people close to Ava. These are statements from her sister Myra Gardner Pearce, the wardrobe mistress Franka, actress Arlène Dahl, and above all Ava's friend and trusted companion, Mearene Jordan. This autobiography, though apparently lacking in enthusiasm, confirms rather than alters our vision of Ava Gardner.

Jane E. Wayne *Ava's Men: The Private Life of Ava Gardner* (St. Martin's Press, New York, 1990).
The death of Ava Gardner, in January 1990, would necessarily give rise to new book, above all, the kind that saw in this event a commercial potential. From this point of view, Ava Gardner could be considered a true godsend. *Ava's Men: The Private Life of Ava Gardner* ignores Ava the actress. Its author seems interested only in repeating details of what never ceased to fire the public's interest: Ava's dissolute life. The fact that this book is no longer available is further proof of its popularity.

Karin J. Fowler, *Ava Gardner: A Bio-Bibliography* (Greenwood Press, New York, 1990).
This work, which appeared after Ava Gardner's death, was the fruit of a researcher's study: a brief biographical summary, chronological outline, and filmography. The distinguishing feature of this book, however, is its exhaustive bibliography. Karin J. Fowler classifies, and also often annotates the English-language books and periodicals that carry any mention of Ava Gardner and/or her films.
Unfortunately, errors and regrettable omissions discredit the work. The filmography omits some of her earliest films, such as *Calling Dr. Gillespie*, and then fails to mention *Regina Roma* (1982) or *Maggie* (1986). It then mentions Ava in a film in which she never appeared, confusing *This Time for Keeps* directed by Richard Thorpe (1947) and the film directed by Charles Riesner (1941). Two out of the nine photos reproduced have erroneous captions, (stating "Ava in *The Killers*" when in fact it is *The Bribe*; or "Ava in the sixties", for a photo of a costumed Ava in *Bhowani Junction* made in 1955). A pity, since the work aspires to be serious and exhaustive. It is also the only work to contain all of Ava Gardner's radio appearances and recordings.

Grabtown Girl: Ava Gardner's North Carolina Childhood and Her Enduring Ties to Home (Down Home Press, 2001).
Now here is a book that bears a title that will shed some light on the most obscure period of Ava Gardner's life: her childhood and adolescence. Journalists and MGM always wanted to relate a poverty-stricken upbringing, just to make the "Hollywood dream come true" even more convincing. Here we are introduced to her family and intimate circle of friends, aspects that are usually missing from biographies which prefer the stormier parts of Ava's life. Here we meet Ava's sisters, brother, nephew, nieces and classmates who make Ava human and remind us that, though a star, she was not less of a woman for it. *Grabtown Girl* stresses the bonds Ava kept all through life with her origins. It relates her regular trips back to her cherished hometown. The author devotes a few pages (with supporting photos) to the class reunion at Rock Ridge School in 1978 when Ava was reunited with her girlfriend Alberta. In fact, they exchanged letters until the last days of Ava's life.
Of course, this undertaking is well overdue and many of the people close to Ava are no longer alive. Nor does the portrait of Ava as a young girl, which the journalist attempts to reconstruct, necessarily throw light upon the person she eventually became. Were her poor taste in shoes or her independent spirit, as seen through Ava's childhood escapades, enough to explain the character of the "barefoot contessa"? Nothing seems to truly relate the child to the adult woman and indeed it would seem that Ava's true nature was created in Hollywood.
Allenberg, Bert 96, 97